DAD THE FAMILY
COACH

◆

DAVE SIMMONS

D0168218

VICTOR BOOKS®
A DIVISION OF SCRIPTURE PRESS PUBLICATIONS INC.
USA CANADA ENGLAND

SERIES

Dad, The Family Shepherd
P.O. Box 21445
Little Rock, AR 72221
(501) 221-1102

Unless otherwise indicated all Scripture references are from the *New American Stan-dard Bible,* © the Lockman Foundation 1960, 1962, 1963, 1968, 1971, 1972, 1973, 1975, 1977. Used by permission. Other references are from the *Holy Bible, New Inter-national Version* (NIV), © 1973, 1978, 1984, International Bible Society. Used by per-mission of Zondervan Bible Publishers.

Library of Congress Cataloging-in-Publication Data

Simmons, Dave.
　　Dad the family coach / Dave Simmons.
　　　　p.　　　cm. — (Dad the family shepherd)
　　ISBN 0-89693-946-4
　　1. Fathers—United States—Religious life. 2. Fatherhood (Christian theology)
　　I. Title. II. Series: Simmons, Dave. Dad the family shepherd.
　　BV4843.556　　1991　　　　　　　　　　　　　　　　　　　　91-21582
　　306.874'2—dc20　　　　　　　　　　　　　　　　　　　　　　　CIP

Contents

DAD THE FAMILY SHEPHERD SERIES

WISDOM

PHILOSOPHY

WHAT YOU MUST KNOW		WHAT YOU MUST BE		FUNCTIONS			
SIGNIFICANCE		SCOPE		SURVEY OF FUNCTIONS			
1	2	3	4	5	6	7	8

VOLUME 1 — DAD the FAMILY COACH

PRACTICAL

TECHNIQUES — WHAT YOU MUST DO

COACHING TIPS

LOVE		BOND		LEAD			
1	2	3	4	5	6	7	8

VOLUME 2 — DAD the FAMILY COUNSELOR

EQUIP

TEACH		TRAIN		TRACK		TEND	
1	2	3	4	5	6	7	8

VOLUME 3 — DAD the FAMILY MENTOR

Dedication

To my father:
Major Amos E. Simmons

World War II ● Korea ● Vietnam

He did the best he could
with what he had

Coaching Tips:
How to get the most from this book

Coaching Tip One: START AN E-TEAM.
Real Men need Real Men

Dad, the Family Shepherd
E-TEAM

Iron sharpens iron, so one man sharpens another.

—Proverbs 27:17

For best results, this course on fatherhood should be:

1. Ingested internally at the rate of 1 chapter per week.
2. Digested in the company of a few trusted men, an E-Team.
3. Invested in the lives of your family slowly but surely.

This calls for an E-Team (Encouragement Team), a small group of three–five men who meet weekly to study family-life principles and to motivate each other to apply what they learn. An E-Team functions as a vehicle to get you from the valley of intention to the plateau of success. An E-Team converts ambition to action. It transfers desire for better fatherhood to changed behavior patterns in the home.

An E-Team is the only way I know to guarantee steady progress. There are no shortcuts. Progress requires men committed to help each other work hard at fatherhood over a long period of time.

Take the initiative and recruit an E-Team to go through this course with you. Turn to Appendix A and study the E-Team Captain's Guide to learn all you need to know to run a successful E-Team.

An E-Team gives a man:

Encouragement
Understanding
Inspiration
Solutions
Challenge
Accountability

E-TEAM INSTRUCTIONS

In order to establish an E-Team and successfully lead it through this course, follow these steps.

1. READ THE E-TEAM CAPTAIN'S GUIDE IN THE APPENDIX.

2. RECRUIT YOUR TEAM.

Challenge four to six other men to meet together with you for eight weeks to complete the course. Mention that each meeting has a reading assignment that must be completed beforehand and there will be a brief, practical, useful application project following each session. Make sure each man gets a copy of the book in time to prepare for the first meeting. Be sure they know the exact time, place, and assignment for the first meeting.

3. MAKE ASSIGNMENTS.

Instruct each man to read "The Scouting Report" and "Chapter One: Father Power" before the first meeting. Remind them to bring the book, note paper, and pencil to the meeting. Call them a couple of days before the first meeting to remind them of everything.

4. FOLLOW THE E-TEAM GUIDE AT THE END OF EACH SESSION.

Coaching Tip Two: SCHEDULE A VIDEO CONFERENCE.

Dave Simmons' message on fatherhood is available on video. The video package contains the exact same eight hours of the Dad the Family Shepherd live conference that Dave has given throughout the nation since 1984.

The video package is designed to be used for conferences and is not for sale. It is the convenient alternative to a live conference and has been proven to be just as effective as the live conference. (For information on how to sponsor a video conference in your church, see Appendix B.)

Coaching Tip Three: START A FATHERHOOD INSTITUTE.

Consider these questions. Does your church have:

A fatherhood basic training process?
A fatherhood wellness and enhancement process?
A fatherhood diagnostic and remedial training process?
A fatherhood crisis center and an intensive care unit?

The Fatherhood Institute is a comprehensive fatherhood training package specifically designed so a church can easily insert it intact and equip their men to become more effective family shepherds. It features a system of set courses based on a tri-semester format with courses offered in the fall, winter, and spring. (For more information on the Fatherhood Institute, see Appendix C.)

Foreword

Throughout my career in football as a player and as a coach, I considered one of my greatest leadership roles not to be on the football field but in the home. In our present culture, too many families are splintering because of the lack of male leadership in the home. There will be serious consequences for our nation if present trends continue. Dr. James Dobson writes: "Our very survival as a people will depend on the presence or absence of masculine leadership in millions of homes."

There are definite reasons for the decline of excellence in fatherhood. Too few young fathers are aware of the significance and skills of fatherhood. We need a clear precise statement on fatherhood and a basic primer that covers what a father does, how to do it, and how well it must be done.

Dave Simmons, a former player of mine with the Dallas Cowboys, has provided such a work. I have followed Dave and his ministry since he left the Cowboys and believe he has the message and the heart to effectively equip men to become more effective family shepherds.

After working with fathers just like you since 1975 and after surveying the literature in the family and fathering field, Dave saw the need to provide a foundation book on fathering that starts with the basics and clearly explains fathering techniques. Dave has crafted a "Fatherhood Primer," the first resource on fathering a man should read.

Dave has distilled the essence of fatherhood into a three-volume series called *Dad the Family Shepherd*. This series touches all the bases of fatherhood and serves as a text and guide for fathers to learn and perfect basic fathercraft skills.

This volume, *Dad the Family Coach*, establishes the significance of fatherhood by showing how your father power can affect not only your family but your descendants for as long as four generations. It helps clear up the confusion about the role of the father by presenting a fatherhood job description and gives detailed coaching tips on how to perform the Four Fatherhood Functions with excellence.

This book is the coaching playbook for all fathers. It should be the first book on fatherhood that every father-to-be, father, and grandfather should read. It will help build a foundation on which all other fatherhood helps can stand.

Every father needs to know the principles in this book. And remember, a wise man once said,

> You pay for what you need
> whether you have it or not.

Coach Tom Landry

The Scouting Report

"All happy families resemble one another. Every
unhappy family is unhappy in its own way."
— *Leo Tolstoy*

FLEETING FATHERHOOD

Raising children is like the 100-meter high hurdles race.

My son, Brandon, was a high school decathlete. He first entered
the state decathlon as a freshman and worked hard for four years
with the goal of winning it his senior year. His last decathlon finally
rolled around, and the papers tabbed him as one of the favorites to
win.

On a bright May day with the Arkansas heat shimmering above
the stadium, Brandon reported and weighed in his shot-put and
discus. The 100-meter high hurdles race is the second event on the
first day. Brandon had just finished his high jump and topped out
at 6'2". After stretching and warming up for the hurdles, he jogged
over to me and said, "Dad, this is the last hurdles race I'll ever run
in my life. I want you to anchor the blocks for me."

On the track team, his specialty had been the 300-meter high
hurdles race in which he had set a school record. I think the
hurdles are the most elegant of all track events. Nothing has ever
fired my blood more than to watch my son rip out of the blocks,
glide down his lane, float over the thirty-nine inch hurdles, and
strain for the finish wire.

Now, at the end of his track career, my son wanted me to anchor
the blocks for his last hurdles race. I considered this my highest
honor. What you do is stand on the starting blocks and anchor

them firmly to the ground so the runner can get a good solid start without any give.

After they called Brandon's flight to the starting line, we measured his blocks from the starting line with a tape measure and secured them. He crouched down at the line in a starting position and carefully fitted his cleats on the blocks. He practiced a couple of starts and then stood, shaking his arms, legs, and neck to stay loose. I could smell the sweat that popped out on his forehead. He was ready.

This was his last hurdles race. My baby boy had grown up and was facing his last hurdles race. And I got to anchor his blocks. I wanted to burn this scene into my mind and never forget it.

"On your mark!" the umpire called out.

As Brandon initiated his ritual by coiling up from the blocks and poising his fingers on the starting line, I leaned over and whispered, "Run with God's speed, my son."

"OK, Dad."

"Get set!"

Brandon's butt arched up as he held the launch position. I could see the muscles knotted in bunches along his back and arms. Adrenaline shot through his heart. The blood vessels in his neck pulsed. His whole body trembled as he strained against some invisible force holding him in place. This is my son. This is his last race. I am anchoring his blocks.

POW! The starter fired the .22-revolver cartridge, and the race started.

Brandon was gone. He was gone! He exploded out of the blocks and left me standing there. He bolted toward the first hurdle.

Time seemed to stop. My keyed-up mind leapt into high gear and slowed the race down to a crawl. I looked at my boy as if his frame was frozen. In super slow motion, he neared the first hurdle. Thoughts raced through my mind. "Look at him try. Wow! He sure is trying. He can't try any harder. Nothing in the whole world exists for him right now except those ten hurdles and the finish tape. Look how hard he is trying. He really wants to win this last hurdles race. Watch him kick up his left toe. See him lunge. Now, tuck your right leg and drag it over. Pump. Pump. Pump. Get back into your stride." Like a dream runner, he ghosted over the first hurdle and floated off for the second.

With a jolt, I realized I had the worst seat in the stadium. I stood on the starting blocks and saw the race develop from the rear. They were moving away from me, and I could not see the runners in relation to one another. Normally, I stand at the last hurdle where I can see who has the lead going into the stretch. I can see who crosses the finish line, and I am there to catch Brandon and help him walk off the track.

The only way I could see his progress now was when he came to a hurdle, he would zip up and down. Between the hurdles, when he ran smoothly, I could not discern his advancement. And, if he tarried or fell, I could not reach him to help. I could not encourage him. He had to run the race without me. He had to do it alone. I had anchored the blocks, but now I was out of the race. In fact, I couldn't even see the finish.

Raising children is like the 100-meter high hurdles race. If a kid wants a good start in life, he needs his dad to anchor the blocks. He needs a solid family shepherd standing firmly in the home. He needs the dominant male authority figure in his life standing behind him as he lunges out of the home and races off into his future. He needs you, Mr. Dad, to stand there to love and watch him. He needs a whisper from you. He needs you to care deeply and hope desperately for him.

You may not have the best seat in the stadium. You must watch his life from the rear. You won't know about his problems until you see him bounce over the hurdles of life. His progress in between hurdles will be imperceptible. If he falters or falls, he must get up and keep going. You can't do it for him. It's his race. And you may not even be around to watch him cross the finish line.

Your kid wants you to anchor the blocks more than anything in the world. That is your proper duty and role. Coach him. Work with him. Get him in shape. Train and condition him. Teach him the techniques. Help him with strategy. Warn him of problems and dangers. Walk him to the starting blocks and anchor his plunge into life. Let him loose. Watch him fly. Watch him run the race.

THE THREAT TO FATHERHOOD

Leo Tolstoy starts his classic novel *Anna Karenina* with these opening lines: "All happy families resemble one another. Every unhappy family is unhappy in its own way."

Maybe so in 1876, but nowadays an incredible number of unhappy families are unhappy in the same way—they suffer from paternal deprivation. Hordes of kids have no dad to anchor the blocks. Kids can't run without a care-giving father standing on the starting blocks.

Phantom Fatherhood

We live in the land of stealth fathers, phantom fathers, fathers who are not effectual. Paternal deprivation, like the grim reaper, respects no class and plays no favorite. Destitute homes and affluent homes are unhappy in the same way. Professor Max Lerner has written:

> The vanishing father is perhaps the central fact of the changing American family structure today.

Even when the family remains intact, many dads circle frequently but seldom land. They rarely deviate from their ritual of dawn departure, dusk drag-in, and diminishing personal focus. Here we have brain-dead dads, and we see the incredible shrinking father. Everywhere we hear of disappearing dads. Imagine, the Late Great Dad.

Toxic Fatherhood

Fatherhood can be worse than neutral:

The Times, Seattle.

"A 13-year-old boy in Lenexa, Kansas, has invented a toy robot that punches you in the face and kicks you with a boot—and calls it a 'Portable Dad.' "

New York Times Magazine

"The Youth Board realized it had penetrated into a world where there is no father. The welfare world of New York is a fatherless world. The father is an impregnator. He vanishes after he has planted his seed. He is frightened by the bloom."

Knight News Service

"Hug them and they won't hug you back. Smile at them and a blankness glazes their eyes. Pick them up and they may be as stiff as plywood. They are the kids without a conscience, and there are

THE LATE GREAT DAD

Men are baffled by the conflicting role expectations shouted at them from different authorities. In our culture, there no longer exists a specific universal concept of the role of the adult male in the family. Men are confused because they can't find a clear job description and instruction manual. Many men have gotten out of step not because they march to the beat of a different drum, no one beats the drum for them at all.

Read how prominent authorities have summarized the male's plight:

James Levine—"After countless books about the condition of women that have been published in the last decade, we are now getting a spate of studies about men. One theme comes through loud and clear: the male is in crisis. Buffeted by the woman's movement, constrained by a traditional and internalized definition of masculinity, men literally don't know who they are, what women want from them, or even what they want from themselves" (*Psychology Today*, Nov. 1979, vol. 13 no. 6, p. 147).

Peter Stearns—"Never before in the history of the species have groups of women attacked men with more verbal violence than during the past decade of the United States. Never before have the conventions of gender differentiation been so thoroughly challenged. The initiative in the rhetoric of gender relationships is clearly now in the women's hands. Men can seem badly on the defensive. Some feminists enjoy amazonian games, attacking men as unnecessary and masculinity even as dangerous" (*Be a Man* [New York: Homes and Meyer, 1990], 116, 124).

Weldon Hardenbrook—"The lack of adequate models of American masculinity, the increasing numbers of passive and withdrawn fathers, and the feminized approach to the major areas of education have combined to produce modern males who are bastions of passivity and irresponsibility" (*Missing in Action* [Nashville, Tenn.: Thomas Nelson, 1987], 105).

You can't make vast changes in the gender role of one sex without dramatically affecting the other. If the women are confused, the men are dumbfounded. Males don't like to be made fools of, and they don't like to fail. If they wonder who they are and don't know what to do, they are effectively neutralized. Our homes are filled with too many neutered fathers.

more of them than ever in America. We're at a crossroads. We need to attend to the crib, not the criminal, to the playpen, not the state pen."
Newsweek

"The early adolescent years are no longer the wonder years. One quarter of all junior-high-school students are involved in some combination of smoking, drinking, drug use and unprotected sex: half are involved in at least one of these activities."
Daily Telegraph, London

"Entire neighbourhoods will probably become dominated by an 'underclass' of young delinquents within the next decade. The scale of 'contamination' by crime, violence and drug-taking could easily surpass that which has already devastated American cities. The fewer fathers in a community, the more the children would run wild."

Talk to the police in any major city, and you will hear tales like the Detroit kid shot dead for his goosedown parka, the Manhattan kid knifed for his tennis shoes, or the fourteen-year-old in Massachusetts who took his friend into the woods and beat him to death with a baseball bat because he wanted to see what it was like to watch someone die. What about the kids in New York who went "wilding" in Central Park and beat and raped a female jogger? What about the group of teenage boys in New Jersey who lured a retarded girl into a room and raped her with a broomstick?

Our youth are out of control. More of them are getting worse at a faster rate. Why? Toxic fatherhood.

Fathers are abusing children, and the incidence and seriousness of paternal abuse is rising at a geometric rate. Child killings, beatings, and sexual abuse is skyrocketing.

If you charted the increase in the frequency and viciousness of child behavior in our nation, you will find that it corresponds exactly with the rate of increase in dysfunctional fatherhood. As child abuse increases, youth violence increases. It's simply a case of "biting the hand that beats you." Mean dads make mean kids.

Toxic fatherhood creeps across the land and pollutes the "seed corn" of the next generation. In my years of work and study in the field of fatherhood, I see these percentages of fathers falling into these different categories:

1. Excellent Fathers (10 percent)

These fathers are mature men of good character with high ethical standards. They are congruent and focus on the needs of others. They know their position well and enjoy strong gender security. They spend time with their children and perform the Four Fatherhood Functions with excellence.

2. Satisfactory Fathers (15 percent)

These fathers get the job done in a bland sort of way. They manage to get by because of raw ability more than from serious commitment and dedication. They come from satisfactory homes and are content to coast in fatherhood. They are not willing to throw their hearts into their children.

3. Overcoming Fathers (20 percent)

These fathers come from dysfunctional homes and have suffered the difficulties thereof, but they are determined to break the cycle. They demonstrate commitment to overcome their own personal deficiencies and master the skills of the Four Fatherhood Functions. They started at the bottom, but they are aiming for the top.

4. Deteriorating Fathers (15 percent)

These fathers come from adequate homes but have chosen not to make fatherhood a priority. They are sliding downward. They have mild personality disorders and do not perform the Four Fatherhood Functions. They squeeze other family members into compensating roles, thereby causing dysfunctional families.

5. Inadequate Fathers (25 percent)

These dysfunctional fathers are noticeable by their absence. They are the passive, neglectful, uninvolved, inconsistent fathers. They have notable personality disorders. They do not know their responsibilities, or they refuse to carry them out. They cause much damage by what they withhold, not by what they commit. They may be passive/aggressive or covertly abusive.

6. Abusive Fathers (15 percent)

These dysfunctional fathers cause severe emotional and psychological damage to their children by overt physical, verbal, and sexual abuse. They suffer serious personality disorders. They almost always come from a home where they suffered under an abusive or inadequate father. They force family members to play dangerously distorted roles.

FUNCTIONAL		MARGINALLY DYSFUNCTIONAL	TERMINALLY DYSFUNCTIONAL		
ROBUST FAMILY	SATISFACTORY FAMILY	OVERCOMING FAMILY	FRAGMENTED FAMILIES		
EXCELLENT DADS	ADEQUATE DADS	OVERCOMING DADS	DETERIORATING DADS	INADEQUATE DADS	ABUSIVE DADS
10%	15%	20%	15%	25%	15%

0 10 20 30 40 50 60 70 80 90 100

This breakdown classifies 55 percent of American fathers in a dysfunctional mode. What if America were a company and 55 percent of our work stations produced defective products and released them to the market? Would you buy stock in a company like that? Would you buy their products? These families are spewing troubled kids into our society, and we will all pay a price if it continues. Malachi 4:6 says: "And he will restore the hearts of the fathers to their children, and the hearts of the children to their fathers, lest I come and smite the land with a curse."

Only 45 percent of the fathers do satisfactory work or better. What can we hope for if only 10 percent of the fathers in America are raising future competent leadership material?

Something must be done. America needs to restore fatherhood to the lofty status that God intended it to have. Samuel Liebowitz, New York criminal court judge for many years, prescribes this remedy for juvenile delinquency: "Put father back at the head of the family" (Cited by Dave Sunde at Family Life Conference).

Because of the breakdown in fatherhood and the warning from Malachi, I have started a ministry, Dad the Family Shepherd, to sound the bugle call for fathering excellence. Dad the Family Shepherd exists to help local churches establish a fatherhood training program to equip their men to be more effective family shepherds.

THE CALL TO FATHERHOOD

The purpose of the *Dad the Family Shepherd* series is to help fathers see the seriousness of fatherhood, understand the details of their assignment, and master the techniques of fathercraft. As you go through this course, it will help if you know the perspective from which I write.

Confessional Fatherhood

I write in pain. I write to you not as the epitome of a family shepherd or as a successful father. I write to you as a man who suffered an agonizing childhood of father deprivation and abuse. I write to you as a camp director (twenty years at Kings Arrow Ranch with exposure to 8,000 campers), who has seen the jetsam and flotsam of ruined children wash up on our "camp shores" from the shipwrecked families that abound in our culture.

I write to you as a father who failed in my early years as a father. But, I saw my malfeasance, recovered, and made fathering a top priority in my life. I write to you, then, as a rehabilitated dad who studied, practiced, trained, and learned the hard way. I learned many intellectual, academic, theoretical things that wasted my time. But I also learned practical truths that made application reasonable and success possible.

I believe most men are like me and can benefit from a common sense approach that lends itself to easy application and measurable positive results.

I don't know you and probably never will, but if I had the privilege of personally meeting with you and transferring what I think are the essential lessons on fathering, I would tell you that the principles and techniques in this book changed my life. They worked for me. And because I think we are a lot alike in many ways, I predict you will make significant advances in your family shepherding skills if you study this book—especially if you study it with a small team of men.

Wellness Fatherhood

I write on family construction—how to build it right the first time. A primary book on fathering would naturally deal with the ideal family and the fathering techniques that build a healthy stable family. It could not possibly address all of the unique family pathologies to which dysfunctional families are prone. It deals with how to take the essential steps to keep your family well and avoid serious problems on down the line.

Of course, correction and rehabilitation of fathering demands mastering the wellness steps as part of the solution. For serious childhood problems that require more sophisticated therapy and reclamation techniques, I refer you to your pastor or close friends.

If you take fatherhood seriously and study this book with a few other good men, you will capture the essence of fatherhood and master the techniques of basic family shepherding.

Optimistic Fatherhood

Most men share the common trait of feeling guilty after they do serious thinking about their fatherhood performance. Guilt and regret seem almost unavoidable when you compare your track record with the high standards and ideals that many speakers and authors present. Be warned. Anticipate guilt feelings and be prepared to shake them off. The last thing I want is for you to be discouraged or laden with guilt. These morbid shackles have destroyed the efforts of many a good man.

Conviction, however, is another thing. I hope you get your socks convicted off. Conviction points to the future with hope and motivates positive changes. Guilt looks backward and dwells on discouraging negatives. Therefore, acquire conviction and shun guilt.

Be comforted. I will present some pitiful personal illustrations that will make you feel like a superdad by comparison. Most men approach me after a conference and gleefully confide, "Gee, Dave, thanks. I sure learned a lot from your stupid mistakes. You have no idea how much you encouraged me."

Remember, also, that God is on your side. In Jeremiah 29:11, He says, " 'For I know the plans that I have for you,' declares the Lord, 'plans for welfare and not for calamity to give you a future and a hope.' "

Claim this promise for yourself and your family. God wants you to learn from your mistakes and failures and go on to be a successful family shepherd. Discard the past. Don't let it hold you down. You can't change the past, but you can change the future it was headed for. Stop now and make a commitment to follow God's master plan for fatherhood and secure a future of hope and welfare.

Incremental Fatherhood

When I played middle linebacker for the New Orleans Saints, I wanted to make All-Pro; so I figured I needed to become more self-disciplined. If I could discipline myself better, I would condition myself better, recognize offensive formations faster, call audibles more effectively, and attack the point of the ball quicker. I went to a psychiatrist to see whether he could help me.

My shrink told me to relate freely about my childhood. After forty-five minutes, he interrupted me with this question: "Dave, what do you do with your clothes at night?"

Maybe I need to counsel this guy, I thought. "Well," I replied, "being a man of God, I peel 'em off, throw 'em in the air, and where

God wants 'em, He puts 'em. No. Just kidding. Seriously, I don't do anything with my clothes. I just kinda molt and hit the sack."

"Dave," he said, "I want you to go home and discipline yourself about your clothes. Each night this week, hang up what you can and throw the rest in the hamper."

I accepted his challenge, paid his secretary $75, went home, and became the master of my clothes. In one week, I had become the champion of my clothes. Sandy was awed.

The following week, he asked me to talk about my childhood for fifty minutes. Then he asked me, "Dave, what does your car look like?" I took the hint; his secretary took my $75. I went home and sanitized and polished my car.

A week later, he endured my childhood discourse and asked about my desk. I volunteered to clean out my desk with my weed-eater, and his secretary volunteered to take another $75.

This routine went on for another seven weeks before I got a flash of insight and realized that he was charging me $75 a week just to assign me one area of my life at a time to get me fixed up. For only $750, I learned the secret of self-improvement: ONE PLAY AT A TIME. Don't try to do it all at once. Just run one play until you get it down, then go on to the next.

Beware of instantaneous MEGADAD conversions. No one becomes Superdad overnight. Your family will not enjoy family shepherd whiplash. Just take it easy and try running one play per week. Get into your E-Team huddle, call a play, execute it until you get it down. Then huddle up and call another play. Now, send me $750.

Gratifying Fatherhood
Yes, Leo Tolstoy would start his book differently in the twilight of the twentieth century. He would have probably written: All happy families resemble one another. Most unhappy families are unhappy in the throes of paternal deprivation.

As I look back over the last twenty-two years, my natural tendency is to focus on the mistakes I made with Helen and Brandon. In my studies and counseling, I often think, "Wow! If I had only known this twenty years ago!" Or, "Gosh! Think how much better off Helen and Brandon would be if only I had done this (or not done that)!" I never think, "I spent too much time with my kids" or, "The quality of my life was diminished because of the distraction of my children."

No. Men don't feel good about their lives when they poorly father their children. No matter how successful the terms of the world measure a man, he will not feel significant unless he has fathered with dignity and excellence.

On the other hand, there is no greater sensation a man can ever feel than the gratification that comes when fathering is done well.

I admire my good friend, Dr. Barry Sorrells, former Chief Surgeon of Baptist Hospital in Little Rock, Arkansas. I wish more men could say what Barry said after he lost his oldest son, Barry Jr., in a tragic airplane crash. Not many men can make this world class statement: "No regrets. Dave, I look back over my time with my son and have no regrets. I was the best father I could be. I have no regrets."

Prophetic Fatherhood
The secret motivation I have for dedicating my life to the cause of fatherhood lies in the words written by a fatherhood advocate, one of the earliest fathers, hundreds of years before Christ was born. Malachi received a special message about one of the signs to look for that would indicate the coming of the Messiah. Malachi 4:5-6: "Behold, I am going to send you Elijah the prophet before the coming of the great and terrible Day of the Lord. And he will restore the hearts of the fathers to their children, and the hearts of the children to their fathers, lest I come and smite the land with a curse."

This passage refers to that period of time just before Christ returns as conquering King, still yet to happen. Malachi says there will be a revival of fatherhood.

Therefore, I know that all of us — and there are many of us called to promote fatherhood — have the privilege of working directly on a task actually predicted thousands of years ago to happen in the future. It gives me a sense of destiny. And of confidence. I challenge you to join the cause and be a part of this prophetic movement.

The Wisdom
of Fatherhood

Chapter One
Father Power

"The principal danger to fatherhood today is that fathers do not have the vital sense of father power that they have had in the past. Because of a host of pressures from society, the father has lost the confidence that he is naturally important to his children—that he has the power to affect children, guide them, help them grow. He isn't confident that fatherhood is a basic part of being masculine and the legitimate focus of his life."
—Dr. Henry Biller

We buried Dad, Major Amos E. Simmons (Ret.), in the family cemetery by a country road about one-half mile from where he was born and raised. The soldiers came from Ft. Polk, draped an American flag over his silver-blue casket, and saluted him with rifle fire. A solitary trooper played taps on his bugle. We prayed. I cried.

I cried because I had loved him for only three years. I had hated him for twenty-five years and had liked him for eight years. I felt cheated. I wanted my dad back. We were busy building good memories to replace the painful ones.

They were painful because he did not know much about fathering, and I did not know much about "sonning." It took me thirty-three years to mature enough to make the effort to understand Dad and start being a good son.

THE AMOS CONNECTION

The Amos Generation
He was born into a family of lumberjacks in Tangipahoe Parish, Louisiana. He left home at seventeen, joined the army as a private,

and with several battlefield promotions and hard work, worked his way up to the rank of major. He was on the administrative staff of General George S. Patton, Commander of the Third Army during World War II. He was a powerful man: tall, stiff-backed, with ice blue eyes and prematurely snow-white hair. He was the arm wrestling champ of several army bases.

But he had doubts about his ability to raise a son. I now understand why. His father, "ole man" Luther, had the awesome job of keeping the family of nine children together during the depression without a wife. Dad's mother died when he was four years old. Times were tough, men were tough, and they weren't soft on kids. My grandfather once ran a 1927 Ford Model T touring car into the back of one of his logging trucks and tore the radiator loose. He drove it home anyway, parked it, got an ax, and chopped it to pieces. That was the way he did things, and that was the way he raised kids.

I've heard that he beat my dad the most because he was the biggest and bellowed the loudest. One gruesome habit of "ole man" Luther was to wait until the family had company and call my dad in and whip him in front of everybody. "Ole man" Luther kept a selection of seasoned hickory switches in the gun rack by the front door for easy access. Not noted for his delicate touch, he did well, nevertheless, to squeeze nine kids through childhood during the Great Depression.

The Amos Technique

With a track record of fathering like this one in his blood, no wonder Dad was worried about how he was going to raise me. He had three goals: he wanted me to love him, to be hard-nosed and aggressive, and to be a high achiever. His heart was right. His intentions were OK. But his philosophy and methodology were a little suspect. From the moment I was born, he had me in a training program.

To make me tough, he would walk me out to the playground and actually pick fights for me. I remember once in Berlin, Germany Dad looked out the window and saw three German boys walking by our house. He ran over, threw open the door and said, "Get out there and whip those boys, and if you don't, I'm going to whip you."

Father Power

To develop me into an outstanding achiever, he employed several techniques. A favorite was to set impossible goals. One time, while we were living in Ft. Riley, Kansas, I got a bicycle for Christmas. It came unassembled, and Dad said, "Son, you wanna ride it? Put it together." He gave me the parts, the tools, and the directions. I couldn't read yet, so I did the best I could by looking at the pictures. Shortly, I was hopelessly lost and started crying. He brusquely knocked me aside and said, "Get away, stupid, I knew you couldn't do it." His theory was that if I had such high goals, I could never accomplish them, and in frustration, I would make even greater efforts to achieve. The key was to keep me on the leading edge of a high intensity effort.

A variation of this technique was to nudge the goals higher if I started to get close. I didn't start playing football until my junior year at Austin High in El Paso, Texas. Dad challenged me to make the starting team my first year. I did. Then he challenged me to make All-District. I did. Then, after the season was over, he wanted to know why I didn't make All-State.

Every ball game I ever played in high school, I played twice: once at the stadium or gym and then again at home in the backyard. Dad would get me out back and go over every mistake I made. It didn't matter how bruised and bleeding I was; every game presented more opportunities to learn from mistakes. This technique of improving was by focusing on the negatives. Concentrate on the mistakes. The idea was to never let me think I did a good job because I might relax. Don't ever get satisfied. Don't let up. The pack will catch up.

What if there are no negatives to focus on? What if you overcome mistakes, do a great job, and accomplish a significant goal? Then you simply get negative about the goal. You ridicule the accomplishment. I made several second string All-American teams my junior year at Georgia Tech, and Dad wanted to know why I didn't make first team on every All-American team. The St. Louis Cardinals drafted me in the second round, and Dad wanted to know what it felt like to be only second. (Joe Namath was their first-round choice.) I played in three college All-Star games, was a cocaptain of the South Team in the Senior Bowl, and was linebacker with Dick Butkus in the Chicago All-Star game, and Dad was curious as to why they interviewed him at halftime on national TV and not me.

Another ploy to make me successful was to goad me into a frenzied temper tantrum and, flying high on an adrenaline overdose, I could blast through any barrier to new heights. Just pitch a fit. Get mad. Go crazy. It didn't matter who or what I got mad at. The trick was to get me angry at myself, at him, or anything, and then redirect my fury toward my task. (If only I had an ax, I could chop a Model T to pieces.)

The Amos Project

I had three choices why I could feel like a failure: because I did not reach impossible goals; because the goals I did reach were not significant; or because I acted so silly in the process. In any case, I was bound to feel like a failure. I never experienced the feelings of success. I was in a lot of pain, and I associated this pain with my dad.

I seethed with bitterness and rebellion toward Dad. I could not confront him openly (I tried once and he broke my nose), so I struck back in sneaky ways that I couldn't get caught and punished for. I deliberately sabotaged things and failed at things just to watch him blow up. I withheld the only things Dad needed from me: love and respect. I never told him I loved or respected him, and I never asked for advice or went to him with a problem. I deprived him of all the rewards of fatherhood.

My greatest blow of revenge on Dad came when I chose where to play college football. I had scholarship offers from all over the nation, including his beloved LSU and West Point, either of which would have been his crowning reward for fatherhood. I decided to play for coach Bobby Dodd at Georgia Tech because it was 1,500 miles from him. I had to get away from him. I didn't want him to ever see me play another ball game. He saw only three of my college games in four years. This racked his soul.

But I didn't leave Dad behind when I left home, and he didn't leave me behind when he died. Our fathers never leave us. They hang around in our minds for the rest of our lives, and their voices keep repeating all the things we heard as we grew up.

To this day, I can't capture the feeling of a job well done. I constantly focus on my mistakes and am negative toward all that I do. I set goals too high and fail. I sabotage things and fail. I get angry and emotional, and I fail. I resent and rebel against authority and fail. I go to ridiculous lengths to reach perfection in order to get compliments and recognition for my work, but then I can't accept appreciation and feel like a failure. I carry the voice of Major Amos E. Simmons, the Commander, in my heart. He speaks to me through my emotions and I still believe everything he told me. Even though all the facts say I am successful, my emotions convince me that I am a failure. My dad still exercises formidable power in my life.

Nothing is more powerful in a person's life than a father. Father power can be positive or negative; it can make the difference between success and failure. Negative father power left me twisted and bent. Not only did it disable me, but I saw the same destructive father power flowing from me to my children. "Ole man" John gave it to "ole man" Luther, who passed it on to Amos, who deposited it in me, and I am determined to stop the flow. The cycle must be broken.

I realized I needed to convert destructive father power into constructive father power. To start this conversion process, I had to deal with Dad. With a supporting wife and some professional counseling, I recognized my own share of the fault and took responsibility for it. It wasn't until I was 33 years old that I finally matured enough to understand Dad and realize that Dad did love me. No father ever loved a son more. He was proud of me, amazed even, and no one wanted to have a son love him back as much as he did. He simply did not know how to express his love and pride. He was severely handicapped: no mother, childhood lumberjack, battlefield trauma, army life, and his dad chopped up cars and abused him. All he knew about fathering had been passed down through the Simmons' bloodline. The cycle at work.

I saw that Dad hated his imperfections and mistakes more than I did. He was a prisoner trapped behind his own personality and didn't know how to break out. HE WANTED TO BREAK THE CYCLE TOO. And he tried. He just never learned how. He did not know how to be a family shepherd and transfer positive father power.

If we were ever to salvage our relationship, I had to take the initiative. I experimented with different techniques on love and discovered some amazingly successful principles that are covered in chapter 7. As a result of these secret love techniques, Dad and I inaugurated a great love relationship that thrived until his death.

Our love grew. I looked forward to going home. I would drive up, honk the horn, get out of the car, and Dad would come out, grab me in a smothering bear hug and lift me right off the ground. He would tell me how good is was to see me and say, "Son, I sure love you and am proud of you."

We were breaking the cycle. You can't break the cycle at the link between you and your children. You must go back and break the cycle at the link between you and your dad. I am convinced that if you do not repair your paternal cords, you will never be fully released to give your own children all that you could. The first step in providing my children with positive, constructive father power is to get things right with my dad. Then, I can begin to be a balanced family shepherd.

However, there is never a clean break in the cycle. There is a turbulent generation to work through. One man in the genealogy chain will have to pay the transition costs. He will struggle with the massive task of breaking up the old patterns that he received from his early family influence and his genetic endowment. He will also struggle with the massive task of grafting in new ones that he takes the initiative to search out and absorb. It will take at least one generation to complete the break, sometimes two. It requires enormous energy and commitment to shift from negative to positive father power in a family line.

Unfortunately, shifting from positive to negative father power is like breathing: it is natural, automatic, and anyone can take in fresh air and exhale dead air without even thinking about it. An old American proverb: "From shirt sleeves to tuxedo in two generations and back again in one." It is a laborious climb up the ladder and a slick ride down. I wish I could tell you that it has been easy for me and that overnight I experienced startling success simply by willing it. But in my life, the pendulum makes wide swings: I win lopsided victories and lose with great flourish.

The Amos Cycle
Take Brandon for instance. Brandon went out for basketball in the eighth grade and made the team. I went bananas. My boy! Playing

ball! Big game tonight! I showed up thirty minutes before warm-ups and staked out a section for me and my photography equipment. I scouted the gym to locate the best camera angles, erected my tripod, arranged my telephoto lenses, and started drawing up my rebound charts and shot charts.

I took some magnificent photos during warm-ups. Luckily, I was also able to slip the coach a few last minute strategy ideas before the tip-off. It was loads of fun being a typical father in the stands.

The game started, and it didn't take long before I put down my cameras. I folded my tripod and forgot about the rebound and shot charts. I got depressed and angry. Brandon was a spectacular flop.

Oh, he got lots of rebounds and points, but it was evident that he was out there fooling around trying to have fun. He acted as if it were a sport or recreational game. He didn't crash the boards for rebounds. He never once dived for a loose ball. He loped around impervious to fast breaks, filling lanes, and following shots. I was mortified. Humiliated! He acted as if he didn't know he had to go out and win and take a shot at the record books. He was my son. He was representing me out there.

I could not wait to get him in the car after the game. With my wife Sandy, sitting quietly in the front seat, I yelled at him all the way home, "Where is your pride, boy? Don't you care? You didn't hustle. You didn't try. You were terrible. I'll tell you what: I don't care what your coach says, what you say, or what the other players say—you are off the team if I ever again catch you not giving it all you've got. Either you hustle or you quit."

We drove up our driveway, and when I got out, I saw Brandon sitting in the backseat, quietly crying. I walked up the stairs, opened the door, and stepped back to let Sandy in. As she walked by, she shot me a smoldering glance and said one word, a thunderbolt word that electrified my heart... "Amos!"

My mouth fell open with a shock. I couldn't believe it. She was right. After all those years with my dad harping on me about sports, I was doing the same thing to my son, and I KNEW BETTER AND HAD SWORN THAT I WOULD NEVER DO TO MY SON WHAT MY DAD DID TO ME. I was just like Amos. Destructive father power bleeds through generation after generation. All I had to do to fail was relax and do what came naturally. It takes commitment and exertion over the long haul to convert father power to an asset. We have enough 100-yard-dash dads: we need more cross country fathers. The cycle must be broken.

THE FOURTH GENERATION RULE

Your influence goes far beyond the immediate members of your family and their lifetimes. You will have a dynamic impact on your descendants for as far as four generations. You will help shape the generation that will provide the leadership for the middle of the *twenty-second century.*

Who and how you are determines the character of your family which influences how your children turn out, who they marry, the health of their families and how their children turn out. You will be felt down through the generations just like Major Amos E. Simmons will impact his descendants for four generations. This is true because of the Fourth Generation Rule which I will explain using the Simmons' bloodlines.

Amos Will Hang Around for Generations

They buried my dad with a flag, a rifle salute, a lonely, solitary bugle tune, and a son saturated with regret. But that wasn't the end of my dad. He is still very much around. Amos lives on in me because of father power. I constantly hear Dad whispering his old messages to my inner soul. He abides in Helen and Brandon as well and will continue to manifest himself as he flows downstream in his genetic bloodline.

There is a lot of ole Amos in me and I bet you have noticed a lot of your dad in you. If you haven't, your wife will gladly point it out to you. Your dad had an incredible impact on your life. Because of father power, we all tote our dads around inside for the rest of our lives.

Not only do we observe father power at work in our families, we find it documented in Genesis, the first book of the Bible. It shows up in the dynamics of the very first family.

"When Adam had lived one hundred and thirty years, he became the father of a son in his own likeness, according to his image, and named him Seth." Genesis 5:3.

This verse tells us that Adam demonstrated the effects of father power when he produced a son named Seth who bore his likeness and image. The words likeness and image refer to far more than a physical resemblance: they allude to personality traits, behavior patterns and character qualities. Father power transferred the essence of Adam into his child and has done the same in every generational transfer since.

Positive and Negative Father Power

Father power strikes deeper than one generation. It not only injects you into your children, it projects you through your genetic lines as far down as your fourth generation.

The Fourth Generation Rule is derived from two passages but there is a disturbing feature about it: it is value-free. It does not distinguish between good and evil. The energy of father power picks up the heart of a man, good or evil, and hurtles it down through his seed. So father power can be negative or positive. The Bible specifically describes each:

Negative Father Power

Yet He [God] will by no means leave the guilty unpunished, visiting the iniquity of fathers on the children and on the grandchildren to the third and fourth generations.

Exodus 34:7

Positive Father Power

For He established a testimony in Jacob, and appointed a law in Israel, which He commanded our fathers, that they should teach them to their children:
    That the generation to come might know, even the children yet born, that they may arise and tell them to their children.

Psalm 78:5-6

Father power, therefore, can act as a negative force or a positive force. A father can send the light of God down through the next four generations, or he can send the darkness of sin down through the next four generations.

God wants His truth and light to pass from one generation to another so He established an automatic device to fit into the family to insure His wishes. He created father power with the strength to span four generations and inserted it into the hearts of fathers. Father power is like a tool, a claw hammer, to extract the truth about God out of one generation and pound it into the next generation, and the third and the fourth.

This process works beautifully when the father is a man of God. Take, for instance, the case study of Jonathan Edwards and the impact he had on a span of four generations (a 4-G Span). His fatherhood left a legacy of 300 clergymen, missionaries, and theology professors, 120 college professors, 110 lawyers, 30 judges, 60 authors of books, 14 university presidents, 3 United States Congressmen, and one Vice President of the United States. The legacy this one man left can give us a perspective of the significance of the Fourth Generation Rule when used in a positive way.

On the other hand, great destruction can come down through the generations when negative father power is used. For example, consider the progeny of one man who lived in New York City, Max Jukes (from whose name the term "juke" was coined which means to fake or deceive). Among his known descendants, 1,200 were researched and here is his negative father power legacy: 310 were vagrants, 440 had their lives physically wrecked by debauchery and uncleanliness, 130 were sent to prison for an average of 13 years each, 7 were murderers, 100 were alcoholics, 60 were habitual thieves, and there were 190 prostitutes. They collectively cost the state of New York over $1.2 million in a 4-G Span that overlapped the 1700s and 1800s.

The Scope of Father Power

With these documented examples of father power in action, I am convinced that the most important contribution I make to the world will not be what I do with my life but what my next few generations do with their lives as a result of my influence. Consider now yourself and the legacy you will leave over the next 4-G Span. What kind of legacy will father power extract from you and inject into the next four generations? How significant does this make your performance as a father? What kind of world will your descendants inherit in the twenty-second century?

To gain a dramatic perspective of the magnitude of your fatherhood and how strategic your legacy over the next four generations is, take the Simmons family as an example and examine the 4-G Span issuing forth from me into the future and view it with the 4-G Span beginning with my dad and going backward.

The Civil War Fourth Generation Span

My dad, Amos Simmons, was the fourth generation out of John Richardson Simmons (1816–1885) who reached his peak during the War between the States. The following table shows John Richardson Simmons' "4-G Span" and the major events that occurred over this single 4-G Span.

The Fourth Generation Span of John Richardson Simmons: 1816–1885		
1st Generation	1846–1904	Thomas Jefferson Simmons
2nd Generation	1867–1927	John Thomas Simmons
3rd Generation	1889–1969	Luther Franklin Simmons
4th Generation	1922–1978	Amos Eldredge Simmons

These men witnessed profound events during their "4-G Span." Our nation fought the War between the States, World War I, World War II, the Korean Conflict and the Vietnam War. They saw the birth of totalitarianistic communism and its attempt to break up and swallow the Western empires. The United States cut its moorings as a republic (law is king) and started drifting into a democracy (man is king) in its long slide toward socialism (the elite is king). The family splintered, and the individual became the new political/cultural unit — adolescence as a class was invented and women defined themselves as a distinctive group for legislative purposes.

Men turned their hearts away from their families as their primary priority and the nuclear family began to wobble. To rescue the family, an army of social scientists, in league with a growing welfare state, marched on the scene and began to tinker with the institution of the family and gender roles. The nuclear family as a norm vanished and its functions (education, worship, economic production, welfare, and charity) were assumed by secondary institutions. The pathology of the family increased and the social scientists and socialists pronounced the need for more federal funding for research to solve the problems they themselves were promulgating.

The notion that the Bible is merely a rendering of men's perception of God and not explicitly God's accurate, infallible revelation to man crept out of Europe's theological centers, invaded American mainline seminaries, and finally worked its way out into the mainstream of all denominations, separating Christians into warring camps of moderates (liberals) and conservatives (fundamentalists).

The Star Wars Fourth Generation Span

I was born August 3, 1943 and, since a man achieves the peak of his leadership/wisdom/governing powers between 60 and 70 years of age, I will reach the pinnacle of my influence between the years of 2000–2015. The tables below show the years of peak influence of my descendants and the extent of the Fourth Generation Rule in my descendants. If you are my age, look at this chart on our legacy to the twenty-second century.

The Fourth Generation Span of My Generation	
Generation	Window of Peak Influence
Our Generation	2000–2015
Our Children	2030–2045
Our Grandchildren	2060–2080
Our Great-Grandchildren	2095–2115
Our Great-Great-Grandchildren	2130–2150

Our fourth generation will be commanding the areas of government, business, commerce, and religion when the human race enters the twenty-second century after Christ. Think of it: you will leave your mark on the leaders of the twenty-second century.

All in all, the "4-G Span" that ended with my dad saw incredible changes. Their "4-G Span" convinces me that the only thing we can know for sure about the events of the next "4-G Span" is that all trends will continue; only the pace will change—it will accelerate. And there will be new problems our nation has never faced before during the next four generations: serious fossil fuel depletion, ozone dissipation and world warming trends, possible terrorists' wielding of nuclear power, the ever-creeping socialist state, the point of no return on deficit government spending, economic isolationism, AIDS, and other problems that we can't begin to imagine.

How will the next generation respond to these problems? Take a look at the nearest high school and analyze the political mind-set and social responsibility quotient of the average high school student. How are they handling their own set of problems—drugs, alcohol, sex, and suicide? What kind of education are they getting? What kind of valueless and situational ethics and morals are they being taught? What are they learning about capital formation, wealth production and re-distribution, and management and economic principles? What kind of political indoctrination are they bombarded with from the media.

Here's a sobering thought: when all the children who are products from today's dysfunctional families start having children, what kind of family lives will they establish? What kind of child products do you think they will produce? What will the families of their grandchildren be like? What kind of people and culture will their great-grandchildren create?

Few fathers have stopped to consider these issues. When you contemplate the nature of the world environment that your next four generations of descendants must face, how do you feel about the task of child-raising?

When your little baby came along, did you think your job consisted merely of feeding, clothing, and getting him off to school, and married? Well, there's a little more to it than that. You, sir, will be held responsible for equipping your children to raise the grandparents of the leaders of the twenty-second century.

This means that the most important and significant task of your life is to perform the functions of fatherhood with excellence. You were called to the profession of fatherhood. You and I are members of the Brotherhood of Fatherhood. We must do whatever it takes to allow father power to send a positive influence down to the leaders of the twenty-second century.

ESTABLISH YOUR DYNASTY

Men, we cannot allow the use of negative father power to continue to muddy the stream of our descendants. We must each guard our own lives and protect our children from the devastating effects. Our nation doesn't need any more phantom fathers and domino dads. We need to take the initiative and start now to spawn a Christian dynasty of effective family shepherds down through the generations.

Some Must Continue the Cycle

Many of us must continue the cycle. For those who had a great family shepherd, you need to continue the great legacy you inherited.

To the rest of us, however, life is not fair. James Dobson got all the luck. Every time I hear him or read him, he always talks about his fantastic world class dad. It's "Dad this" and "Dad that." It's not fair.

Seriously, even though I don't personally know either man, I love Dr. Dobson, but I love Ole Man Dobson even more. What an outstanding father. Just think of the job he did with his son. Through his son, Ole Man Dobson is reaching the world for building better families.

I admire the Dobson family. We need millions of fathers like Old Man Dobson. James Junior came out of his family and hit the ground running. He leaped immediately into the battle because he was mentally and emotionally equipped with great maturity and functioned as an extremely useful tool in God's hands.

We cannot afford more situations like me: I came out of a family crippled and not fit for service. It took God seventeen years of working on me day and night deep in the pine forest (the wilderness) of southern Mississippi before I became qualified for service. We can't afford any more seventeen-year gaps between the generations. Things are moving too fast. The situation is too critical. You need to train your troops and get them on the field when they emerge from your family. Initial training is far more effective than rehabilitation and reclamation projects like me.

Some Must Break the Cycle
Some of us need to break the cycle. We need to start a new legacy. And it can be done!

When we moved to Little Rock in 1983, Brandon tried out for the junior high football team, and he made it. He came home and made the tragic announcement that he was a quarterback. This news was terrible. As an old linebacker, I hate quarterbacks.

Anyway, the kid had an arm. He could fire the ball.

The season started, and he came out passing. He did great. He moved the team right down the field, and I was proud. That was my boy out there.

About the fourth game, however, he broke down and went to pieces. He played terrible. He fumbled the snap several times; he tossed a couple of pitchouts over the halfback's head and effortlessly completed interceptions. He single-handedly lost the game for us.

In the stands, I began to get embarrassed. Then disgusted. Finally, I got so angry that, at halftime, I sat back, folded my arms across my chest, and started getting psyched up.

Then, all of a sudden, I realized what was happening. I stopped and thought of Major Amos. I thought of myself and the fourth generation rule. I remembered I wanted to break the cycle and not do what was so natural for me to do. So, I prayed.

During the second half, Brandon played no better. But I deliberately concentrated on my attitude and emotions. I forced myself to withdraw emotionally from the game. I backed out of the contest and prevented myself from getting psyched up. I prepared myself for my meeting with Brandon after the game.

The game was a lopsided catastrophe. Sandy, Helen, and I waited in the car for Brandon to come out of the locker room. The car was blanketed in silence. Brandon eventually shuffled out and climbed into the backseat.

We drove homeward and eventually came to our street. I asked the girls if they wanted to go home or, as was our custom, drive on into Little Rock and get some frozen yogurt. Since they wanted to go home, I wheeled up our driveway and dropped them off.

Brandon and I drove to town, parked, walked into the store, got our frozen yogurt and sat down. Not a word had passed. When we were almost done, Brandon put down his spoon, looked searchingly at me, and asked, "Dad, why are you doing this?"

I said, "Well, Son, I'll tell ya. I just want you to know that I love you and accept you totally. Just as you are. I love you whether you're the football hero or whether you play terrible. I love you because you're Brandon and not because you're number ten on the football squad."

Brandon's face lit up, and he burst out with all kinds of comments about the game. He eventually got around to the big question: "Come on, Dad. Tell me. What did you really think of the game? Tell me how you really think I did."

Fantastic, I thought. *Now, he's really asking for it. I can blast him now!* But I didn't. I paused and asked him, "Well, Brandon, what do you think? How did you play?"

And he proceeded to tell me exactly how he did. He listed every mistake and explained how he made it and what he needed to do to correct it. He understood it all.

Men, we don't need to follow our kids around pointing out every mistake or informing them of all their shortcomings. They know. They are quite aware. They need a family shepherd dedicated to building them up and encouraging them. One who believes in them and will bring out the best in them.

Later, as we drove home, Brandon's spirits soared, and he got carried away. Before I knew it, he said something that I will never forget. It was the highest compliment I have ever received.

"Dad, you know what I wish?" he asked. "I wish you and me could be on the same team. Wouldn't it be great if, on offense, I could be the quarterback, and you could be the tight end, and, on defense, we could both be linebackers together? Dad, I wish we could play on the same high school team, then play at Georgia Tech together and go on and play for the Dallas Cowboys. Dad, I sure wish we could play on the same team."

After a long pause, Brandon must have thought he might have

offended me because he rushed in with this consoling disclaimer: "But, Dad, even if we were brothers, I would still want you for a dad!"

He wanted us to play on the same team. I think back to August of 1961, when a young man left El Paso, Texas by train and traveled all the way to Georgia Tech in Atlanta to get as far away from his dad as possible to play college football. He didn't want his dad in the same state during a football game! Now comes Brandon one generation later, and he wants his dad in the same huddle.

Father power. Father power can be negative or positive. It affects generations. Who and what you are will be stamped into your children and will be passed down through the generations, to the second, third, and fourth generations.

Men, I proclaim to you that the cycle can be broken. You can stop a negative legacy and initiate a positive legacy. The cycle can be broken.

E-TEAM HUDDLE GUIDE
CHAPTER ONE: FATHER POWER

Dad, the Family Shepherd
E-TEAM

> After coffee and fellowship, allow each man to cover the following:
> 1. Tell the E-Team your name, occupation, and phone number.
> 2. Tell the E-Team your wife's name and the names and ages of your children. Record their family information below.

Team Member	His Wife	Phone	Children
1. _____	_____	Of _____	_____
		Ho _____	
2. _____	_____	Of _____	_____
		Ho _____	
3. _____	_____	Of _____	_____
		Ho _____	
4. _____	_____	Of _____	_____
		Ho _____	
5. _____	_____	Of _____	_____
		Ho _____	
6. _____	_____	Of _____	_____
		Ho _____	

E-TEAM DISCUSSION
50–60 minutes

> This part allows you to discuss the key concepts in this chapter and relate them to your individual lives. Be sure to leave time to complete the Workout and Encouragement sections.

THE PRINCIPLES (Check the text for help)
1. In your opinion, what is the most interesting idea in this chapter?
2. What is the purpose of father power?
3. How does the Fourth Generation Rule work?

THE IMPLICATIONS: (Why are these ideas significant?)
4. Discuss the importance of fatherhood in light of the positive and negative aspect of father power.
5. How have you seen these principles at work in our nation?

THE APPLICATION (How do these ideas affect me?)
6. Tell the E-Team about your father.
7. Tell the E-Team how your father has affected your fathering style.

E-TEAM WORKOUT
10–15 minutes

Allow each man to choose one of the project options (plays) to perform during the week. If so desired, design your own project. Note: it is essential that each man leave having made a definite commitment to a specific project.

1st PLAY:
Make an appointment with your dad and discuss Father Power and the Fourth Generation Rule.

2nd PLAY:
Make an appointment with your wife and tell her all about your father. Ask her to tell you all about her father. Discuss the principle of Father Power and the Fourth Generation Rule with her.

3rd PLAY:
Get alone with God and talk to Him about your father and your fathering style. Ask for insight into the dynamics of your family and wisdom to provide quality leadership in your home.

E-TEAM ENCOURAGEMENT
5–10 minutes

Close the meeting in prayer for each other and your families. Include in your prayer a specific request for spiritual power to successfully complete your project.

BREAK THE HUDDLE, GO HOME AND RUN THE PLAY!

Chapter Two
Family Forces

"All family members, offspring and parents, are
caught up in reciprocal victimizing and rescuing
processes in which they are all
tragically enmeshed."

—*Lyman Wynne*

This man's book is for men, and I see no need to prance around rough and rugged issues. I write to you man-to-man and tell you things I would say if we were sitting down and having a cup of coffee together. Try to imagine this is not a book but you and I having a serious talk about sobering issues. I won't pull any punches, and I won't waste your time.

This next story is tragic but true, and it opens the window on some deep and personal secrets of a troubled family. It's in the book to show you how bad things can get and still turn out OK.

THE RELUCTANT SEDUCTION

Down in the West Texas town of El Paso, a boy's mother found his *Playboy* magazines hidden in a cowboy boot box in his bedroom. The mother, an old-fashioned virtuous woman of great character and integrity, confronted her son, Alan, who thereupon was filled with extreme shame and embarrassment. Alan could not look his mother in the eye for weeks. To have her know just crushed him. When she told his father, he was crushed a lot more, but the incident apparently blew over.

A few months later, the mother left town for a week to visit her parents back East. Meanwhile, the father had been pondering the typical symptoms of adolescence in his fourteen-year-old son and determined that, since the boy was getting interested in girls, it was time to perform his fatherly function and equip the boy: teach him about sex.

A little father/son talk on the birds and bees? Hardly. The father, being bold and dashing, wanted to equip his boy properly. Why wimp around? Let's get to it. So, what do you do in a high desert town on the Mexican border? The dad decided to help his son ease out of boyhood and into manhood by taking him to a whorehouse.

The father loaded the boy into the car and drove off across the Rio Grande to do his duty to educate his son. In a few moments, the father told the boy where they were headed, and the boy's stomach knotted up with fear and anxiety. When they arrived, it was noisy and gaudy. A musty aroma that smelled like a mop bucket carried about the sharper odors of stale alcohol and tobacco smoke.

The boy sat self-consciously at a two-chair table in a dark corner. His eyes were cast down from a pale face wet with sweat. He watched furtively as his father scouted out the women and made the arrangements. His father came to fetch him, and the boy pleaded to cancel the nightmare and go back home. The dad said, "No, Son, you're getting to be a man and it's time."

After the man pushed his boy toward the bar, a smiling woman led him by the hand down a long hallway. At the end of the hall sat an ancient bedraggled woman, the nurse, who administered a perfunctory "inspection" of the boy, and then he was in a small room with the door shut. The girl began to undress and get ready. Alan just stood and gaped. The girl waited. After an eternity of degrading silence, Alan blurted out that he didn't really want to do anything. Maybe just talk.

The boy stood with his back pressed against the door while the girl coyly tried to coax the boy to accept her delights. The boy stood paralyzed and just stared at the naked teenager. She finally understood. She laughed at the boy, leaned back on the bed, and lit a cigarette. After about 15 minutes, she dressed and led the disgraced boy back.

As they drove back home, the father proudly joked around and welcomed his son into the fraternity of manhood. The irony is that the dad actually intended this project to make Alan feel grown-up, proud, and masculine. He thought it would make the boy grateful and bond himself to his boy. For months afterward, the dad would mumble something suggestive and shoot the boy an exaggerated wink as if the boy had been initiated into a privileged order reserved for "real men."

Alan found the experience devastating. The mysterious secrets of the opposite sex fascinated him, and he was just as eager as any young boy to investigate further. However, the suddenness of being tossed into a room with a girl the same age and expected to perform traumatized him. All of the excitement and titillating emotions he had always imagined would be there at that poignant moment did not materialize. Instead, he was shot through with fear, horror, and dread.

And there was something much deeper and more damaging. He felt like a sexual failure and a fool. Rather than a lesson on the male "rites of passage," the experience was supposed to be, it raised more questions than ever about his manhood. He felt guilty and angry for acting like a frightened mouse. Even worse, while he was with the girl, he had not gotten biologically prepared. This failure raised serious questions about his ability to perform like a man. "What's wrong with me?" he thought. "I am a man, and that's what men do? I'm a failure!"

At fourteen, he already had enough trouble trying to figure out what a man is. Now this experience, which was supposed to give him confidence and "blood" him into manhood, only clubbed him into more confusion. The father's attempt to mature the boy and instill masculine pride and confidence backfired. It produced the opposite. The boy felt shamed and confused. He experienced feelings of alienation, and his fear of his impotency grew. He felt as if he didn't measure up. "If Dad knew I didn't do anything," he thought, "he would be disgusted with me."

The father shredded Alan's heart and shattered his confidence in a well-meaning, but perverse attempt to help him into manhood. Instead of feeling manly, the boy felt crushed and lost even more self-esteem because he had struck out one more time in life. I know. That boy was me, David Alan.

Caution: Please don't judge me and my dad too quickly—him for doing it and me for writing about it. Before he died, Dad and I became friends and talked about the whorehouse incident and many other sad events in our life together. We started the long process of confession and forgiveness in an attempt to build a rich fellowship with each other. (This process is described in Volume 2, *Dad the Family Counselor.*)

My purpose for exposing our personal family problems is not to put Dad down but to let others learn from our suffering. If he could have known that he and I could be used in the cause for fatherhood and help families have less suffering by telling our story, I feel sure he would be honored. I have dedicated both our lives to the purpose of uplifting fatherhood.

The case of the reluctant seduction illustrates how a family can get completely off track and use its powerful internal forces in destructive ways. The boy had problems. The father had problems. The family, as a system, had defects. The result: a dysfunctional family that spread pain to all its members and to offspring yet to be born.

A family with troubled people and/or faulty systems that damages its members or seriously hampers them from reaching their full potential is called a dysfunctional family. It contains at least one member who manifests some type of personality disorder that adversely affects other members and disrupts normal healthy operational patterns.

In a functional family, the parents have healthy self-concepts, know how to get their needs met in appropriate ways, and are secure enough to be others-oriented. The children are accepted in the process of maturation. They need not be mature, just on schedule. The environment consists of open, honest, loving communication, and a system of dependable governing and supporting systems.

This chapter deals with the powerful dynamics of family systems and explains forces that work on the family and its members.

THE FAMILY ENTITY

Family historian Ed Shorter suspects that the familiar family forms are phasing out:

> In the 1960s and 1970s the entire structure of the family has begun to shift. The nuclear family is crumbling — to be replaced, I think, by the free floating couple, a marital dyad subject to dramatic fissions and fusions, and without the orbiting satellites of pubertal children, close friends or neighbors . . . just the relatives, hovering in the background, friendly

smiles on their faces (*The Making of the Modern Family* [New York: Basic Books, Inc., 1977], 280).

Abnormal families have become the norm. The average American family hurts so much that one out of every two recent marriages will end in divorce (terminal dysfunction). You, as Dad the Family Shepherd, must master the field of family dynamics and harness this energy to your advantage or risk a family meltdown.

The Family Is an Organism

Each family is a living organism, a unique entity, a personal life-form with a distinct personality and character derived from its two major components—the roles (the people) and the rules (the systems). The family is like an atom: it appears as crisp little parts revolving in tight narrow orbits with no hint of the cataclysmic powers that make things work. A vortex of mysterious forces and undercurrents swirl around the parts and operations of a family.

Each family has its own identity, social system, structure, secrets, rules, ethics, and habits. Each one has its own way of facing adversity, coping with stress, resolving conflict, solving problems, and defending itself. Each one has its own habits of hygiene, recreation, and revitalization. They all age and die in their own way. Together, these elements give the family its own peculiar personality.

The family gets its personality from the members, and the members get their personality from the family. The family is both the cause and the result: The members contribute to the formation of the whole, and the whole clearly marks the individual. A person is not an isolated object, but a part of a set. A man is not an island—he is an archipelago. Family expert John Bradshaw writes:

> Any family system is composed of connecting relationships. To study the family as a system, one must see the various connections between the individualized persons and how they interact. Each person in the system relates to every other one in a similar fashion. Each is partly a whole and wholly a part. Each person within the system has his own unique systemic individuality as well as carrying an imprint of the whole family system. I am my family as well as whatever uniqueness I have actualized as a person. I am individual and group simultaneously (*Bradshaw on: The Family* [Deerfield Beach, Fla.: Health Communications, Inc., 1988], 28).

The Bible emphasizes this principle of oneness and wholeness in Matthew 19:5-6:

"For this cause a man shall leave his father and mother, and shall cleave to his wife; and the two shall become one flesh. Consequently they are no more two, but one flesh. What therefore God has joined together, let no man separate."

A family is like a mobile. All parts are individual pieces that hang together in a delicately balanced equilibrium. Each member is separate and self-contained with unique individuality, but is interconnected with all the others to form a whole. Any force that touches one part causes an energy transfer to all other parts and change results throughout the whole structure. There is no independent action and no isolated unaffected parts. The whole works its will on each part, and each part determines the whole.

The Family Is a Laboratory

The family is a research and development laboratory that introduces brand-new humans to initial training in life and survival skills. The little know-nothings pop into the world totally dependent on other family members to teach them everything they need to know about living. A child arrives with an empty "tool box" and relies on the family to fill up the "tool box" with all the tools required for constructing a healthy productive life. The child needs a whole set of tools and years of experimentation and practice before being unleashed on life.

Children need years of experience with relationship tools. They develop their basic identity from family relationships. They learn about gender roles and marriage systems. They develop social and communication skills.

A family is like a cold-remedy capsule with tiny time-release pellets; it lets out pain in the system in small dosages so the child can learn how to process it. Pain happens. You are born in pain, live in pain, and die in pain. Pain cannot be avoided; pain must be processed. A child is born learning how to deal with pain and experiments furiously in early life to learn how to resolve pain. God designed the family as a laboratory to provide ample painful situations to accommodate the child's need to encounter and experiment with techniques to master pain.

The family exists as a living organism of people and systems with the whole worth more than the sum of the parts. The members help each other reach full potential and fulfillment—when things go right. For many dysfunctional families, however, things go wrong, and the members do great damage to each other.

The Family Is a Matched Set

My son, Brandon, just got his first set of golf clubs last week and promptly challenged me to a golf match. We tied but he was ecstatic because he sliced seven strokes off his lowest previous score. He loves his new sticks and fiddled and fondled them all around the golf course. He got a putter, a pitching wedge, 2 through 9 irons, and three metal woods—a perfect matched set. Each club looked a lot like the others: you could tell they belonged together but each club is a separate unique distinctive club with a specific purpose.

A family is like a matched set of registered golf clubs. They all fit together to form a distinctive set but, at the same time, each member exists and functions as a self-contained entity with a unique purpose. Each member has specific boundaries and protection: they don't lose themselves in each other.

Dysfunctional families blur the distinction between members and clump together in unhealthy co-dependency. They all stay caught up in each other's dysfunctions. The family becomes a glob like the green gelatinous blob from outer space. It rolls over and cannibalizes each new child and becomes a mucus mess.

My plan to beat Brandon in golf is to melt down his new clubs into a single jumbo lumpy club called a basher. He will have to tee-off with it, chip and putt with it. Just put wheels on it and he won't need a golf bag. He will become a dysfunctional duffer.

The Family Is a Church

The family is a miniature body of Christ. Wherever two or more Christians are gathered together, God is present. The New Testament refers to marriage as a picture of the relationship between Christ (the Groom) and the church (the bride). All of the principles of Christian living are to be learned and applied in the family, the primary circle of believers in a person's life. Church leadership is supposed to be field tested in the family before being assigned.

The Family Is a Public Official
The family and its culture have a reciprocal relationship. The family feeds the culture because it is the seedbed for cultural norms, ethics, values, and law. It also acts as public servant to dispense cultural benefits to each individual.

The family is the smallest public unit. It is the building block of society. It makes a culture what it is and transfers civilization on to the next generation. Cotton Mather, the great Puritan, wrote, "Well-ordered families produce a good order in other societies. When families are under an ill discipline, all other societies will be ill-disciplined" (*A Family Well-Ordered* [Boston, 1699], 3). We say it like this: As the family goes, so goes the nation.

THE DYSFUNCTIONAL FAMILY
Dad was the first to break my nose. I was a high school sophomore, and one day my dad had been drinking heavily. He jumped me for talking back to him, threw me down, got me in a headlock, and WHAM! My nose crumpled and left the field of play.

My family of origin is like a broken nose; it bled a lot and didn't smell good.

A Case Study
Dad and I were both born and bred in similar unhealthy family systems (dysfunctional families) that left blistering scars on us. We each developed a serious problem in the deepest core of our being; we each developed an extremely negative shameful self-concept. As a result of this root problem, we both struggled with the character imperfections and chemical dependency that naturally flows out of a shame-based self-concept. We both suffered intensely from the inability to establish healthy intimate relationships. We were so bad, in fact, we didn't even love our loved ones!

My dad broke my nose because he did not learn self-control. He had these deep inner conflicts that switched him into behavior patterns that were destructive to the whole family. He seemed to be open to the influence of powerful internal compulsions and addictions that made him think and act in ways that alienated those closest to him.

He grew up not knowing how to deal with people. He had to

guess as to what is appropriate behavior. Problems arose because he didn't always guess correctly, and, if he did, he didn't have the strength necessary to follow through. He would start withdrawing from the family, become moody, and start drinking, which soon led to unpredictable explosions. Dad was dysfunctional. To control his moods and take away the constant pain of his dreadful self-esteem, he became dependent on alcohol, anger, sorrow, self-pity, and more.

Dad was a victim of abusive parenting. His depression-era, alcoholic father struggled just to keep the eleven-member family alive, and he had little time for family niceties. Ole man Luther frequently abused Dad physically, and Dad's mother died when he was four years old. Because of Dad's difficult childhood and the abuse he suffered, he grew up without his needs for love being met. He suffered from overt and covert rejection, and the toxic level of his shame skyrocketed.

Dad had to spend his energy trying to get his own meganeeds satisfied that should have been met when he was an infant. Consequently, he had little energy left over to fulfill the needs of his children. My dad turned out just like his dad.

And I turned out like Amos. Amos broke more than my nose. He broke my confidence, bruised my heart, and tore my soul. Even though he loved me, he had no clue as to how to communicate his love. He allowed me to think that he hated and rejected me. He constantly told me how inadequate I was. My nickname was "Stupe"—short for stupid—and I heard it often, but especially when it came to sports. I felt abandoned and cut off. The end result: Dad convinced me that I was defective, and I became deeply ashamed of my core person. I developed a shame-based self-concept.

But my mother rescued me. She was perhaps the most outstanding person I have ever met. To me, she represented the epitome of nobility, integrity, duty, and honor. After my abusive bouts with Dad, she would sneak into my room at night to administer succor and solace. She would hold me and try to do damage control. She tried to fill the gaping father-hole as best she could. She saw my soul tearing and tried to stitch me up.

She was *too* good. I now see that, virtuous as her efforts were, they proved unhealthy to me. Mother became my safety net; she always salvaged me. She acted as an anesthetic to numb my pain. I relied on her to fix my suffering and failed to develop the coping skills a young man needs to face the rigors of life. Mother was a classic enabler—in her attempt to help, she inadvertently made it easy for me and Dad to avoid facing and overcoming our problems.

Dad's dependency affected every member of our family. It reached through Dad, grabbed us, and jerked us into unhealthy patterns. We adapted damaging coping mechanisms to adjust to our dysfunctional leader. We became secondary victims of his dependencies—we were co-dependents. Our whole family became trapped in a family system with defective rules and destructive roles.

I grew up thinking that we had the only unhappy family. I thought we had some rare family affliction that all other families were vaccinated against. They all seemed so healthy and happy. It never occurred to me that the greater the dysfunction, the greater the family tries to hide it. Many other families hid their anguish and agony behind carefully constructed masks just like ours.

Dysfunctional Dynamics

There is no such thing as a black sheep in a family. When one member appears dysfunctional, it's only because the rest of the members force him to act out the symptoms.

A family is an organism. When it gets sick, the whole entity is sick, not just one part. Family interconnectedness causes the health of the family and its members to be mutually reciprocal. A person is only as healthy as the family, and the family is only as healthy as all its members. The family can make itself sick or healthy. Family experts document this principle well.

> In family psychiatry a family is not regarded as a background to help the present patient along. Family psychiatry accepts the family itself as the patient, the presenting member being viewed as a sign of family psychopathology. (John Howells, quoted in John Bradshaw, *Bradshaw on: The Family* [Deerfield Beach, Fla.: Health Communications, Inc., 1988], 25.)

For a family to be healthy, it requires the marriage of two healthy mature people with competent operational systems, who bring each newborn child into the family in a healthy way. Dysfunctional families occur when two people bring unresolved childhood conflicts into the marriage with them and cannot establish healthy operational systems. When each child arrives, it occupies a distorted position and gets sucked into faulty relationship patterns.

John Bradshaw says it this way:

> Two people, carrying unresolved conflicts with their parents, get married. As intimacy voltage rises in the marriage, these conflicts become more intense. The partners try to settle these issues with an emotional divorce, "a marked emotional distance." When a child is born, it is "triangled" into the system. The child becomes the focus of the relationship. The child is locked into the system and finds it virtually impossible to leave the family. This child often becomes emotionally disturbed and is the identified patient who is sent to therapy. Actually, the identified patient is only a symptom of the emotionally disturbed marriage. And the patient's so-called emotional illness can be seen and understood only in relation to the emotional system of which he is a part (*Bradshaw on: The Family* [Deerfield Beach, Fla.: Health Communications, Inc., 1988], 25).

This analysis means that anyone in your family with problems is a signal that the whole family needs adjusting. The family organism infects the symptom-member: he or she functions like a thermometer that shows the degree of dysfunction in the family. The rest of the family may appear to be healthy, but sooner or later they all pay the price and keep the presenting problem person from full recovery. They all became sick together; they all need to become well together.

THE VICTIMIZED CHILDREN

My family of origin didn't work right. My father and mother did not establish healthy family relationships. They took some unhealthy personal behaviors and some destructive operational patterns and processed them continuously through the family system. Dad acted out hostility, and mother held it in. It seemed to me that Dad hated me and Mother loved me.

I developed a strong male-avoidance and female-attachment bias because of this punitive-father and pampering-mother dyad. It became difficult for me to relate to both men and women because of my fantasy expectations from each; I expected men to strike me and women to stroke me. All my life, I've had incredible anxiety while near a male authority figure. I've never figured out how to feel right

FUNCTIONAL and DYSFUNCTIONAL FAMILIES CONTRASTED

	FUNCTIONAL FAMILY	DYSFUNCTIONAL FAMILY
SUMMARY	Open, flexible, moderate, boundaries, justice, honor-based self-esteem.	Hidden, rigid, extremes, interference, abuse, and shame-based self-concept.
ROLES: FAMILY MEMBERS	1. Members are real. They are open, transparent, and congruent. What you see is what you get. Reality and truth prevail. 2. Communication on all subjects is welcome, honest, truthful but tactful. 3. Gender roles are firm but flexible. 4. Attitude consists of love, acceptance, forgiveness, encouragement, affirmation, support, and respect. 5. Members know how to deal with pain and get needs met in healthy ways. 6. Members feel significant, belongingness, competency, and a strong sense of identity. 7. Members operate on an honor-based self-concept.	1. Members hide themselves and play roles. They are closed and throw up layers of protection and hiddenness. Deceit and denial prevail. Inconsistency and explosiveness rule the day. 2. Communication is controlled: there are many forbidden subjects. Permission to communicate certain opinions and emotions is not universal and some topics are smothered with untruth and unreality. 3. Gender roles are artificial, rigid, and brittle. 4. Attitude consists of selfishness, suspicion, paranoia, condemnation, blame, punishment, and abuse. 5. Members promote and store pain causing them to look for quick-fix pain killers that lead to addictions, compulsions, and obsessions. 6. Members feel worthless, alone, helpless, and confused about identity. 7. Members operate on a shame-based self-concept.
RULES: FAMILY SYSTEMS	1. Boundaries, authority, policies, and organization are well-defined, just, and understood by all. They are firm and consistent but flexible. This builds stability. 2. Rules promote unity while allowing personal freedom. 3. People are allowed own feelings, opinions, and freedom of expression. 4. Anger, conflict, and difficult decisions are faced and handled quickly, fairly, and effectively with specific systems. 5. Problems and crises are treated as opportunities to grow and are resolved by systems. 6. Family had adequate provisions and equitable distribution of goods and services based on good budget. 7. Family actively involved in public, government, and religious activities and has healthy social intimacy with others.	1. Boundaries, authority, policies, and organization are confusing, unfair, and continually fluctuate. The stated rules do not match the rules in reality. This breeds confusion and fear. 2. The rules make people feel trapped and enmeshed into each other with no healthy personal distinction. 3. People are not allowed own feelings, opinions, and freedom of expression. 4. Anger and conflict either denied or exist as a permanent state of affairs. Resolution seldom achieved. 5. No systematic approach exists for crisis management and decision-making. Power and force determine outcome. This causes blame and demoralization. 6. Goods and resources distributed unfairly and members do not know how to feel content no matter what the level of provision. 7. Family stays withdrawn and hidden from all outsiders and discourages social contact.

or do right around one. I've always been confused about women. It astonishes me whenever a woman doesn't dart in to pamper me like Mom did.

I grew up dysfunctional, just like Dad. I had a dependent/addictive personality and no inner strength or self-control. Outside factors determined my inside feelings and behaviors. I became an alcoholic, and all normal bodily needs screamed for compulsive excessive gratification that I found impossible to delay. I was a food addict. I was prone to depression. I was subject to wild mood swings. I seethed with rage and lost my temper over almost anything. Personal relationships remained a mystery to me. Intimacy was an abstract concept. I lived in a wasteland swept by gusts of pain. Just like Amos. Just like Luther.

Born to Win

It's not an accident that father power and family forces work the way they do. Dysfunctional parents produce troubled children who grow up and start new dysfunctional families because God designed the system to enable parents to pass themselves on. A child picks up the parents' problems automatically in order to learn how to win at life. The child comes with nothing and must figure out a way to stay alive physically and get the four basic psychological needs met.

The four needs and the functions that provide them are listed below:

Psychological Needs	Functions
1. Significance	LOVE
2. Belongingness	BOND
3. Identity	LEAD
4. Competence	EQUIP

To get these psychological needs met, the newborn infant is driven to find and attach to The-One-Who-Knows-About-Life, who can do the four functions. To help the child make the attachment, he is born with two unquenchable drives: to find the Truth and to copy the Truth. The child then begins the duplication process so he or she can eventually reach maturity and perform the four functions for his or her children.

Born to Lose
This survival instinct to attach and copy contains incredible energy, but it has one serious defect: It is value free. It does not distinguish between truth and untruth, good and evil, productive and destructive. It causes a child to blindly attach to whatever parent figure is there—for good or bad. The child then starts copying, for good or bad.

This attachment is called a "fantasy bond" or "irrational love." It is totally blind faith. To the child, the parents are like gods—Shakespeare called parents "God's Lieutenants." They created the child and represent the only link to life. A child is only a moment from death without constant parental care. Therefore, the child will lock onto the parents for dear life.

They will stick to the primary caregivers and totally believe anything the parents say even if it proves to be destructive for them over the long run. Their instinct for short-term survival overrides long-range considerations. Also, they are not mentally and morally mature enough to conceptualize these things and make rational decisions. They operate on blind instinct. Since all parents are human and bear the pain and scars from their childhood, it is impossible for children not to pick up a lot of damaging characteristics.

Born to Fight
This dynamic sets up a process that determines much of the behavior of the child for life. The patterns learned in these first few years become riveted to the steel plate of a child's heart and make up the child's basic self-concept and the manner he or she fights to get his or her needs met. The chart on page 64 shows how the process works.

The parents provide input that is stored in the data base of the mind. These thoughts, when believed, stimulate specific emotions that affect the will. The will, driven by emotions, adopts behaviors that bring the most peace (or less pain).

In a functional family (if there really is one), the process looks like this:

YOUR FAMILY	YOUR SOUL		
MESSAGES	MIND	EMOTIONS	WILL
INPUT	DATA BASE	EMOTIONS	BEHAVIORS

YOUR FAMILY	YOUR SOUL		
GOD'S WORD	MIND	EMOTIONS	WILL
TRUTH	HONOR BASE	PEACE	HEALTHY BEHAVIOR

The parents provide truthful positive data. The child develops an honor-based self-concept and feels good about life. The child adopts constructive behavior patterns and has them reinforced by the parents. Steady progress is made toward maturity.

In a dysfunctional family, the process looks like this:

YOUR FAMILY	YOUR SOUL		
FALSE BELIEFS	MIND	EMOTIONS	WILL
LIES	SHAME BASE	PAIN	DESTRUCTIVE BEHAVIORS

The parents lay down a set of negative false beliefs in the child. The child develops a shame-based self-concept that brings much pain. The child frantically searches for behaviors (defense mechanisms) that will dissolve the pain. With dysfunctional parents, the child picks up a set of distorted tools that only hide the pain instead of processing it. The behavior backfires, and it too becomes a source for more pain.

The False Beliefs
The negative parental input consists of all messages, verbal and nonverbal, that are false and lead to a shame-based self-concept. There are thousands of these negative messages, which Robert

McGee has classified into four major thoughts in his book, *Search for Significance* (Houston: Rapha Publishing, 1990), 40:

1. The Performance Trap: I must meet certain standards in order to feel good about myself. This false belief leads to fear of failure.
2. The Approval Addict: I must be approved (accepted) by certain others to feel good about myself. This leads to fear of rejection.
3. The Blame Game: If I fail, I am unworthy of love and deserve to be punished. This leads to fear of punishment.
4. Shame: I am what I am. I cannot change. I am hopeless. This leads to feelings of shame.

The Pain Pool
When parents pound these false beliefs into children, they become permanently fixed in their thinking, and they establish a shame-based self-concept. This process brings massive pain. Their hearts become a reservoir of pain, a giant pool of stagnant pain that weighs them down and brings sorrow to their lives.

Protection from Pain
Life centers on this pain, and in life the main task centers on making the hurt go away. Unfortunately, attention is not put on an attempt to correct false beliefs that caused the pain. How can children correct their parents—their gods? Instead, temporary painkillers are taken. They are mood altering behaviors that become our inner compulsions and addictions. The pattern is the same, but the destructive behaviors vary widely.

The process of encountering pain and developing dysfunctional behaviors is pictured on page 67.

Family Forces

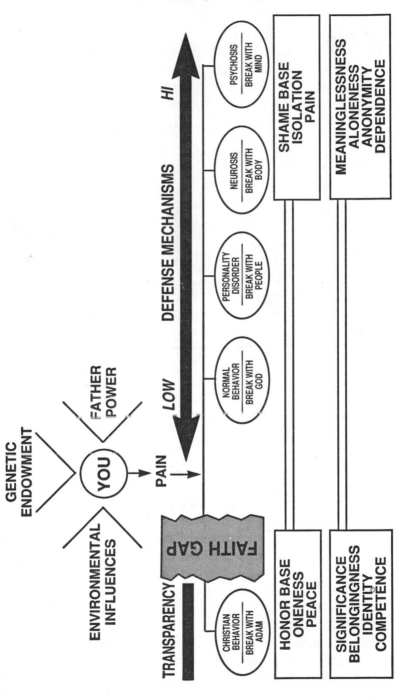

67

Perpetuating Pain

The greater the pain, the more desperate the behavior. As a child moves down the scale to more intense defensive mechanisms, the more dysfunctional he or she becomes. This process brings more rejection, and the pain pool continues to fill.

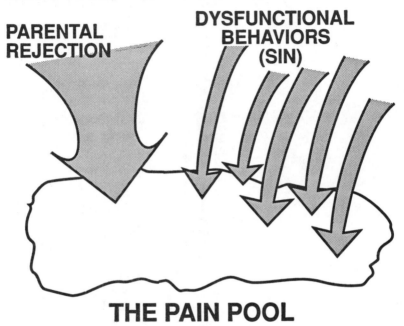

PARENTAL REJECTION

DYSFUNCTIONAL BEHAVIORS (SIN)

THE PAIN POOL

When children get locked into this system and become trapped, they are in bondage.

This model of how a dysfunctional family produces a child with great pain is the story of my life. It happened to me, my dad, and his dad. It traveled down the bloodlines from generation to generation. I was determined to break the cycle and make the dysfunction stop with me and not flow on into the families of my children.

In order to do that, I had to master the secrets of fathering skills, but I also needed something else. Learning techniques was not enough. I needed a new heart. I had to switch out of the old shame-based system and its painful dead end into a completely new honor-based system with hope. How I did it is the subject of the next chapter. Why I did it has a lot to do with a visit to a graveyard.

A MESSAGE FROM THE GRAVE

About a year after my mother died, Sandy and I drove to Chesbrough, Louisiana, to see my relatives and visit my parents' grave site. The private family cemetery, about the size of a basketball court, sits off the road about a hundred yards and is bordered by a thicket of ancient oak and pine trees on the back and a little creek branch on the left.

I circled around my parents' graves, reading the different tombstones, dreading and postponing my confrontation with their marble markers. Finally, I saw the tombstone. A tremendous pain shot through my heart. I felt intense sorrow. It was grief.

There were several reasons why I was stunned by the grief. It was the first time I had been back after Mom's burial. It was the first time I had seen the new double tombstone. It hit me that both parents were gone. I was the designated elder of my line. I grieved because of the good times I would miss: playing golf and watching football with Dad, going fishing with Mom, getting up early with her alone and having her special carrot cake and chicory coffee for breakfast together. It really hurt.

But, do you know what hurt the most? The most painful thing of all was thinking of the good times we could have had if we had only known how to work out of our dysfunction. I also grieved because I had not been a good son. I could have loved Dad earlier and played college ball closer to home. I could have washed his car and mowed the grass just a few times without forcing him to make it an order. I could have called Mom once a week instead of once a month after Dad died. I should have made Mom retire and come live with us and get to know her grandchildren. And a million other things.

As I stood there, I reflected on their difficult, turbulent lives. I thought back as far as I could; and for each Army base we had lived on, I tried to capture a memory of them. The sharpest memories were extreme: either great or tragic. They had lived, struggled, hoped, loved, and faced that brief, awful moment of holocaust before death. And now their remains were deep in the ground before me, still and quiet, separated from each other by two feet of earth; it had all come down through the years to this. What was it all for? What significance is there to life?

What did they leave behind? Strangers lived in the homes they built. People took over their jobs within a day after they died. They left a few personal effects that had value only to their children. They left very little, but they left everything.

They left one thing of eternal significance: their children. They reproduced human life in their own image, in the likeness of Amos and Helen. They left Margaret, Gracella, Douglas, and me. We are what is left of Major and Mrs. Amos E. Simmons, and they are extended even further through their grandchildren, Helen and Brandon, their images carried one step further.

I gained a new awareness of the significance of children and what they represent. I realized, like never before, the importance of being a good son. I kneeled down, put my left hand above Dad's head and my right hand above Mom's head, and looked up. I spoke to them softly:

"Dad and Mom, I'm sorry. Forgive me. I know that I was not a very good son. I know that you are with the Lord now and have perfect peace, and I can never make it up to you. Now that you are gone, the best son I can be is the best father I can be. I promise to shepherd your grandchildren and provide them with positive, constructive father power."

I lingered for a while as the evening shadows glided over the tombstones as if drawing up bedcovers for the night. I reflected on the enigma of death, the purpose of life, and the role of intergenerational relationships.

Father power. You have it. That's not the question. You are stuck with it whether you like it or not. The question is, "What are you going to do with it?" Will you use it in a positive way or a negative way? Will you make fatherhood a priority in your life and establish a positive Christian dynasty that will last into the middle of the twenty-first century? It's your choice. Go for it!

E-TEAM HUDDLE GUIDE
CHAPTER TWO: FAMILY FORCES

E-TEAM REVIEW
10–15 minutes

Dad, the Family Shepherd
E-TEAM

> Allow the men to tell about the results of last week's project. Be firm with each other and encourage everyone to complete the projects. If anyone encountered difficulty or had a family problem arise, pause and pray.

E-TEAM DISCUSSION
50–60 minutes

> This part allows you to discuss the key concepts in this chapter and relate them to your individual lives.

THE PRINCIPLES (Check the text for help.)
1. According to the text, what is a family? Give several answers.
2. Look over the section *The Dysfunctional Family* and answer this: Why is there no such thing as a "black sheep"?
3. Discuss the difference in the way functional and dysfunctional families train a child to get natural needs met.

THE IMPLICATIONS (Why are these ideas significant?)
4. Discuss the importance of fatherhood in light of the information on dysfunctional families.
5. Discuss the effectiveness of most of the institutional and governmental solutions to family and youth problems.
6. What are the symptoms of someone with a large pain pool?

THE APPLICATION (How do these ideas affect me?)
7. Does anyone identify with Dave's pain in his family of origin?
8. What would your wife say about your pain pool? Would she say you had a large one?

E-TEAM WORKOUT
10–15 minutes

Allow each man to choose one of the project options (plays) to perform during the week. If so desired, design your own project. Note: It is essential that each man leave having made a definite commitment to a specific project.

1st PLAY:
Make an appointment with your wife and discuss the concept of the pain pool. Discuss each person in the family in terms of the pain pool. How big a pain pool does each member have? What keeps adding to it? How can you drain some of it away?

2nd PLAY:
Make an appointment with one of the men in the E-Team to get together (try breakfast or lunch) and talk about your families in terms of the characteristics on the functional/dysfunctional chart.

3rd PLAY:
Make an appointment with each child who is old enough and ask them:
1. Is there anything bothering you that you have never told me about that you would like to talk over with me?
2. Are there any problems you would like to discuss with me but feel like it is "against the rules" to talk to me about?
3. What suggestions do you have that would help our family?
4. How can you and I make our relationship better?

E-TEAM ENCOURAGEMENT
5–10 minutes

Close the meeting in prayer for each other and your families. Include in your prayer a specific request for spiritual power to successfully complete your project.

BREAK THE HUDDLE, GO HOME AND RUN THE PLAY!

Chapter Three
The Man

*"You must live with people to know their problems;
and live with God in order to solve them."*

—*P.T. Forsyth*

HALFTIME IN THE LOCKER ROOM

The greatest thrill in my pro football career occurred at 31,000 feet above sea level. It was my second year with the New Orleans Saints. We had just played the Rams in L.A., our fourth exhibition game of the early 1968 season, and we were flying back to New Orleans. As I sat near the rear of the chartered United Airlines Boeing 247, I happened to pick up a copy of the *New Orleans Times-Picayune* and turned to the sports section.

There, cruising high over the Grand Canyon at hundreds of miles per hour, I read that I had been traded to the Dallas Cowboys for an offensive guard and a future draft choice. I couldn't believe my eyes.

After we landed in New Orleans, I hopped another jet and flew back to the West Coast to Thousand Oaks, California, where the Cowboys still had one week of preseason camp left. What a thrill to be able to play for Tom Landry and his Cowboys!

The Saints vs. the Cowboys

A situation that best describes the contrast between the two teams was the different way the two coaches approached halftime and the adjustments that always have to be made for the second half. The Saints' coach would herd us in and, at the top of his lungs, bellow things like: "You girls aren't hitting. You sissies aren't tackling. You tomatoes aren't running hard."

With this brilliant technical analysis of our first half perfor-mance, he roared on with these ingenious instructions for the sec-ond half, "I want you guys to get out there and hit harder, tackle harder, and run harder! Now, get outta my sight and go out there and prove to the fans that you don't wear skirts."

With supreme feelings of invincibility, rosy feelings of self-esteem, and magnificent confidence in our game plan, we ran onto the gridiron, screaming for blood and slavering for opportunities to rip off their heads and suck out their brains. Naturally, our opponents would delicately dissect us with cool surgical precision and finesse us inside out. Like skunks, we always stunk up the last half.

How different to be in the locker room with Landry. The Cowboys would file in, take a break, and get comfortable. Landry would call our attention to the one or two offensive plays that were hurting us the most; such as on third and long, the ball on the left hash mark with the strong side on the short side of the field in a pro split formation, the halfback in motion with the fullback delay flare to the wide side. In his Texas drawl and his MBA style, Landry would give us an audible option that would throw us into a strong side rotation and allow the weak linebacker to take the fullback into the flat, the middle linebacker feather back to the weak hook, and the strong backer and safety inside/outside on the tight end.

Everyone knew how the enemy was hurting us and what to do to stop it. It was a question of playing smarter, not harder. Football is a game of inches, angles, and fractions of seconds. It's not the team with more brutish animalistic slobberers. All NFL players are big, strong, and fast. It's the team that knows where to line up, what angle to charge, and how to perform the proper techniques that makes it to the playoffs.

In the same way, fathers don't need anyone yelling at them, "You sissies need to get out there and father! Father! Father!" We need to father smarter. We need to relate better, pay more attention, and communicate better. I've never yet met a man who wanted to fail miserably as a husband and a father.

Two Sides of the Coin
To introduce the subject of the Fatherhood Job Description, I must make one of the most important points of the entire book. There are

two sides to fatherhood: Who you are and what you do. Your character and personhood matters just as much as your fathercraft and daddy techniques. A family shepherd is careful to *be* the right man as well as *do* the right things.

In Psalm 78:72, the Bible clearly points out this double responsibility: "So he shepherded them according to the integrity of his heart, and guided them with his skillful hands."

Competent shepherding entails two essential aspects: your heart and your skills. You must have a heart of integrity; that is, you must *be* a certain kind of man. And you must *do* specific activities that require a skillful hand.

It's not enough just to tackle the skills and techniques and bypass the development of your character. A man can be dysfunctional and master the Four Fatherhood Functions. He then can wonder why his family comes crashing down around him.

Therefore, before we focus on the position of fatherhood and discuss the Four Fatherhood Functions in the next chapter, we will first discuss how to develop a fatherhood heart in this chapter. These two chapters serve as the foundation for the rest of the entire Dad the Family Shepherd series because they lay down the basic requirements and job description of the family shepherd.

CLOSE ENCOUNTERS OF A SPIRITUAL KIND

I give you now a major point of my concept of fatherhood: Children do what you are, not what you say. Who you are, the kind of man you are, is more important than all of your tasks, techniques, and talks. Children play with your words but work off your heart. Out of your heart come the issues of life, and that's the true source of wisdom to a child.

You need to make sure your heart is right with God. You must know God personally through Jesus Christ and allow His Spirit, the Holy Spirit, to change your heart and empower you to reach your full potential for fatherhood. The best father you can be is the best son you can be. You must be a son of God to be the best father for your child.

This news was bad for me. If my children were going to copy my heart, they were headed for trouble. I hated to think that father power would transfer Dave Simmons down through four generations. Father power and the Fourth Generation Rule had worked from Luther, through Major Amos, and into me. It was time to stop one dynasty and start another. My only hope was to have a heart transplant. I needed to get rid of the old Dave Simmons and get a new one. Something dramatic would have to happen to me to change my heart into the kind that good fatherhood requires.

The Ramblin' Wreck from Georgia Tech
It happened at Georgia Tech. I got a spiritual heart transplant and started the process of being refathered.

The 1963 Georgia Tech Yellow Jackets won their first seven ball games, and they were rolling along rated number eight in the nation. As we were preparing to play Alabama, coach Bobby Dodd dismissed practice early Thursday afternoon, and I ended up down at the Sigma Chi house on Techwood Ave.

I picked up the paper and read an article about a young Communist student who had been killed in West Berlin, Germany. He had stolen some secret files and, while trying to escape back into East Germany, the guards fired warning shots. One of the shots fell low and hit him in the back. As he lay dying on the cobblestone street, he cried out to the soldiers, who rushed up, "I am dying for communism; what are you living for?"

Although I detest Marxism and the totally discredited communist form of government, I admired the resolute courage this man displayed. For the first time in my life, it made me wonder whether there really were things worth living and dying for.

I examined my life and did not like what I saw. In high school I brimmed with hostility and experienced periods of ferocious rage. I started serious drinking and frequented wormy little joints in Juarez, Mexico, just across the Rio Grande from El Paso. I drank ten-cent shots of tequila and licked limes until the wee hours. I let a Mexican tattoo a Georgia Tech Yellow Jacket on the inside of my left ankle. Once, the Mexican police chased me across the Mexican red-tiled roof tops and fired a shot at me. I smuggled ole Thunderbird wine into school and drank at assemblies. We cruised the alleys of Mexican slums looking for fights. We ambushed the Army GIs from Ft. Bliss who came into our territory on overnight passes.

In college, the football team and the Georgia Tech high academic load cramped my style. They toned me down on the outside, but I still screamed on the inside. I had difficulty developing friendships and remained confused about life. And women. I treated women like objects. I had not the faintest idea of how to relate to women. Georgia Tech had no female students at the time so I was spared the tension of constant association with them. My only contact with them was sporadic encounters with Atlanta working girls and the good-time girls who cruised Techwood Drive on the Georgia Tech campus.

This young communist zealot died for communism. I had nothing important enough in my life for which I would be willing to die. I wouldn't die for football, my teammates, for Georgia Tech, for good grades, for my dating life, or for Sigma Chi, my fraternity. It dawned on me that if I had nothing for which to die, I had nothing for which to live.

I took stock of my life. Where was I? Where had I come from? Where was I headed? Father power had hurtled down through the Simmons clan and deposited many weaknesses and strictures in my life. I had inherited many incapacities and, in just eighteen years, managed to cultivate the bad into much worse. I was becoming the kind of man that makes a horrible husband and a despicable father.

I was headed toward becoming the terminal link in the Simmons chain. I was poisoning the stream that would kill off my gene pool. Frankly, I would have ruined any woman that tried to cope with me, and no children could have survived the ravages of dysfunction that father power would have transferred from me.

I started asking "the big questions" about life that we all eventually address. How do you know what is really important in life? How do you determine values and priorities? How can a young man find out the secrets of maximizing his life? Is there a God and a spiritual world existing outside the natural ken of men, and, if so, how do you establish contact? Do I want to establish contact?

It Takes More than Desire

When I thought about it, I wanted to be a good man. I desired to be a successful husband and an effective father. But I had no hope. I was not only a man who constantly made mistakes—I was a mistake. I was defective, not normal, different than others. It would take a miracle to rescue me, rehabilitate me, and equip me to be a good family shepherd.

Unfortunately, it takes more than desire and wishful thinking to make a competent family shepherd. You must become a certain type of man, learn certain truths about life and families, and master certain techniques and skills to excel as a family shepherd.

I needed a miracle, and I got one. I needed to be totally reparented, raised all over again, and it happened. I needed years of training, learning, and practice. And guess what? God can make a family shepherd out of any old guy.

If only I had known these things before I struggled through my early years of fatherhood, Helen and Brandon would carry fewer scars today. It takes a desire to be a good father (which you must have or you wouldn't be reading this book), but it takes more. You not only must have desire, you must *be* a certain kind of man, *know* certain truths, and *do* certain tasks.

To raise children with God's methods for God's purposes, you must be God's man for the job. Before you focus on the why, what, and how, you must make sure you know Christ. You must be rightly related to God. The most crucial experience of my life, personally trusting Christ as my Savior, occurred late in my junior season at Georgia Tech.

John Battle had just become my roommate, and, even though he was the strongest man on the Georgia Tech team and quick like a cat, the most unusual thing about John was his faith in God. In the middle of the twentieth century, he walked around the Georgia Institute of Technology, home of engineers, and said weird things like, "I can relate to God because I know Jesus Christ!" and "Jesus was killed but didn't stay dead because He was resurrected!" and "Jesus is the Son of God, and you can personally know Him!"

The worst thing about having a religious nut like John for a roommate was that I soon discovered that one of his greatest goals in life was to get me to think like him and believe all that stuff in the Bible. He developed the amazing knack of being able to take a conversation on any subject and eventually turn it to the Bible and Jesus. For survival, I had to jump alertly ahead of him and nullify his chain of thought. I learned to beat him to the pass and head him off.

The Man

The bother of fending John off didn't matter much until the Alabama game because we were all riding high on our undefeated season. When we rolled into Birmingham, however, we had to face Bear Bryant and the Crimson Tide who were sky high because of our seven to six upset on Grant Field the year before. They were ranked number four in the nation and, after a long painful afternoon of trying to stop Joe Namath, Alabama was still ranked number four.

It seemed that all the color drained out of life as I returned to Georgia in a terrible mood. To make things worse, my Saturday night date stood me up. The plan called for her to meet me at the airport and go out to celebrate our victory over Alabama. I ended up hitchhiking back to the Georgia Tech campus. This was not my idea of a great college weekend.

In that context, John continued his religious chatter. I blew up and screamed at him. I told him I was sick of him and his Christ, and I didn't want to hear any more.

John Battle's Reinforcements

Undaunted, but more tactful, John decided to shuttle me over to his good friend who was on the Campus Crusade staff. Jon Braun came across town late Tuesday night during a driving Georgia rain and walked into my room. Battle introduced me, and Braun soon ended up sharing some thoughts from the Bible with me. He called his little presentation "The Four Spiritual Laws."

Braun presented a powerful airtight case with only one major flaw that I could spot: He based everything he said on the Bible. He would read a few Scriptures, summarize with a pithy principle, and illustrate with clever diagrams. I have to admit that he made a lot of sense; his logic seemed flawless. But, his undoing was citing Scripture as unquestionable authority. I regarded the Bible as a collection of profound short stories, legends, myths, and biographies that contained useful ideas and encouragement to do good and be nice—not much pragmatic stuff for a middle linebacker roaming downtown Atlanta during his free time.

Braun drew his pitch to a close with this question, "Dave, what do you think?"

With studied neutrality, I said, "Well, that was very nice."

Encouraged, he went on, "Dave, did it make sense?"

"Yes," I responded.

"Then, Dave," Braun said, "is there any reason you would not want to accept Christ right now?"

"Yes," I answered. "There is a good reason why I can't do that. Everything you said came from the Bible, and I don't believe the Bible."

Wrestling for the Truth

I then made it obvious that further discussion would be inappropriate and the great Last Resort Presentation came to an end. Braun left, Battle and I went to bed, but I could not sleep. I kept thinking about what Braun said and Battle's sincerity and force of convictions. I reviewed what I knew to be absolutely true about life and realized I had only three things I knew absolutely for sure:

1. I knew that I did not know God. No evidence proved His existence to me. No miracles. No voices. No encounters of a third kind. I was positive that I did not know God.

2. I could not rule out the possibility of God. How could I say that in all the world of knowledge and experience that existed outside of my limited parameters that there is no God. I had to admit the possibility of His existence.

3. If God existed and is knowable, I certainly wanted to know Him. If the whole purpose of life is to be born and die and, during the brief snap-of-the-fingers life span, we are supposed to meet God, link up with Him, and spend eternity with Him, then what a tragedy to miss Him. I wanted to get in on knowing God if He was really there.

My brain kept reviewing the Four Spiritual Laws that Jon Braun explained to me. They made so much sense and were so logical. And beautiful. I kept thinking how much I wished they were true. The four laws seemed so clear:

Law 1. God loves you. Even if you don't believe in God, He exists and knows you and wants you to know Him and enjoy a relationship with Him.

Law 2. Man is sinful. All of us are born with a common rebellion and resistance toward God. We strive to find meaning and purpose in life in just about anything except a personal knowable Supreme Being—God.

Law 3. Jesus Christ is God's only provision for man's sin. The penalty for our sin is not to know God, that is, to live in spiritual death. Christ experienced spiritual death on the cross for our sin. He became a sacrificial substitute for us.

Law 4. We must individually trust Jesus Christ as our Savior. To become a Christian, we must believe that Jesus is Christ, and His work on the cross is sufficient to take away our sin. At the point of belief, Christ's Holy Spirit enters our life, and we become "born again." We pass from the state of spiritual death and ignorance into a new eternal spiritual life.

I looked at the lighted dial on my clock. It read 4 A.M. I was so tired of this struggle that I decided to try an experiment. I would test the prayer they recommended. If I asked Christ to come into my life, He would or He would not. If He did, I would get all the benefits. If nothing happened, then I would know that God didn't exist, Jesus was not His Son, and I could rest easy and know all those Christians were as silly as I had always thought they were.

Not being one with faith to move mountains, I tentatively started my prayer with the word, *If.* I prayed, "If You are really there, Jesus, and God exists like the Bible says, then I want You to come into my life." That's all I prayed. Then, I fell asleep.

The Amazing Thoughts of an Atheist
The next morning, I struggled out of bed, showered, shaved, shuffled up the hill to class, and nodded my way through my economics class. I had forgotten the whole incident from the night before. All of a sudden, as I watched my professor, a strange alien thought popped into my head: a thought I had never thought before—a weird thought for an atheist. "I wonder if he [the prof] knows God like I do?" I thought.

That afternoon, at practice, the defensive coach had us doing warm-ups and agilities. After a period of this exercise, Coach Bobby

Dodd blew his whistle, and we jogged by his tower on the way to another field for skeleton drill with the backs and receivers. As I passed by Coach Dodd, another strange thought popped into my head: "I wonder if Coach Dodd knows God like I do?"

Oblivious to the significance of those strange new thoughts, I continued through the day in a sleepy daze, but those thoughts kept squirming through my mind. What was happening finally dawned on me after practice while I was walking from the Rose Bowl practice field back to the Georgia Tech locker room underneath Grant Field. I made the connection between the alarming new thoughts coursing through my mind and the prayer I had prayed in the early hours that morning.

In the locker room, as I was cutting off my ankle tape, I leaned over toward Battle, who was shelling off his shoulder pads, and said, "Oh, Battle, by the way, I prayed that prayer last night, and I guess I have become one of you guys."

John was ecstatic. I was relieved. Maybe he would ease up on me for a while.

As I think back, I must tell you, I would die for John Battle. I love that guy. Night after night, he laid awake praying for Dave Simmons. He prayed that somehow, someway, God would open my eyes and I would see the truth and act on it. It was the prayers of a Christian college football player that brought me into a personal relationship with the God of the universe and started me on the path that would eventually help me break the Simmons' dysfunctional family cycle and turn out my children with a new heritage — a heritage with Christ in their hearts and a destiny with God forever.

Applied Faith

How can you be a family shepherd for God if you have never established a personal relationship with God through Jesus Christ? For some of you, the first step you need to take is the essential step of trusting Christ as your Savior.

I urge you to trust Christ right now, before you go on with this book. You can never know whether there is even a God or not, much less know Him personally, until you decide to take a big step of faith. Trust Christ's work on the cross on your behalf. Choose Christ. Jim Elliot, a missionary killed in the line of duty, said, "He is no fool who gives what he cannot keep to obtain what he cannot lose."

Simply pray a prayer like the following to indicate to God your heart's desire:

Dear God,

Thank You for revealing the truth about Yourself to me and allowing me to understand how I can know You in a personal way. I realize I can never be good enough or earn my way into Your presence. I know the basis of my relationship with You is my trust in Christ and His work on the cross as a sufficient payment for all of my sins. With my sins canceled, there is nothing to separate me from You. Therefore, I accept Christ as my Savior. Jesus, please enter my life and give me eternal spiritual life.

Thank You,
(your name)

It's Who You Know, Not What You Do

If you prayed this prayer (or one like it: God cares about the desires of your heart more than your word choice), then God will send Christ's Spirit, the Holy Spirit, to reside in your life. You will become a new creature, a Christian who has been born again into a completely new kind of existence. You will begin the incredible journey of getting to know God better through Christ, and your life will gradually begin to change from the inside out as God brings you to maturity in Christ.

Read these selected verses: "The one who believes in the Son of God has the witness in himself; the one who does not believe God has made Him a liar, because he has not believed in the witness that God has borne concerning His Son. And the witness is this, that God has given us eternal life, and this life is in His Son. He who has the Son has the life; he who does not have the Son of God does not have the life. These things I have written to you who believe in the name of the Son of God, in order that you may know that you have eternal life" (1 John 5:10-13).

Notice in verse 13: "I have written ... that you may *know* you have eternal life." What an assurance and comfort to me. I don't have to depend on feelings, or circumstances, or my own logic and wisdom. I can take God's Word at face value and simply believe.

Some things have to be believed to be seen. My professors at Georgia Tech trained me to believe nothing unless it could be proved. Before you believe something, you must prove it, prove it, prove it, prove it, and prove it. Then you may believe it. With God, however, you believe it first. You believe it. Then God adds proof after proof. Read Hebrews 11:6: "And without faith it is impossible to please Him, for he who comes to God must believe that He is, and that He is a rewarder of those who seek Him."

For a long time, I didn't believe in God, didn't want to, and tried not to seek Him. But, through the prayers of John Battle and the efforts of Jon Braun, my eyes were opened and early that morning, I came to the point where I honestly sought Him. He brought me to Himself, and my life has been changing ever since.

GROWTH ENCOUNTERS OF A SPIRITUAL KIND
Notice, I said, "changing ever since." At the point when I trusted Christ, my sins were forgiven, my old self died, I became a new creation with eternal life, and the Holy Spirit came to live inside me. Then, the maturity process started, and God began His project of refathering me. It takes time to grow to maturity in Christ.

The Benefits
When you trust Christ, you are adopted out of the family of man and into the family of God (by a blood adoption). You get a new father with a completely different set of life benefits. I like the way the Rapha declaration says it (Robert McGee, Personal conversation, January 1991):

> Because of Christ's redemption,
> I am a new creation of infinite worth.
>
> I am deeply loved,
> I am completely forgiven,
> I am fully pleasing,
> I am totally accepted by God.
> I am absolutely complete in Christ.

You are now connected with God, who is a Trinity, and you are a

part of the church. Because of this, you can get your psychological
needs met in a gratifying way like never before.

Need	Provision	Means
Significance	LOVE	Jesus died for you.
Belongingness	BOND	You have a niche in the church.
Identity	LEAD	God adopted you as a son.
Competency	EQUIP	The Holy Spirit gives you gifts.

In addition to meeting your basic psychological needs, God also
provides solutions for the fears that arise from the Four False
Beliefs, as taught by Rapha (Robert McGee, *The Search for Significance* [Houston: Rapha Publishing, 1990], 40).

UTILIZING YOUR BENEFITS
The growth process is simply a matter of incorporating these great
benefits into your life. The process is described below:

And do not be conformed to this world, but be transformed by the renew-
ing of your mind, that you may prove what the will of God is, that which is
good and acceptable and perfect. — Romans 12:2

That, in reference to your former manner of life, you lay aside the old self,
which is being corrupted in accordance with the lusts of deceit, and that
you be renewed in the spirit of your mind, and put on the new self, which
in the likeness of God has been created in righteousness and holiness of
the truth. — Ephesians 4:22-24

Basically, these passages tell us that you used to have a corrupted self but it is now replaced by a new self totally acceptable to
God. To grow in Christ, you must break down the old thought
patterns in your mind and replace them with the incredible declaration of the Scriptures—you are a new awesome creature in the
likeness of God. In other words, your mind needs to be repro-
grammed with the truth about your new standing with God and His
acceptance of you.

The Fears	God's Answer
The Performance Trap: The Fear of Failure	**Justification:** God has forgiven our sins and granted us the righteousness of Christ (Romans 5:1).
The Approval Addict: The Fear of Rejection	**Reconciliation:** At one time, I was hostile to God; but now I am forgiven and accepted by Him (Colossians 1:21-22).
The Blame Game: The Fear of Punishment	**Propitiation:** Christ satisfied God's wrath on the cross: therefore I am deeply loved by Christ (1 John 4:9-11).
Shame: Feelings of Shame	**Regeneration:** I am a new creature in Christ (John 3:3-6).

Protecting the Benefits

Problems arise when we forget who we are in Christ and allow sin to work through our minds, emotions, and wills so that our behavior conforms to what it was before we became Christians. In that case, we need to use the "Christian bar of soap," 1 John 1:9, and wash ourselves clean again: "If we confess our sins, He is faithful and righteous to forgive us our sins and to cleanse us from all unrighteousness."

When we sin, God does not get mad at us. He totally expended His wrath for our sin at the cross. He grieves when we sin. Our sin makes Him sorrowful because it cuts us off from fellowship with

Him and the enjoyment of His benefits. After He has gone to the trouble to send His Son, Jesus, to die for our sin, He certainly grieves to see us discard the benefits of our new identity. He wants us to be quick to confess our sins so our fellowship can be restored.

After confession, God wants us to walk in faith again. He wants us to allow the Holy Spirit to work through our minds, emotions, and wills to produce spiritual traits described in Galatians: "If we live by the Spirit, let us also walk by the Spirit. . . . The fruit of the Spirit is love, joy, peace, patience, kindness, goodness, faithfulness, gentleness, self-control" (Gal. 5:25, 22-23).

Prayer is a good way to tell God you agree with Him about your sin. When you pray, tell God all about your sin and thank Him for the forgiveness He has already provided for your sin by means of the cross. Then, thank Him for the Holy Spirit who resides in you and tell Him you would like to resume your life with the Holy Spirit in control.

Perpetuating the Benefits

We have a God who wants us to seek Him and know Him. Bill Smith, an investment consultant, has written, "God wants us to know Him. It's staggering to think that the God of the universe could actually want to know me, and want me to know Him, but it's true. He has said so in many ways" (*Quiet Time* [Little Rock, Ark.: Dad the Family Shepherd, 1988], 10). Bill points out this verse to make his point: "Now this is eternal life: that they may know You, the only true God, and Jesus Christ, whom You have sent" (John 17:3).

God delights in us knowing Him, and Jesus Christ actually prayed for you to know God. So meeting God when you first trust Him as Savior is just the beginning. After He enters your life, you must spend time with Him and get to know Him. (Remember, Jesus and God are one.) The only way to grow in your knowledge and understanding of God and His ways is to spend personal time with Him on a regular basis.

We call this personal time with God "quiet time." This time is an essential part of growing and maturing in Christ.

Note: For the most outstanding teaching on quiet time (its purpose, mechanics, procedures, and benefits), get the booklet *Quiet*

Time, by Bill Smith, published by Dad the Family Shepherd.

THE ANSWER

I can now answer the young communist, who asked, "I'm dying for communism. What are you living for?" I am living for Jesus Christ. I live for Him and would die for Him. I would die for John Battle. Night after night, he lay in his bunk praying for me. He earnestly prayed that somehow, some way, the eyes of Dave Simmons would be opened and I would see the truth and respond to it. I would die for Sandy, Helen, and Brandon. Yes, I now have so much for which to live. I have a question for the challenging misguided young communist: "I'm living for Christ. What is the world dying for?"

E-TEAM HUDDLE GUIDE
CHAPTER THREE: THE MAN

Dad, the Family Shepherd
E-TEAM

E-TEAM REVIEW
10–15 minutes

After coffee and fellowship, take 10–15 minutes to allow the men to tell about the results of last week's project. This is the accountability part. Be firm with each other and encourage everyone to complete the projects. If anyone encountered difficulty or had a family problem arise, pause to allow the E-Team to pray.

E-TEAM DISCUSSION
50–60 minutes

This part allows you to discuss the key concepts in this chapter and relate them to your individual lives. Be sure to leave time to complete the Workout and Encouragement section.

THE PRINCIPLES (Check the text for help.)
1. What are the Four Spiritual Laws?
2. Why is 1 John 5.10-13 significant?
3. What solution does God have for the Four False Beliefs?

THE IMPLICATIONS (Why are these ideas significant?)
4. Discuss the difference between trusting Jesus Christ's work to become a Christian and trusting your own works to become a Christian.
5. When one becomes a Christian, he gets adopted into the family of God and gets a new Father—God, the Father. Discuss how this affects his fathering potential.
6. Discuss why you think Dave inserted this chapter here in front of the chapters covering fathering skills and techniques.

THE APPLICATION (How do these ideas affect me?)
7. Volunteer request: Have each man tell the E-Team how he became a Christian.

E-TEAM WORKOUT
10–15 minutes

Allow each man to choose one of the project options (plays) to perform during the week. If so desired, design your own project. Note: it is essential that each man leave having made a definite commitment to a specific project.

1st PLAY:
If you have not trusted Jesus Christ as your Savior yet, read the chapter again and also read John 3:1-9. Then make an appointment with one of the Christians in the E-Team and ask him to answer your questions and handle your objections.

2nd PLAY:
If anyone in your family has not trusted Jesus Christ, explain to that person how he can and see if he would like to do it. If you need help, ask a Christian in your E-Team to help you make the explanation. Perhaps your wife would benefit from reading this chapter.

3rd PLAY:
Read the fourth Gospel, the Book of John.

E-TEAM ENCOURAGEMENT
5–10 minutes

Close the meeting in prayer for one another and your families. Include in your prayer a specific request for spiritual power to successfully complete your project.

BREAK THE HUDDLE, GO HOME AND RUN THE PLAY!

Chapter Four
The Task

"Our very survival as a people will
depend on the presence or absence of
masculine leadership in millions of homes."
— James Dobson

A FATHER'S PLACE IS UNDER THE BED

Most men want to excel. The problem is that confusion on fatherhood runs rampant in our culture. The big questions are: What is the father's place in the family? What is a father? What position do you play? Where do you line up? What are your assignments? What are your techniques and coaching tips?

These questions were not asked a generation or two ago. Men just knew. Fatherlore and fathercraft passed down through the centuries from father to son. We live in a confusing age, however, when the signals from the past fathers have grown weak and are drowned out by confusing concepts from desperate people.

One of the best pictures I've ever seen on the current confusion on the placement of fathers comes from Erma Bombeck. She paints a portrait of a little girl who loved her dad but wasn't sure what Dads do:

> One morning my father didn't get up and go to work. He went to the hospital and died the next day.
>
> I hadn't thought that much about him before. He was just someone who left and came home and seemed glad to see everyone at night. He opened the jar of pickles when no one else could. He was the only one in the house who wasn't afraid to go into the basement by himself.
>
> He cut himself shaving, but no one kissed it or got excited about it. It

91

was understood when it rained, he got the car and brought it around to the door. When anyone was sick, he went out to get the prescription filled. He took lots of pictures . . . but he was never in them.

Whenever I played house, the mother doll had a lot to do. I never knew what to do with the daddy doll, so I had him say, "I'm going off to work now," and threw him under the bed.

The funeral was in our living room and a lot of people came and brought all kinds of good food and cakes. We had never had so much company before.

I went to my room and felt under the bed for the daddy doll. When I found him, I dusted him off and put him on my bed.

He never did anything. I didn't know his leaving would hurt so much (*Family — The Ties that Bind . . . and Gag!* [New York: Fawcett Books, 1988], 2).

What a picture of the modern American dad! He exists mainly in some mysterious place called "work." When occasionally found at home, he acts confused and out of place and stays out of the mainstream. He putters around without much purpose, hides in remote areas collecting dust, and functions mainly as a ghost-like backstage handyman.

Most modern fathers feel awkward in the home zone. They feel confused about the role that the family and society expects them to play. Most have a strong desire to excel as a family shepherd; they are just not sure where they fit and what exact responsibilities they must tackle.

Fathers need an official job description. Of course, the Bible doesn't spell out perfect family job descriptions, organization charts, and position focus sheets. But, it talks about the family from Genesis to Revelation, and this information can be collected, categorized, and put into forms suited for easy learning and practical use. I have studied the Scriptures on the family, especially fatherhood, for years, and I have developed some family management tools that help me see my role and responsibilities clearly.

This chapter provides you with the Dad the Family Shepherd Job Description. The first section deals with the foundation of your job; the second section introduces you to the Four Fatherhood Functions—Love, Bond, Lead, and Equip.

This chapter is pivotal: The first three chapters of this volume tell you the why of fatherhood; this one tells you what; and the last four chapters give you a good introduction to each of the Four Fatherhood Functions. The next two volumes of the Dad the Family Shepherd series go into careful details on how to perform these functions with excellence.

THE FOUNDATION OF YOUR JOB

Before we look at the Four Fatherhood Functions, it will be helpful to set the foundation on which these responsibilities rest.

The Context of Fatherhood

Nothing has a meaning without a context. To grasp the meaning and implications of your job description of fatherhood, you need to see how it fits into God's overall plan for the family.

God has purpose, planning, objectives, and strategies. Since He is in control, He has a plan for the world. By His very nature, He establishes order and eliminates chaos. You can depend on Him to keep things on track and work out His plans. He wants people to work through His strategies in an organized fashion. The Bible tells us about His plans and strategies on almost every page, but He specifically comforts us with His management power: "Declaring the end from the beginning and from ancient times things which have not been done, saying, 'My purpose will be established, and I will accomplish all My good pleasure' . . . Truly I have spoken; truly I will bring it to pass. I have planned it, surely I will do it" (Isa. 46:10, 11).

The nation of Israel, the church, the nations, and even the family are caught up in His plan, and He has strategies for all. The family plays a unique part in His grand design. This section introduces you to God's blueprint for the family.

The Big Picture

God has four primary objectives for the family, and each one has its own specific strategy. The chart on page 94 paints the big picture of God's plan for the family. Volume 2 contains a more detailed treatment.

Listed across in the first row are God's four basic objectives for the family. Each objective has the primary strategy needed for its accomplishment right below it (row 2). Continuing down from each

		To Reflect a Godly Image	To Conduct a Godly Government	To Multiply a Godly Heritage	To Nurture a Godly People
FAMILY	**OBJECTIVES**	To Reflect a Godly Image	To Conduct a Godly Government	To Multiply a Godly Heritage	To Nurture a Godly People
	STRATEGY	To Establish Identity	To Establish Harmony	To Establish Intimacy	To Establish Security
GENDER ROLES	**MALE**	To Lead Your Family	To Bond Your Family	To Love Your Family	To Equip Your Family
	FEMALE	To Report to You	To Complete You	To Respond to You	To Amplify You

objective and strategy, you will find the male gender role and the female gender role. Together they will develop the strategy that reaches the objective. This chart helps you see how your job description fits into God's overall plan for the family.

The Fatherhood MasterPlan Arrow (from Bobb Biehl)
I have extracted your role from the information above and formatted it into a form called the MasterPlan Arrow on page 95.

The Fatherhood MasterPlan Arrow explains the philosophy and tasks of your position. The philosophy forms the target, and the arrow contains the four major fields of activities for which you are

OBJECTIVE	STRATEGY	PURPOSE	NEED

TO REFLECT A GODLY IMAGE	BY ESTABLISHING **IDENTITY**		
TO CONDUCT A GODLY GOVERNMENT	BY ESTABLISHING **HARMONY**	TO FUNCTION AS GOD'S SMALLEST BATTLE FORMATION	IN GOD'S CONFLICT WITH SATAN, WE ARE LOSING TOO MANY FAMILIES
TO MULTIPLY A GODLY HERITAGE	BY ESTABLISHING **INTIMACY**		
TO NURTURE A GODLY PEOPLE	BY ESTABLISHING **SECURITY**		

THE FAMILY MASTERPLAN ARROW*

*This arrow has been adapted, with permission, from a "Masterplanning Arrow" made available by Masterplanning Group International. For information and instructions on the complete "Masterplanning Arrow" call 1-800-443-1976.

responsible—which I call the Four Fatherhood Functions.

THE PHILOSOPHY OF FATHERHOOD

In philosophy, the question must be asked Why. This question must also be answered because the Why provides the motivation needed to accomplish the How. Your job's existence is justified because the need for it is identified and its purpose is defined in philosophy.

The Need for Fatherhood

Too many families are failing due to the lack of strong effective male leadership in the home.

The Purpose of Fatherhood
The purpose of a father is to establish and maintain the family as an effective operational battle formation for Jesus Christ by creating the environment where each family member can reach full maturity and maximum potential.

THE STYLE OF YOUR FATHERHOOD
Amos had his unique fathering style. So do I. So do you. No one has a fathering personality exactly like yours. You are unique. And that's great. There is plenty of flexibility in fathering personality. God made a variety of father flavors. We should not all be alike — God does not intend cookie-cutter dads. Your fatherhood style is your unique pattern of exercising the Four Fatherhood Functions determined by your peculiar mix of personality traits.

Personality
The only rule I put forth on fathering style is, "To thine own self be true." Be who you are and don't try to be someone else. No one is like you, and no one fathers like you. You neither need to try to copy another's style nor compare yourself with him. Don't play roles. Your fatherhood style comes out of your personality.

For example, if you are a laid-back accountant type, you should not try to be a showbiz car salesman type dad. If you are a calculating engineer type, you should not try to be an artsy-craftsy type dad. If you are an outgoing backslapping gregarious dad, you shouldn't try to be a hermit monk specializing in the study of postexilic martyred prophets. Your children want your fathering style to match your personality.

Character
Character is much different than personality. Character carries with it the seriousness of values, ethics, and convictions. The Bible definitely approves of some character traits and condemns others based on whether they damage or improve your relationships with God, family, and friends. Incredible flexibility is in the type of personality you have, but an excellent father demonstrates the Judeo-Christian virtues and morals in his life. Don't compromise your character.

The Task

Influences

Your fatherhood personality materializes out of a swirl of influences that bear on you throughout your life. Here are some of the influences that affect your fathering style:

1. Your temperament. Fathering personality should be true to your temperament. You should not fake it or play roles.

2. Your dominant father model. You will father like your father. Sometimes, a father model is ultranegative, which causes a man to reverse himself and father opposite his father model.

3. Your environment. Depression dads of the thirties were different from affluent dads of the eighties. War dads differ from peace dads. Occupations affect fathering personality: doctor dads, salesman dads, coaching dads, machinist dads, construction dads, military dads are all different.

4. Your culture. Fathers extracted from immigrant ancestors differ. Have you noticed the difference in Italian, German, Chinese, African, English, Greek, and Eastern European dads?

5. Your education. Research shows significant differences in fatherhood according to academic achievements.

6. Your religion. Religious fathers are different from atheists and agnostics (not necessarily good or bad). Protestant, Catholic, Jewish, Islamic, New Aged, and Eastern religions impact father style.

7. Your testosterone level. Testosterone dramatically impacts male behavior (and, therefore, fatherhood). Different men have different levels of testosterone, and the levels fluctuate with age. At puberty, boys start feeling the effects. They suffer massive infusions during the seventeen-to-nineteen-age period and then, after this jolting overdose, begin a long steady decline in production of the *Big T*. This biological fact explains the male transition from the "hot and bothered" young turks to the "mellowing" effect in older fathers.

Evidence exists that the selection of occupation may be, in part, hormone-driven. A study done at Georgia State reports that "Testosterone is probably related to career choice through its links in personality . . . actors scored tops . . . followed by football players, physicians, professors, firemen, salesmen and ministers."

8. Your phase in life. As you move through your life cycle, you may mellow or sour with age. The predominant factor that seems to

affect your ease into mid-life and late-life is your ability to develop intimate male friendships. Men who have close friends mellow tastefully. Men who did not develop close male bonds through the years age quicker and become more crotchety with age.

9. Career choice. Research shows that occupation is related to fatherhood effectiveness. Certain jobs attract men with the same characteristics required for good fathering. Others screen out good fathers. Some jobs demand so much energy and emotion that fathers are drained at work and cheat their families — "they gave at the office." Some jobs keep men physically separated from their families; no matter how great the commitment, the fathers simply can't make up for lost time.

10. Personal choice. This factor could be the main influence in fathering style — the basic decision to excel. Men have a free will, and no one can make a man be a good father. It is an option. It requires a decision. You choose your values and establish your own personal priorities. Men do what they want. If a man chooses to excel at fatherhood, he will find a way to succeed.

THE FOUR FATHERHOOD FUNCTIONS

From years of researching the teachings and references to fatherhood in the Scriptures, I have completed a list of all the fatherhood tasks I can find. These can be classified easily into four major categories, which I call the Four Fatherhood Functions: Love, Bond, Lead, and Equip.

Each of the Four Fatherhood Functions has a full spectrum of elements that describe it.

Functions: What you must DO
You must perform these four categories of related activities or tasks.

Roles: What you must BE
You fill these four positions in order to carry out your functions.

Benefits: The primary BLESSINGS
These four essential attributes are established in a child when the father successfully performs the corresponding function.

Penalties: The primary CURSE
The child must pay these four penalties when the father does not perform the corresponding function.

In this section, only the function and PFP dimensions will be explained. The rest of the elements for each function will be covered in the next four chapters.

The Fatherhood Function of Loving

LOVE	
Role	Be a PRIEST.
Benefit	To give SIGNIFICANCE.
Penalty	MEANINGLESSNESS.
Introduction	This Volume: Chapter 5
Coaching Tips & Techniques	Volume Two: *Dad the Family Counselor*

You are to love your family with the same kind of love with which Christ loved the church. He acted out His love as a living sacrifice, nourishing, cherishing, and eventually dying for the sake of the church. His love is unique and not possible for mere humans. Since He is the only source for this kind of love, the only way you can ever acquire and use it is to become a Christian. When Christ comes into your heart, He brings His unique love with Him, and you can begin to use it with your family.

In my opinion, the greatest passage in the Bible on love is Philippians 2:5-8: "Have this attitude in yourselves which was also in Christ Jesus, who, although He existed in the form of God, did not regard equality with God a thing to be grasped, but emptied Himself, taking the form of a bondservant, and being made in the likeness of men. And being found in appearance as a man, He humbled Himself by becoming obedient to the point of death, even death on a cross."

This passage tells us about the kind of love that Christ has. It starts as an attitude, and because of His unselfishness, works itself out into action that benefited us and cost Him great loss. From this description, I get my definition of love.

The Fatherhood Function LOVE	Love is a mind-set that chooses to give the gift of self for the benefit of others regardless of their performance.

THE FATHERHOOD FUNCTION OF BONDING

BOND	
Role Benefit Penalty	Be a COACH. To give BELONGINGNESS. ALONENESS.
Introduction Coaching Tips & Techniques	This Volume: Chapter 6 Volume Two: *Dad the Family Counselor*

Bonding allows the father to help his family know that they belong and fit in a special place in the family. You are like a coach who helps his players know where they belong and how to work together like a team. You, as Dad the Family Coach, are responsible for the depth and quality of family bonding. It starts with the quality of your relationship with your wife and carries over to parent/child bonding.

Bonding is the creative art of deep knowing and skillful placing of each person into a special niche to form a whole. It comes from the meaning of the word *manage* in 1 Timothy 3:4-5: "He must be one who *manages* his own household well, keeping his children under control with all dignity (but if a man does not know how to *manage* his own household, how will he take care of the church of God?)."

The Greek word for manage is *proistemi*. It has two meanings that describe the function of bonding.

1. It means "to preside over; to maintain unity; harmony, and purpose." It's like a museum curator who organizes and arranges each display in a pattern to show it off at its best. A curator takes each display and harmonizes all the shapes, textures, hues, and light to form a complete unified whole.

You are Dad the family curator. You are responsible for bonding your family together in a perfect pattern of togetherness. You preside over the unification of the family and make sure each member fits into the whole and feels belongingness.

2. It means "to care, to protect, to meet sacrificially the total needs of another; to give aid." It is the same word used in the Parable of the Good Samaritan. The Samaritan took a mugged victim to an inn, nurtured him, and before departing, told the innkeeper to "do whatever it takes to help the victim recover and send the bill to me."

You are Dad the Family Samaritan who sacrificially meets the needs of each member. You keep them going and make them feel they are part of the team.

Therefore, the explanation for bonding is:

The Fatherhood Function BONDING	Bonding is the creative art of deep knowing and skillful placing of each person into a special niche to form a whole where everyone's needs for belongingness are met.

THE FATHERHOOD FUNCTION OF LEADING

LEAD	
PFP Dimension	With CONSISTENCY.
Role	Be a MAN.
Benefit	To give IDENTITY.
Penalty	ANONYMITY.

Introduction	This Volume: Chapter 7
Coaching Tips & Techniques	Volume Two: *Dad the Family Counselor*

You represent the family anchor. You are the fixed point on the x and y axis of a graph that every other family member uses for self-location. They take their bearings from you. You are the North Pole, the North Star, the fixed point that keeps everybody from flying off in every direction. A consistent leader maintains a certain level of predictability and regularity. People know what to expect.

You hold the family position that insures that the family stays on track and functions as God's smallest battle formation. The biblical term for this leadership position is *head* as described in Ephesians 5:23: "For the husband is the head of the wife, as Christ also is the Head of the church, He Himself being the Savior of the body."

The Greek word for head is *kephale*, and it has three shades of meaning:

1. It means "prime source" or "chief cause." You are the prime authority in your home because God delegated His authority to you. You represent God to the family and exercise leadership on His behalf.

2. It means "that which is to be seized or grasped; door handle or doorknob." You are God's steering wheel for the family. You are His control instrument. When He wants to touch your family, He reaches for you. Whoever or whatever has a hold of you has a grip on the family.

3. It means "to govern or oversee." You are the family *face* who sees the family's vision and purpose. You make sure the family follows God's plans and progresses in the right direction.

You are assigned the prime authority in your home. You are God's steering wheel for the family, His control instrument. You are the family *face* who sees the family's vision and purpose. You are the model for the family who demonstrates how to live. A consistent leader maintains a certain level of predictability and regularity. People know what to expect.

Another key term for leadership is responsibility. Responsibility has two directions:

The Task

1. You are obligated to a higher authority; therefore, you exercise delegated power.

2. You are obligated to those who report to you. You must do what is required to make them successful.

This function ensures that the family stays on track and functions as God's smallest battle formation. My explanation for leadership is:

The Fatherhood Function LEAD	A leader is one under authority who provides stability, knows what to do next, and can motivate his team to work together to accomplish a task with maximum efficiency while building unity.

THE FATHERHOOD FUNCTION OF EQUIPPING

EQUIP	
Role Benefit Penalty	Be a MENTOR. To give COMPETENCE. DEPENDENCE.
Introduction	This Volume: Chapter 8
Coaching Tips & Techniques	Volume Three: *Dad the Family Mentor*

The father has the primary responsibility to provide everything a child needs to reach maturity in a healthy, productive way. He must provide the right environment that allows maximum growth, and he must provide the right enlightenment to help them learn to cope. He does not have to do everything himself; he can delegate, but he must assume the responsibility that it will be done.

My concept of a family shepherd's function to equip comes from Psalm 23:

The Lord is my Shepherd,
I shall not want.
He makes me lie down in green pastures;

103

He leads me beside quiet waters.
He restores my soul;
He guides me in the paths of righteousness
for His name's sake.
Even though I walk through the valley of the shadow of death,
I fear no evil; for Thou art with me;
Thy rod and Thy staff, they comfort me.
Thou dost prepare a table before me in the presence of my enemies;
Thou hast anointed my head with oil;
My cup overflows.
Surely goodness and loving-kindness will follow me all the days of my life,
And I will dwell in the house of the Lord forever.

This classic passage tells us many things about the Great Shepherd who is the model for a family shepherd. A shepherd takes care of mental and spiritual needs. He offers protection and provisions. His purpose is to ensure that his charge will stay united with the Lord forever and enjoy the best fruits of life while on this earth. In short, a shepherd provides what a child needs to be successful and feel competent.

Therefore, my explanation for Equipping is:

The Fatherhood Function EQUIPPING	Equipping is the diligent labor that provides children with the right environment and enlightenment required to cope successfully with life.

ONE PLAY AT A TIME

You have just received a management tool that I crafted out of the information I have gleaned from the Bible. It is my best attempt to consolidate all your responsibilities into a practical management tool with which you are familiar. You need to make your own study and modify this tool as you feel led.

However you see your job description, be careful not to be overwhelmed by it. I suggest that you see it as something to grow slowly into, not as a law with which to beat yourself over the head and lay on the guilt. Take it easy, and take it one play at a time.

THE FATHERHOOD MASTERPLAN ARROW

The Task

OBJECTIVES	STRATEGY	PURPOSE	NEED

WE ARE LOSING TOO MANY FAMILIES DUE TO LACK OF MALE LEADER-SHIP

TO FUNCTION AS GOD'S SMALLEST BATTLE FORMATION

TO REFLECT A GODLY IMAGE	BY ESTABLISHING	IDENTITY
TO CONDUCT A GODLY GOVERNMENT	BY ESTABLISHING	HARMONY
TO MULTIPLY A GODLY HERITAGE	BY ESTABLISHING	INTIMACY
TO NURTURE GODLY PEOPLE	BY ESTABLISHING	SECURITY

I paid a psychologist $75/hour for ten weeks just to learn that you can't make massive changes all at once. You have to take it one step at a time.

Huddle up with your E-Team each week, discuss the playbook, call a play, break the huddle, go home, and run the play until you get it down. ONE PLAY AT A TIME.

Job Description for the Head of the Home

Position title:

    The Family Shepherd

Mode of operation:

    Committed servant

Purpose:

    To establish and maintain the family as an effective operational battle formation for Christ.

Major functions	P.F.P. dimensions	Gifts to wife
To LEAD my family	CONSISTENCY	To HONOR her
To BOND my family	AWARENESS	To UNDERSTAND her
To LOVE my family	NURTURANCE	To LOVE her
To EQUIP my family	INVOLVEMENT	To PRAISE her

Priorities:

Mission Priorities

People — Eternal

Things — Temporal

Relationships / Christians / Non-Christians / Family / YOU / GOD / Time / Body / Capital / Vocation

Resource Priorities

Strategy:

    To pray.

    To walk in Christ, and the power of the Holy Spirit.

    To equip myself with scriptural principles.

    To make myself accountable to a small team of men (an E-Team).

Reporting Relationships:

    I report to God and my church leaders.

    I work closely with other fathers and my church's youth director.

    Reporting to me are my wife and children.

E-TEAM HUDDLE GUIDE
CHAPTER FOUR: THE TASK

Dad, the Family Shepherd
E-TEAM

E-TEAM REVIEW
10–15 minutes

After coffee and fellowship, take 10–15 minutes to allow the men to tell about the results of last week's project. This is the accountability part. Be firm with each other and encourage everyone to complete the projects. If anyone encountered difficulty or had a family problem arise, pause to allow the E-Team to address the problem and pray.

E-TEAM DISCUSSION
50–60 minutes

This part allows you to discuss the key concepts in this chapter and relate them to your individual lives. Be sure to leave time to complete the Workout and Encouragement section.

THE PRINCIPLES (Check the text for help.)
1. Define each of the Four Fatherhood Functions—Love, Bond, Lead, and Equip.
2. What are the major influences that affect a man's fathering style?

THE IMPLICATIONS (Why are these ideas significant?)
3. What advantage is it to have a specific Dad the Family Shepherd Job Description?
4. What dangers do you see in having a specific Dad the Family Shepherd Job Description?
5. Describe the difference in the quality of life between two children where one had a father who concentrated on the Four Fatherhood Functions and the other child's father did not practice them. What future would you predict for each of the two children?

THE APPLICATION (How do these ideas affect me?)
6. Take out your PFP reports and tell the E-team which functions/dimensions you want to work on the most.

7. Describe to the E-Team how you feel about your fathering style in light of this job description.

8. Discuss ways that you can help each other avoid feeling guilty about past mistakes and how you can encourage each other to feel hopeful and positive about the future of your fathering style.

E-TEAM WORKOUT
10–15 minutes

There is only one project (play) this week—get up fifteen minutes earlier on at least four mornings and pray for your family. Pray for your wife and each child. Pray for yourself. Ask God for wisdom, insight, and power to perform your responsibilities as a father. Pray for your E-Team members and their families by name.

E-TEAM ENCOURAGEMENT
5–10 minutes

Close the meeting in prayer for each other and your families. Include in your prayer a specific request for spiritual power to successfully complete your project.

BREAK THE HUDDLE,
GO HOME AND RUN THE PLAY!

The Functions
of Fatherhood

Chapter Five
Loving Your Children

*"The physical and psychological welfare of a child
is largely a product of affectionate, demonstrative
love received in infancy."*

—*Dr. Lee Salk*

THE CHARRED STEAK AFFAIR

It had been one of the roughest weeks ever at Kings Arrow Ranch. Everything had gone wrong: We had a few tyrant kids; the temperature and humidity hovered around the high nineties; we were shorthanded; and the water system had gone out. This situation meant that bucket brigades with lake water had to be used to flush commodes for 140 people. I was not a happy camper.

Coping with adversity in my old nature, I became sullen and grouchy, mostly with Sandy. In public, however, I tried to act nice.

Instead of responding in the same way, Sandy surprised me. She put her arm around me and said, "Dave, it has been a tough week. I want to do something special for you. Let's let tonight be your night. We can take the family to Hattiesburg for dinner, and I want you to get a big steak. We need to cheer you up."

I eagerly agreed, and we left the Kings Arrow Ranch as soon as I could delegate and bolt everything down. After we arrived at our favorite local steakhouse, we stood in line and looked over the pictured menu on the wall. Sandy nudged me and said, "Dave, go ahead and order the best steak they have. This night is for you!"

"Anything you say, dear," I replied dutifully. I then ordered the big sirloin strip. After giving our order, we raided the salad bar and found a table. When I saw my steak, however, I couldn't believe my eyes. It was the worst piece of meat I had ever seen. It was burned and leathery, blackened and curled on its edges. One of my shoe tongues looked more appetizing.

Suddenly, it disappeared. Sandy had jabbed it with her fork, whisked it away, and dumped her chopped steak in my plate. I shot her a curious look, and she explained, "I meant it. Tonight is your special night. I want you to have the best meal."

And then she quoted the Simmons family motto, "Love is Action!"

I reached out, took her hand, and tried to think of a way to say thanks when I noticed our children, Helen (eight years old) and Brandon (five years old), staring at us with big, wide eyes. "Did you kids see what your mom did? She gave me her dinner." Then, I repeated the Simmons family motto, "Love is Action."

Brandon snapped out of it, grabbed all of his french fries, dropped them on Helen's plate, and exclaimed, "Love is Action!" Brandon has weird tastes; he likes parsley. So Helen reciprocated with all the parsley on the table, announcing, "Love is Action!"

This family incident paints a colorful picture of the biblical concept of love, one of the Four Fatherhood Functions. Love is care for others put into action. It is showing concern and support with deliberate behaviors. The Bible says it this way: "Let us not love with word or with tongue, but in deed and truth" (1 John 3:18).

Using this verse, I have established the Simmons' Family Motto, "Love is Action" and have adopted the following definition for love: Love is a mind-set that chooses to give the gift of self for the benefit of others regardless of their performance.

THE ANALYSIS OF LOVING

The Fatherhood Function of Loving

Function	LOVE your family.
Role	Be a PRIEST.
Benefit	To give SIGNIFICANCE.
Penalty	MEANINGLESSNESS.

The Fatherhood Function: Loving
Love is a mind-set that chooses to give the gift of self for the benefit of others regardless of their performance.

The Role: Dad the Family Priest
God created children as love seekers with a built-in urgent need for love. He also assigned you the function of meeting this need. You plan love, cultivate it, nourish it, and harvest it in your family. Love is a priest's dominant characteristic. Jesus, the High Priest, so loved the church that He gave Himself up for her. In a similar manner, Dad the Family Shepherd functions as a loving priest.

As a priest, you preside over the family as God's representative and as a petitioner to God for the family. Spiritual traffic must pass through you, the intercessor between God and home. Your priesthood functions are emphasized in the instructions given for the Passover in Exodus 12:3, 23: "Each one [is] to take a lamb for themselves, according to their fathers' households, a lamb for each household. And when He sees the blood on the lintel and on the two doorposts, the Lord will pass over the door and will not allow the destroyer to come into your house to smite you."

In this passage, the father acts as a priest for his own family. What he does determines the fate of his entire family. Andrew Murray says it this way:

> All this teaches that God lays down a fundamental law in the Passover and the blood-sprinkling: "I deal with you not as individuals but as families. As I chose and blessed you, the seed of your father Abraham, so I still bless every household through the believing father, who sprinkles the blood in obedience to my command . . . " In the hands of the father, God thus places the destiny and the safety of the whole house *(How to Raise Your Children for Christ* [Springdale, Penn.: Whitaker House, 1984], 58).

In the New Testament, we also see the father's role as the family priest. In Acts 16:30, Paul's jailer urgently asked, "What must I do to be saved?" Paul replies in verse 31: "And they said, 'Believe in the Lord Jesus, and you shall be saved, you and your household.' "

The jailer's family soon heard the message of truth and responded with faith, and the whole family was baptized. The family members didn't actually become Christians directly as a result of the family shepherd's faith, because each person had to believe individually. But, since the jailer believed and because of his testimony and actions, his family came to the point of saving faith.

In summary, let me quote Andrew Murray once again:

> The father must regard himself as the appointed channel through whom the blessings of nature and providence must reach the child. And he may count upon God's help. But the parental relation has a nobler destiny: for the eternal life, too, with its blessings, the believing father is to regard himself as the appointed channel and steward of the grace of God.

The Benefit: Significance

Love establishes significance. At the steakhouse, when Sandy gave me her steak, she made me feel valuable. When she suggested going to get a steak and then reminded me to order the best steak, I felt important. Just to know that another human being had been concentrating on me made me feel special. All her comments and actions proved to me that she had been concerned about me deep in her heart, wanting things to go better for me. She reached out and touched me; she anticipated something that would please me and cheer me up, or at least get my mind off the numbing problems at the Ranch. She made me feel significant.

When you love, the other person increases in value and worth. Love transfers your significance to the other person. For example, Jesus loves you and died for you, which makes you extremely valuable and significant.

God established your significance by His sacrificial act on the cross. The Crucifixion establishes your value in the world. You were originally born and lived in darkness, and your sin held you captive. But God came to the *marketplace* and wanted to purchase you out of darkness and bring you into His light. Your price tag was death. God did not flinch. He sent His Son to pay the price on the cross and bought you (redeemed you) with Christ's blood.

God acquired you by spending His blood on you. This act assigns value to you. You are worth Christ's blood. Since value is inversely proportionate to supply, nothing has more value than Christ's blood — there are only a few quarts of it in the entire universe. This means there is nothing more valuable than you.

How sad that so many people lurch through life trying to conjure up feelings of significance by attaching to worldly things. They scurry to and from all the worldly things that promise significance to wind up only an empty shell with no meaning or value. Sin is the effort of going through life seeking meaning and significance apart from God.

When you, as family shepherd, humble yourself and love your children, you assign significance to your children. Your unconditional love acknowledges the importance and worth of family members. It allows them to develop a stable, positive self-esteem and builds their confidence. Love and acceptance helps remove fear of rejection. Nothing makes them feel more significant and valuable than your love.

Nothing else can make them feel as significant as you can. To your children, you are *Mr. Important Person of the Whole Wide World.* ("My dad can lick your dad!") Until children have a significant person demonstrate sacrificial love to them, they will always struggle with feelings of insignificance. Without it, your children may career through life handicapped by poor self-esteem and feelings of insignificance.

So, men, love your children and give them significance. If you don't, they will grow up with feelings of meaninglessness. The function of love affects a child along this continuum:

Significance ⟨ High   LOVE   Low ⟩ Meaninglessness

The Penalty: Meaninglessness
Without perceiving fatherly love, a child will experience feelings of meaninglessness. A neglected child will think, "I am unworthy and lack value. If I were significant, Dad would pay attention to me. I must be defective, blemished, faulty. He ignores me or notices me only when I do something wrong or bad. I will never measure up and be worthy of his attention."

Humans were not meant to feel meaninglessness. God created us as extremely significant beings, higher than angels. Our psyches were not designed to sustain the intolerable pain that results from feelings of meaninglessness. The child who gets no love from Dad, the Family Lover, will try to get it from somewhere else. The unloved child will scramble around and do almost anything to gain feelings of acceptance and significance, which makes him or her prime prey for all sorts of deviant characters and unsavory groups or cults.

Anytime you see a kid acting insanely weird and doing destructive things, you can bet that it is a frantic attempt to gain someone's attention and build feelings of significance. Children are going berserk because they have someone in mind whom they think they are impressing and will give them approval. Unloved children are pitiful victims who will bring their poison to their own family and down their line of descendants until the fourth generation.

THE DYNAMICS OF LOVE

Sandy's steak caper demonstrates the kind of love that holds families together and gives them the deepest kind of gratification. Sandy didn't just stand by and feel gushy emotions of love. Love did not exist in an existentialist subjective burst of feelings contained within her heart and known to me only by her misty, moist, love-saturated eyes.

No. Her love acted. It reached out and tapped me. Love started in her mind, picked up emotions in her heart, leaped out of her by a decision of her will, and smacked into me. Love is a concrete transaction. Love is action that benefits the other person. Love is an attitude converted into the currency of discernible action.

The trick is to implement this concept into your family. Adopt the right attitude—put others first and then think of creative ways to convert this attitude into action. You know it's love when:

1. Parents drag themselves to their kid's soccer game at 8:00 Saturday morning.

2. Mother lets daughter wear her brand-new panty hose.

3. Father lets the family watch a movie instead of "Monday Night Football" (check his temperature).

4. Daughter comes in from school and unloads the dishwasher without being asked.

5. Husband puts down the newspaper, focuses on his wife's eyes, and listens to the latest PTA report.

6. Son gets ready for church on time (mind-boggling)—gets

ready for anything on time (earthshaking).

7. Mom surprises Dad with breakfast in bed on his day off.

8. Son mows the yard without being told (Rapture is near).

9. Father works through the infinite home-repair list that Wife has been drawing up since the Ford presidency.

10. Daughter schedules timely intermissions for distraught family members during her daily morning bathroom occupancy.

So far, I have been talking about a special kind of love. The world actually contains two kinds of love that lie at opposite poles in meaning, expression, and benefits. They are as similar as *give* and *grab*. Unfortunately, humans come by the lesser one naturally; they are born with it. Few discover the existence of the greater one. If they do, it comes across as a little bland at first; so they never capitalize on its heart-blasting potential. Your wife and kids crave one and *ho-hum* the other. I refer to them as Natural Love and Spiritual Love.

All humans are born with Natural Love, which is the greatest kind of love possible for humans. People are stuck with this low-ceiling kind of love. Spiritual Love exists, but it is not an option for regular humans who are not connected with God because He is the only source of it in all the universe. The trick is for an ordinary human to find a way to get God's kind of love inside and begin to use it and reap its benefits.

Natural Love

Natural love is self-oriented. Its focus is on me, not on other people. Its concern is for what benefits accrue to my account. By nature, it takes, grabs, and demands.

With natural love, your emotional attachment to others relates directly to what they can do for you. It says, "You perform for my benefit." Therefore, people must perform to sustain your interest. The more they do for you, the more value they have. Unfortunately, if they also use natural love, they come to the negotiation table with their own list of demands. The relationship then reduces to a contract—as long as I am getting value for value, we can continue. But, if I start giving them more than I get, I start to shop around for a better deal. Natural love always ends up bargaining for a fifty-to-fifty relationship.

119

Examples of ordinary human natural love:

1. A baby says, "Give me the breast, and I'll shut up."
2. A baby says, "Change my diaper, and you get peace."
3. A wife says, "Treat me tender if you want sex."
4. A husband says, "Make me look good in public, and I'll be nice to you."
5. A husband says, "Meet my needs or forget kindness."
6. A dad says, "Make good grades so I can brag."
7. A dad says, "Stay out of trouble so I can relax."

Natural love always fails. When two people focus on self, when they negotiate for advantage over a long period of time, one will begin to win, the other will lose. Competition increases, the stakes rise, the losses pile up, resentment builds, retaliation grows, and, finally, they drift apart in isolation. They don't like each other anymore and want to be away from each other. Natural love retreats to self, and people wrapped up in themselves make mighty small bundles.

Wives and kids will not endure this kind of love. It robs them of significance. Too bad most of them have to settle for it. Since fathers are born with natural love, they have no human options — it's the best men can do on their own. Sadly, even when Spiritual Love becomes available, it's not often made clear, and many fathers overlook it and continue using Natural Love out of default.

Spiritual Love

You can't run a family on Love the Lesser. It does not meet the needs of your family members, and it will not make you capable of meeting biblical standards like those mentioned in Ephesians 5:28-29: "So husbands ought also to love their own wives as their own bodies. He who loves his own wife loves himself; for no one ever hated his own flesh, but nourishes and cherishes it, just as Christ also does the church."

You are to love your family with the same kind of love with which Christ loved the church — Spiritual Love. He acted out His love as a living sacrifice. He nourished, cherished, and eventually died for the sake of the church. His love is unique and not possible with mere humans. Since He is the only source for this kind of love, the only way you can ever acquire and use it is to become a Christian. When

Christ enters your heart, He brings with Him His unique spiritual love, Love the Great. Then you can use God's love in your family.

Spiritual Love is others-oriented. Its focus is on other people, not on me. Its concern is for what benefits accrue to their accounts. By nature it freely gives and demands nothing in return.

With God's love, your emotional attachment to others relates to what you can do for them. It says, "I perform for your benefit. Therefore, people do not have to perform for you to earn your love. The more you do for them, the more value they have and the more significant they feel. Think of the quality of relationship when both people are giving spiritual love. They come together trying to outgive each other. Spiritual love always succeeds because it bargains for a 100-to-100 relationship. Each person gives all they have. Why go anywhere else?

The above definition did not originate with Sandy or me; it comes from Jesus Christ's example. Since no trace of spiritual love naturally exists in man, it must be acquired from an outside source. It becomes available when one trusts Christ as Savior and becomes a Christian. At this time, the Holy Spirit enters one's life and makes spiritual love an option. Galatians 5:22 says that true love is a *fruit* or result of the Holy Spirit working through us.

If you want your family to benefit from this kind of love, you must understand it as demonstrated by Christ and call it forth by faith in the Holy Spirit's ability to display it in your life. Study the Bible's great love passage, Philippians 2:1-8, and gain insight into how spiritual love can revolutionize your family:

> If therefore there is any encouragement in Christ, if there is any consolation of love, if there is any fellowship of the Spirit, if any affection and compassion make my joy complete by being of the same mind, maintaining the same love, united in spirit, intent on one purpose.
>
> Do nothing from selfishness or empty conceit, but with humility of mind lest each of you regard one another as more important than himself; do not merely look out for your own personal interests, but also for the interests of others.
>
> Have this attitude in yourselves which was also in Christ Jesus, who, although He existed in the form of God, did not regard equality with God a thing to be grasped, but emptied Himself, taking the form of a bondservant, and being made in the likeness of men.
>
> And being found in appearance as a man, He humbled Himself by be-

coming obedient to the point of death, even death on a cross.

In verse 5, Paul wrote that Jesus Christ had a certain attitude (mind-set) that all Christians should have. This attitude is characterized by the phrase *humility of mind* found in verse 3. Paul makes three comments about humility of mind:

1. Paul says humility of mind is the essence of Christianity. If there is any encouragement, consolation, fellowship, affection, and compassion in Christianity, then we should achieve the same mind, maintain the same love, unite in spirit, and be intent on one purpose: In other words, the very core, the central issue of Christianity is a concept of love that he calls *humility of mind.*

2. Paul gives a dictionary definition of humility of mind. He wrote that Christianity's essence will produce successful community life, characterized by these three thoughts:

- Do nothing from selfishness or conceit.
- Regard others as more important than yourself.
- Look out for the interests of others.

3. Paul next provided a case study of what humility of mind looks like as it is lived out. He chose the greatest example in history to demonstrate Love is Action. Jesus Christ's sacrificial death on the cross is the epitome of "Love is Action."

Jesus Christ came to earth and became a man. He, who was equal with God (and who exists throughout and beyond all time in community with God, as a Trinity), did not grasp His position of authority and power in heaven. He had humility of mind that caused Him to put His authority and position aside and consider us and our interests before His.

He made a decision to submit His will to the Father. He voluntarily shot His way through life to hit the bull's-eye — the cross. He hit the ground running and never deviated from His goal to reach the cross and die for our sins. He gave His life as a free gift. He served as a sacrificial offering to pay the penalty for our sins.

And He did all those things for people who in no way deserve what He did. We cannot keep the Ten Commandments, observe the Beatitudes, or ever, in any way, earn our way to heaven by being good enough. We cannot achieve heaven by good works or merit salvation by outstanding performances. God, because of His love and grace, distributes salvation as a free gift to anyone who doesn't deserve it but who believes in Jesus Christ.

Jesus had a mind-set that chose to give Himself as a gift for the benefit of others, regardless of their performances. The Scriptures tell us to have the same attitude. We can have and use His kind of love in our family.

Essential Love

The best thing you can ever do for your children is love their mother. Nothing communicates love and security more than for them to see you act out love for your wife. Research has dramatically shown that children feel loved when they see their parents love each other. Nothing else has quite the effect on them as loving your wife.

A QUARTER'S WORTH OF LOVE

Two weeks after the stolen steak deal, I took Helen (eight years old) and Brandon (five years old) to the Cloverleaf Mall in Hattiesburg to do a little shopping. As we drove up, we spotted a Peterbilt eighteen-wheeler parked with a big sign on it that said "Petting Zoo." The kids jumped up in a rush and asked, "Daddy, Daddy. Can we go? Please. Please. Can we go?"

"Sure," I said, flipping them both a quarter before walking into Sears. They bolted away, and I felt free to take my time looking for a scroll saw. A petting zoo consists of a portable fence erected in the mall with about six inches of sawdust and a hundred little furry baby animals of all kinds. Kids pay their money and stay in the enclosure enraptured with the squirmy little critters while their moms and dads shop.

A few minutes later, I turned around and saw Helen walking along behind me. I was shocked to see she preferred the hardware department to the petting zoo. Recognizing my error, I bent down and asked her what was wrong.

She looked up at me with those giant limpid brown eyes and said sadly, "Well, Daddy, it cost fifty cents. So, I gave Brandon my quarter." Then she said the most beautiful thing I ever heard. She repeated the family motto. The family motto is "Love is Action!"

She had given Brandon her quarter, and no one loves cuddly

furry creatures more than Helen. She had watched Sandy take my steak and say, "Love is Action!" She had watched both of us do and say "Love is Action!" for years around the house and Kings Arrow Ranch. She had heard and seen "Love is Action," and now she had incorporated it into her little lifestyle. It had become part of her.

What do you think I did? Well, not what you might think. As soon as I finished my errands, I took Helen to the petting zoo. We stood by the fence and watched Brandon go crazy petting and feeding the animals. Helen stood with her hands and chin resting on the fence and just watched Brandon. I had fifty cents burning a hole in my pocket; I never offered it to Helen, and she never asked for it.

Because she knew the whole family motto. It's not "Love is Action." It's "Love is SACRIFICIAL Action!" Love always pays a price. Love always costs something. Love is expensive. When you love, benefits accrue to another's account. Love is for you, not for me. Love gives; it doesn't grab. Helen gave her quarter to Brandon and wanted to follow through with her lesson. She knew she had to taste the sacrifice. She wanted to experience that total family motto. Love is sacrificial action.

I challenge you to concentrate on putting love into action for your children. Unless your children experience affection from a dominant male authority figure, their potential for happiness may be severely restricted, and they will develop feelings of insignificance. You are Dad, the Family Priest, and your assignment is to love your children and help them establish their significance. Men, just do it!

E-TEAM HUDDLE GUIDE
CHAPTER FIVE: LOVING YOUR CHILDREN

Dad, the Family Shepherd
E-TEAM

After coffee and fellowship, take 10–15 minutes to allow the men to tell about the results of last week's project. This is the accountability part. Be firm with each other and encourage everyone to complete the projects. If anyone encountered difficulty or had a family problem arise, pause to allow the E-Team to address the problem and pray.

E-TEAM DISCUSSION
50–60 minutes

This part allows you to discuss the key concepts in this chapter and relate them to your individual lives. Be sure to leave time to complete the Workout and Encouragement section.

THE PRINCIPLES (Check the text for help.)
1. What is Dave's definition of love?
2. Discuss what it means to be Dad, the Family Priest.
3. Discuss the chief benefit and penalty of this function.

THE IMPLICATIONS (Why are these ideas significant?)
4. Speculate on the difference between a teenager who, when he was a child, had a father who practiced "Love is Action" and a teenager whose dad did not.
5. When teenagers do not feel significant, what are some actions, behaviorisms, values and personality traits they use to try to compensate? When you see one acting out their feelings of meaninglessness, how does it make you feel? What is your natural reaction? How does your reaction make them feel?
6. What can fathers do to interrupt this cycle and make children feel loved and significant?

THE APPLICATION (How do these ideas affect me?)
7. Tell the E-Team how you feel about having the responsibility of being Dad, the Family Priest.
8. Describe one incident in your childhood that stands out as a great illustration of how your dad put love into action for you. Is there one "love action" you always wanted from your dad but never got?
9. Describe some ways you have recently told your wife and children you love them by putting love into action.

E-TEAM WORKOUT
10–15 minutes

Allow each man to choose one of the project options (plays) to perform during the week. If so desired, design your own project. Note: it is essential that each man leave having made a definite commitment to a specific project.

1st PLAY:
Go to your father and prove you love him by a "Love is Action" event.

2nd PLAY:
Go to your wife and each child and prove your love by a "Love is Action" event.

3rd PLAY:
Make an appointment with your wife and study Philippians 2. Look for the many principles in these 30 verses that deal with the practical aspects of love and discuss how to apply them.

E-TEAM ENCOURAGEMENT
5–10 minutes

Close the meeting in prayer for each other and your families. Include in your prayer a specific request for spiritual power to successfully complete your project.

BREAK THE HUDDLE,
GO HOME AND RUN THE PLAY!

Chapter Six
Bonding Your Children

*"God's relationship with humans is one of intimate
bonding, and all human intimacies are
'rehearsals' for the ultimate reunion of humans
with their Creator."*

—Donald M. Joy

In 1964, just before the Christmas of my senior year at Georgia
Tech, I took delivery of my brand-spankin'-new Pontiac Bonne-
ville, which the St. Louis Cardinals gave me for signing with them. I
headed home with a 24" color TV to give Mom and a complete set of
Craftsman tools for Dad. I gave my '57 Chevy to my little sister. It
was going to be my family's biggest Christmas because, as a second-
round draft choice in the NFL, I could afford it.

My plans called for a week at home and then on to Mobile,
Alabama, to play in the Senior Bowl, where Joe Namath and I were
chosen as captains of the South team. It promised to be the best
Christmas ever, but it turned out to be the saddest and loneliest of
my life.

The first few days at home went well. The excitement of my good
fortune in football carried my family along to some good times
without the customary bickering and hassle. But on the fourth day,
after my dad got into his whiskey cache, the holidays started degen-
erating rapidly. My dad was a "mean drunk." Whenever he drank,
he got fighting mad and showed his cruel punitive streak. He picked
on me most of the time, but this time he started criticizing and
demeaning Mom.

After listening to him berate and ridicule Mom all day long, I
reached a breaking point. I jumped up and faced him. I told him to
leave Mom alone. I called him a "dumb drunk" who had to bully

others to make himself feel good.

It was the night before Christmas and all through the house, not a creature was stirring, not even a mouse!

The whole family stood paralyzed waiting in a hush for the explosion. The whole family stood transfixed at my audacity to confront Dad. He slowly turned his red-eyed glare on me in disbelief and found himself so contorted by anger that he couldn't get his mouth to work.

He finally gained control of his mouth. He started screaming and cursing me for getting too big for my britches. He accused me of getting cocky just because I turned pro and now had a little bonus money in my pocket. He reminded me that no one, not even The Great Linebacker, stood in his home and told him what to do.

He kept spewing words at me and swilling his whiskey until he finally passed out in his recliner. The rest of the family had all melted away and gone to bed for the night. I finally went to bed but did not sleep. At 2 A.M., I quietly gathered my things and snuck out to my car, pushed it away from the house, and drove all night to Mobile, crying as I cruised down the Gulf Coast highway.

As I drove through the night along the ocean, I thought my heart would burst from the squeezing pressure I felt in my chest. Our family should have been so happy. This Christmas could have been so great. But, it turned out like all the rest, except I didn't have to stay there and take it.

I arrived in Mobile three days before the reporting date for the Senior Bowl. I found a little room in a local college dorm and spent three days grieving. I had officially been ostracized from my family and was now on my own and by myself. I felt severe loneliness. My spirit felt distressed because my desperate need to belong had been frustrated. The feelings of not belonging that I had carried all my life intensified. I felt like I had no place to fit.

Even when I joined the South team and started preparing for the game with the greatest athletes in the South, I could not get into the spirit of things. I felt miserable throughout the whole experience. In the midst of the all-star hoopla and the excitement of the game, I felt intense loneliness. I had been busted, not bonded.

Make sure you bond your kids into your family. Don't ever abandon them and sit by while they eat out their hearts. They could end up being smack in the middle of an excited throng of merry-making people and feel very alone. Your children were never intended for isolation and loneliness.

You are like a coach who helps his players know where they belong and how to work together to make a good team. You must help your children feel like they fit. Be a father who bonds, not busts.

The ANALYSIS OF BONDING

The Fatherhood Function: Bonding

Bonding is the creative art of deep knowing and skillful placing of each person into a special niche to form a whole where everyone's needs for belongingness are met. It means to form an attachment. It gives someone a place to fit. It makes a child feel closeness, intimacy, uniqueness, and specialness. It develops trust and security.

The Role: Dad the Family Coach

Your family needs a coach. You, the family coach, must be there and focus intently on building your family into a team where they all rest securely in feelings of belongingness.

The magic word in coaching is teamwork. Teamwork wins games. Winning coaches know how to take a group of individual players, put them in exactly the right position, and motivate each to make his or her maximum contribution. The coach must have keen insight into each player, a thorough knowledge of what each position requires, and then match the players to the right positions.

Each player has a place. They know where they fit. They belong. And they know they do best at their position. This knowledge builds the secure foundation of security each player needs. Then, after he or she learns the basics, he or she can concentrate on the game plan.

If a player doesn't feel secure in his or her position and feel confident in his or her ability to perform there, he or she is handicapped and won't help the team much. When the whole team peaks on feelings of belongingness and confidence, we say we have the *Big M*—momentum. And *Big M* is hard to stop. When it shows up, the team surges ahead to accomplish great feats.

Does your family have the *Big M?* It sure needs it. You are the coach. If you don't work on momentum for your family, they simply won't have it. You must know all the family positions and become the world's greatest expert on each family member. You need to earn a doctorate degree on the study of your wife and each child.

When you know each member intimately, you can help them settle into their positions, learn the basics, and start making their maximum contribution to the team.

We first learn about bonding in the family. The family exists as a primary resource to meet our belonging needs while simultaneously serving as a conditioning and training institute to equip people with the skills for bonding.

A child starts learning to bond at birth and needs intensive bonding during the first two or three years. If the child has bonded well by then, he or she will have developed a healthy capacity for feeling belongingness. But, if the child doesn't experience belongingness by then, his or her capacity for feeling it will be stunted, and the child will struggle with feelings of aloneness for the rest of his or her life.

As children move out of the dependence phase into the independence phase, they encounter powerful forces moving in opposite directions. One force, centrifugal force, wants to hurl them out into the world to help them move toward freedom and autonomy. Another force, centripetal force, wants to collapse them inward to coagulate and stay fixed.

A good coach understands the importance of the maturity process and knows what to do in each phase. An infant's bonding thirst must be abundantly quenched in order to become content with belongingness. With this need secure, the child is able to face the pressure required to break into orbit later on. Otherwise, when the time comes to develop individuality and healthy separateness, the unmet needs for belongingness trap the clinging child in the dependent phase. The child can't break out and become a healthy, separate, unique person.

The Benefit: Belongingness
Belongingness is the deep need all of us have for affiliation and attachment. The family starts with a pledge of bonding to establish

belongingness — the bride and groom take vows to never separate. They commit to belong to each other until death dissolves the bonds.

God created us as sentient beings who yearn for attachment. The human soul was never intended to exist feeling loneliness. God wants us to bond with Him, and He created the family as a training exercise with which to perfect bonding skills. Family members bond with each other to avoid the profound despair that comes with isolation.

A child starts learning to bond at birth and has completed much of his or her bonding training course by the age of four or five. If the child has bonded well by then, he or she will have developed a healthy capacity for feeling belongingness. But, if the child doesn't experience belongingness by then, his or her capacity for feeling it will be stunted, and the child will struggle with feelings of aloneness for the rest of his or her life. The function of bonding affects the child along this continuum:

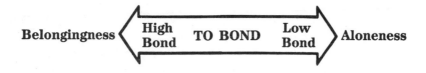

You, the family coach, must be there and focus intently on building your family into a team where they all rest securely in feelings of belongingness. This is the key to instilling your family with the *Big M*.

The Penalty: Aloneness

The ultimate core of the human soul cries out to belong. God made us that way. We were not intended to suffer the separation of soul from our body (earthly death), or the soul from God (spiritual death), or our soul from others (social death). These grim conditions all result because of original sin, which is why God hates sin so much. Our hearts have been clawed and slashed because of destructive attachments and banished to bleak moonscapes of isolation and aloneness.

All of our attempts at relationships are efforts to make contact with others and alleviate the pain of separation. Our ability to bond determines our level of success at relationships. Without a family that bonds and a father who sets the pace for bonding, a child grows up without the experience and model to copy.

Such a child will suffer the effects of isolation more than ever. The child will never feel like he or she belongs. The child will always feel like he or she is on the outside looking in. No matter how many clubs, teams, organizations, groups, or societies his or her name appears on, the child will not feel like he or she belongs. Not only will the child not feel like he or she belongs, the child won't know that something is missing. The child knows that others are different, but he or she won't know how.

Robert McGee, Pat Springle, and Jim Craddock in *Your Parents and You*, list the negative symptoms from poor bonding: " ... shame, depression, self-hatred, emptiness, addictions, fear of being known, loneliness, denial, the inability to perceive and experience reality, feeling attacked, anxiety and fear" (Houston: Word Publishing, 1990, 30). Not a pretty list.

A poorly bonded child will spend megavolts of energy trying to get attached. The child will try anything to gain acceptance and eventually associate with anyone who will befriend him or her. The child will gladly join gangs, cults, radicals, or revolutionists in his or her quest for belongingness.

In his work with families with uncontrollable kids, Dr. Ken Magid *(High Risk: Children without a Conscience,* cited by Bill Scanion "What Causes Bad Kids?" Knight News Service, Oct. 4, 1990*)* reports the number of kids without a conscience is "drastically increasing." He says:

> The teenager who shot a classmate to see what it would look like, the 8 year old who drowned a toddler to find out what it would feel like — no one took time to love these children when they needed it the most. It comes down to a break in primary bonding. Bonding is the glue that holds the child together. It gives a sense of trust in the world, that things are all right and the world is all right.

Lack of bonding tears the soul and causes major destructive behaviors. In poorly bonded homes, children are much more prone to get involved in illegal drugs and premarital intercourse. The risk increases even more when the father moves out of the family. *The Journal of Pediatrics* (cited by Associated Press in *Arkansas Democrat,* Sept. 7, 1989) reports that:

> ... the odds of illicit drug use ran significantly higher—almost twice as high—among students living with only one parent (the mother). The pediatricians discovered a parallel, but even more pronounced pattern for sexual activity. 116 (1990)

Another report from *The Journal of Pediatrics* says that "Youngsters who look after themselves after school for 11 or more hours a week on a regular basis are twice as likely to abuse alcohol, tobacco and marijuana as children who aren't latchkey kids" (cited by Associated Press in *Arkansas Democrat,* Sept. 7, 1989).

Lack of bonding causes pain. Of all the tortures ever devised, many break the body, but the one that eventually breaks the mind is isolation. Prisoners, castaways, sentinels, and astronauts complain most of the haunting fear that comes from choking aloneness.

THE DYNAMICS OF BONDING
God set us loose in the world with an intense psychological drive to attach to others and feel *belongingness.* God designed and built this need, this deep craving to belong, deep in our hearts. We are driven to bond to others—to feel a part of them.

This drive acts like a missile's heat-seeking guidance system that steers us through life, looking for satisfying relationships where we feel *belongingness.* Just as God is a God in community (the Trinity), a man or a woman is a person designed for the community. He or she must develop intimate relationships to capture the feelings of belongingness, or he or she suffers.

Yet, even the most securely bonded and intimate relationships do not totally quench a person's thirst for belonging. People yearn for the belongingness uniquely experienced in fellowship with God. The Scriptures say it this way:

> As the deer pants for water brooks, so my soul **pants** for Thee, O God. . . . My soul **thirsts** for Thee, my flesh yearns for Thee, in a dry and weary land where there is no water. . . . My soul **longs** for Thee, as a parched land.   Psalms 42:1; 63:1; 143:6

God designed humans with a soul that *pants, thirsts,* and *longs* for Him. Nothing can fill that vacuum deep in a person's heart except God made known through Jesus Christ. Back when I became a Christian at Georgia Tech, Jesus Christ entered my life, and I came to know Him. My needs for belongingness started getting satisfied when I started the process of knowing Him.

A person can never rest until he or she knows God and establishes belongingness with Him. Without God, loneliness waits like a vicious set of jaws that clamps on and does not let go. Without a family to provide belongingness, a child feels eaten up with loneliness. Worldwide opinion regards nothing quite so sad as a child with a lonely face.

The Bonding Fields

In our flight toward God, we encounter many people along the way with whom we practice and develop our bonding skills. It's as if human relationships function as a practice field to cultivate the capacity to bond in preparation for the perfect eternal bonding we will enjoy with God. Dr. Donald M. Joy, in his excellent book, *Bonding,* wrote, "The basic thesis of this book is that God's relationship with humans is one of intimate bonding, and that all human intimacies are 'rehearsals' for the ultimate reunion of humans with their Creator" (Waco, Texas: Word Books, ix).

Bonding, therefore, is a fundamental aspect of human nature. Working backward, God wants us to bond with Him because He constructed us with a need for belongingness that can be met only in tightly bonded relationships.

The Bonding Instinct

God puts such a premium on bonding that He built in automatic devices to help us with it. Take a look at the natural bonding helps that God installed in the system.

Pre-Birth Bonding

Communicating acceptance to children begins even before they are born. By careful diet and healthy exercise, a mother ensures the best possible environment for the unborn child in which to weave and spin its little body. Even the emotions of pregnant mothers can affect the unborn's feelings. While the child is in the womb, it can hear, taste, experience, and even learn and feel on a basic level. The unborn child can develop chronic anxiety toward the mother that will scar the baby's personality. The unborn child begins to form a worldview that falls somewhere between these two limits:

1. The world is a good place to be: I feel at home in it. I fit. I am acceptable. Therefore, I feel as if I belong.

2. The world is a bad place to be: I feel like an alien in it. I don't fit. I am not acceptable. Therefore, I feel as if I don't belong.

Birth Bonding

God designed birth to function as a special bonding time between parents and the baby. Dr. Donald M. Joy describes this critical time in great detail in his book, *Bonding*. Here are some selected portions from his book (pp. 114–15):

> There is a period (at birth) of heightened sensitivity to attachment. It seems to last for up to three hours following delivery. Sensitivity to parents or any stimulus tends to wane following that time. . . .
>
> The newborn has a heightened visual acuity, with focusing capacity that matches adult vision, in which a "zoom lens" ability is able to focus on any object near or far. However, within a few hours after birth, the baby's vision will tend to become fixed at a focal length of about ten inches (the distance between breast and mother's face), with all else blurred out of focus. The visual acuity equips the newborn with search ability to locate the object to which to bond . . .
>
> The human mother tends to vocalize at the sight of her newborn, using sounds she does not normally use. These tend to be "helium-like," high-pitched speech to which the newborn is especially responsive. The newborn quickly turns to follow sound as well as sight, with sensitivities and abilities which will recede after the first few hours. . . .
>
> Skin-to-skin contact, literally galvanic connections, appear to have important effects on attachment. Fathers are often advised to remove shirts so that both the warmth of the body and the magic of skin contact can communicate "ownership" and affection to the infant. . . .
>
> The unique aroma of the lanolin-laced lining of the placenta covers the newborn with a gentle skin treatment which has a unique odor. This odor appears to trigger "encompassing" gesturing in the mother, sometimes almost involuntarily—enhancing the desire to hold, to cradle, and to embrace her baby. This odor has been observed to trigger similar responses in other women present at the delivery. . . .
>
> The parents' bodies joined to the infant provide a source of stabiliza-

tion of body temperature during the first few hours of life. The newborn has never had to produce its own body heat alone. . . .

How thoughtful of God to provide these fascinating helps for the bonding process. A baby bonds to the mother for nine months in a special way, then squirts out into the arms of waiting, embracing parents. A small window of time exists at birth for a once-in-a-lifetime bonding experience that will go a long way in establishing the person's capacity to feel belongingness.

Child Bonding

There is no such thing as a chance child. God specifically designed and engineered every child (Ps. 139). God handcrafted your designer child and implanted him or her into your family for a purpose. You are the only ones He chose to take temporary custody of each of your children. Your child is a training project to bring out certain characteristics in you. Therefore, give thanks for your child, no matter what. Make thankfulness to God for your child a bedrock condition of your heart.

> Behold, children are a gift of the Lord; the fruit of the womb is a reward.
> Like arrows in the hand of a warrior, so are the children of one's youth.
> —Psalm 127:3-4

Be thankful for your arrows. You, the Christian hunter with an eye on the fourth generation target, have children like arrows to shoot down through the generations. Your child-arrows bear your markings and featherings. They are an extension of you that hurtles through time to impact the leaders of the twenty-second century. Don't you want to send flaming arrows forward? Kids on fire for Christ?

If your family has this kind of attitude, a child born to you will begin life feeling accepted, and his or her belongingness needs will be tended to. The child will then feel as if he or she fits. The child likes moving along his or her *groove*. The child will also feel as if he or she belongs.

If we don't accept the child's *bent* and try to cram the kid into an artificial mold, the child will experience intense frustration and feel as if he or she is not accepted for who he or she is. The child will feel rejection. "If you don't accept my ways, you don't accept me." "Love me, love my gifts." And the child will not feel as if he or she belongs.

The Bonding Cycle

Children feel bonded when they feel accepted on a nonperformance basis. You need to convey, "I accept you, not the misbehavior, but I love and accept you." (Volume Three, *Dad the Family Mentor*, deals with how to correct misbehavior.)

One of the most common problems strong Christian families have with child acceptance is what I call the maturity lag. The child's actual maturity level lags behind what the parents think it should be. Another way of saying it is that many parents, especially strong evangelistic behavior-oriented parents, expect the child to act much more mature than possible simply because the child is a Christian. "To protect our testimony, we expect such and such behavior!" they think.

You must be careful to accept your child where he or she is in the process of maturing. Let the child be his or her age and act accordingly. You must show acceptance, progressively as the child progresses in maturity.

Two warnings to dads with sons: Don't expect a perfect all-purpose bond and don't expect to keep your son to yourself. By the very nature of your total job assignment, you can't be your son's best *buddy*. You can be buddies, but there is a line that cannot be crossed. You must maintain a deep intimacy along with a command profile that automatically precludes some aspects of being best pals.

There will come a day when you need to transfer your son over to bond with the tribe's other young warriors. He will enter into a different kind of bond, in some ways closer, in some ways not. But it will and must happen, and you must not try to prohibit it. You should encourage it. Don't be jealous. Be thankful you have built a high capacity to bond into your son.

A man has eight crucial bonding points in his lifetime as he moves from total dependence through independence to interdependence. You need to be aware of these as your son moves through them and act accordingly.

The Male Bonding Points

Years	1	1–2	3–13	14–17	18–22	23–44	45+
	Mother	Father	Playmates	Initiates	Warriors	Sons / Mentor	Apprentice

THE MALE BONDING POINTS

For the first few months of his life, a boy starts out bonding with his mother (point 1). But almost from the start, he starts scanning for you, his dad, his second and most important point (point 2). From one until five years of age, you are his primary bonding figure. Then, he gradually moves into bonding relationships with other playmates (point 3) and practices the bonding skills he learned with you.

At puberty (point 4) he lurches out radically to attempt serious bonding with other young bloods, the male initiates, who are on the verge of manhood. He is now honing his skills, getting ready for his *rite of passage* and his acceptance into the brotherhood of tribal warriors (point 5). At the appointed time, he needs to be transferred out of the family matrix and childhood into the system of manhood.

Only a boy can make a man. But only other men in the tribe can bring him into manhood. His mother is totally out of the picture. Even you as his father can't because he will always be your beloved boy. Only the young men can absorb your boy into their ranks of manhood and pronounce him an acceptable male. Your boy must require an audience before the young men, have his masculinity tested, and found approved. He must be confirmed and bonded into the mystic fellowship of single-adult males.

All his life he has been practicing his masculinity with you in the safety of a protective mentor-type bond. Now, he is forced out of the nest and must successfully bond with the strata of men with whom he will process through the life cycle. This pivotal point in his life is awesome. He must succeed, or he will be discarded to the outskirts of the community's male mainstream.

Point 6 finds him bonding with his sons to get them ready for their manhood network. At the same time, he needs to bond with his own mentor (point 7), a father figure who will pick him up and stay with him until his forties. Later in life, he reaches point 8, where he turns to become a mentor for a few young men starting out with families.

The problem is that Americans don't follow the track. They bond well with Mom, and that's as far as many of them ever get. They don't break off from Mom well because Dad is not there to wean them away.

Baby boys do not attach to dads because their dads are not there. Our culture has nipped this bond in the bud. Robert Bly, a poet and prominent thinker on issues of manhood, said:

> Now we don't do bonding with the father well. What did Jeffrey Gore say in *The Americans?* He said, "In order to become an American, it's necessary, first of all, to reject your father." That's about all that is necessary. You don't even attack him, as in Freud; you just regard him as ridiculous, as in all those movies that we're seeing, and all the filmstrips and all the situation comedies in which the men are — the fathers are completely ridiculous ("A Gathering of Men," an interview with Bill Moyers on Public TV, New York, 1990).

Bonding skills are thrown off kilter right from the beginning. Next, boys have trouble bonding with their playmates. They struggle through a school system dominated by female authority figures who stress feminine behavior and bonding patterns.

By the time they get to point 4, the male initiates are confused about their masculinity and harbor distorted ideas about how to bond with peers and what constitutes appropriate *initiation rites*. They are well on their way to becoming dysfunctional. They join clubs, gangs, and cults that have destructive rites. Only a few paternally deprived boys are lucky enough to end up in athletics.

From this point on, the American male remains isolated. In *The Friendless American Male*, David Smith writes, "One serious problem is the friendless condition of the average American male. Men find it hard that they need the fellowship of other men. Even when men are frequently together their social interaction begins and remains at a superficial level" (Ventura Calif.: Regal Books, 1983, 15).

Joseph Mensman, in *Psychology Today*, writes, "In our interviews (with men), friendship was largely noticeable by its absence. Close friendship with a man or a woman is rarely experienced by American men" ("Friendship and Alienation," Oct. 1979).

It all goes back to the father/son bond. This relationship primes the bonding pump. All other bonding relationships stem from this crucial bond. Do it, men.

E-TEAM HUDDLE GUIDE
CHAPTER SIX: BONDING YOUR CHILDREN

Dad, the Family Shepherd
E-TEAM

After coffee and fellowship, take 10–15 minutes to allow the men to tell about the results of last week's project. This is the accountability part. Be firm with each other and encourage everyone to complete the projects. If anyone encountered difficulty or had a family problem arise, pause to allow the E-Team to address the problem and pray.

E-TEAM DISCUSSION
50–60 minutes

This part allows you to discuss the key concepts in this chapter and relate them to your individual lives. Be sure to leave time to complete the Workout and Encouragement section.

THE PRINCIPLES (Check the text for help.)
1. What is Dave's definition of bond?
2. Discuss what it means to be Dad the Family Coach.
3. Discuss the chief benefit and penalty of this function.

THE IMPLICATIONS (Why are these ideas significant?)
4. Explain why a child who did not have strong infant bonding with primary care-givers will have difficulty bonding to God and others later on in life. Do you believe this? Why or why not?
5. Discuss why the strength of father-child bonding is directly proportionate to how well the father knows the child.
6. Speculate on how well you think American fathers know their children. How will this affect their child's bonding capacity? How will this affect our culture in the next generation?

THE APPLICATION (How do these ideas affect me?)
7. With the chart on the Eight Male Bonding Points in mind, tell the E-Team where you are on the chart and which bonding points you

have completed successfully. Which ones do you feel were not accomplished satisfactorily?

8. Describe how you feel about the bond you have with your dad right now. Describe how you feel about the bond you have with your wife and each child.

9. Optional question: Describe the bond you have with God right now.

E-TEAM WORKOUT
10–15 minutes

Allow each man to choose one of the project options (plays) to perform during the week. If so desired, design your own project. Note: it is essential that each man leave having made a definite commitment to a specific project.

1st PLAY:
Make an appointment with your wife and describe the chart on the Eight Male Bonding Points. Describe to her how solid your bonding was at each point that you have been through.

2nd PLAY:
Make an appointment with your wife and study John 17. Look for the many principles in these 26 verses that apply to unity and discuss how you can apply these to improve the bonding in your family.

E-TEAM ENCOURAGEMENT
5–10 minutes

Close the meeting in prayer for each other and your families. Include in your prayer a specific request for spiritual power to successfully complete your project.

BREAK THE HUDDLE,
GO HOME AND RUN THE PLAY!

Chapter Seven
Leading Your Children

*"Our very survival as a people will depend on
the presence or absence of masculine leadership
in millions of homes."*

—James Dobson

BACKWARD FOR A FUTURE

The brand-new gleaming sleek white Delta 88 Oldsmobile came into my life and haunted me. Festooned with sparkling chrome and reeking with rocket engine power, the dream machine shimmered in the driveway seductively so near yet so unapproachable. My dad had just bought it, and no rowdy teenage boy was going to get his lecherous hands on it.

I tried every way in the world to persuade Dad to let me borrow it. My great fantasy in life was to get my little sweetheart in it. I finally asked to borrow it three months in advance so Dad couldn't possibly think of a reason to say no. It worked. "I guess so," he said. "It depends on how you act around here."

There never had been a better teenager. I gave my dad's shoes spitshines, I kept his belt buckle and military silver glittering, and I kept the lawn mowed and the trash carried out. The emotional pressure of being good nearly drove me crazy. But I did it. I earned the car.

Finally, the big night arrived. Dad called me in and said, "OK, Son, you can borrow the car tonight. But you got three rules. One, you can't double-date. I don't want a bunch of teenagers hot roddin' around town showin' off. Two, you gotta be in by 11:00. Three, you can only put twenty miles on the car."

"Yes, Sir," I said. And I bolted for the car.

Dad came out, checked the odometer, and told me again, "Remember, only twenty miles."

I was in trouble before I drove out of the driveway because we lived ten miles out of town.

Of course, I double-dated. Of course, I found myself at the Oasis, the local hangout, at about 11:00. Of course, I saw that I had logged seventeen miles at the halfway point, which meant I was destined to arrive home with thirty-four more miles on the odometer. That was fourteen miles too much. Of course, I realized I was doomed. So I said, "To heck with it! I might as well go for it and enjoy it while I can."

Around midnight, I dropped off the girls, took my buddy home, and began the sobering trip back to face my dad. But, instead of cruising down the highway that went to our housing area, I pulled up to an old gravel road that went clear around Fort Bliss to my home.

If you could have been there back in 1959 standing by that old gravel road, you would have seen a very anxious sixteen-year-old boy barreling down the road at a speed of 35 mph — backward! I had discovered an amazing and useful phenomenon. When you drove the mighty rocket 88 in reverse, it not only didn't record the miles, it subtracted miles. So, I backed home seven miles that didn't register and took off seven miles.

I drove up our driveway, and Dad was waiting on the porch for me. I got out and stood at attention while he inspected me and the car. He knew I had broken curfew but he couldn't prove that I had double-dated. And he *knew* I had tricked him on the mileage somehow. He couldn't find out how, but he remarked that the transmission sure smelled hot. He sniffed around his charmed chariot, glared at me now and then, and muttered to himself for fifteen minutes while the transmission smoked, but he couldn't prove a thing.

Many moons elapsed before I got the Olds again.

This episode shows how a certain leadership style can culminate in the exact opposite of what a father wants. Dad wanted me to be reliable, honest, loyal, respectful, and dependable. Instead, as the Olds story points out, I was deceitful, dishonest, undependable, untrustworthy, and I had a bad attitude.

It wasn't how Dad handled this particular incident that made me that way. My sin nature had a propensity in those directions, and Dad's long-range leadership style activated and encouraged those undesirable traits. It was my faulty heart and Dad's flawed style that gave me my particular set of problems.

Children need the stability and direction that comes with quality, consistent, long-range leadership.

The ANALYSIS OF LEADING

The Fatherhood Function of Leading	
Function	LEAD your family.
Role	Be a MAN.
Benefit	To give IDENTITY.
Penalty	ANONYMITY.

The Fatherhood Function: Leading

A leader is one under authority who provides stability, knows what to do next, and can motivate his team to work together to accomplish a task with maximum efficiency while building unity.

The Role: Dad the Family Man

Be a man: Be a father. Let your wife represent femininity. A man should be a male, and a woman makes a better female, and never the twain shall meet. A child doesn't need a set of androgynous interchangeable bookend parents. A child must be exposed to a masculine father and a feminine mother in order to establish a healthy rewarding gender-identity.

Of course, many functions of fathers and mothers are interchangeable, but a definite maleness and femaleness need emphasis. Who and how you are as a male counts as much as doing the deeds. You are a father, not just a parent. An interesting note about the emphasis the Bible places on fatherhood lies in sheer volume of references to it: There are 1,190 biblical references to fatherhood, 365 to motherhood, and only 36 to parenthood. The chart on page 146 shows the comparison in graphic terms.

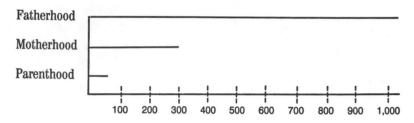

Comparison of Biblical References of Terms for Child Custodians

A major characteristic of manhood is being mature enough to place himself voluntarily into submission to a higher authority. It takes a real man to fit into a chain of command—to exercise authority over some and bear responsibility under another.

In the eighth chapter of Matthew, we read about the centurion who pleased Christ with his insight into authority and submission. He stated that he, like Christ, was a man under authority, and because of his submission to the will of a higher power, he exercised leadership over those under him.

The single most important fact a father should bear in mind is that he is not at the top of the command chain. He is but a link. He exercises authority because he is a man under authority, and his purpose is to impose the will of a higher power, not his own.

This concept of an obedient authority figure magnifies in importance when you consider the major job description of a child: to grow in balanced maturity (Luke 2:52) and learn to fit into a chain of command (Eph. 6:1). A child's job is to learn obedience, and it is best mastered by watching a father walk in obedience to God. Ephesians 6:1 says, "Children, obey your parents in the Lord, for this is right."

That verse states that childhood is a course in obedience taught by parents in obedience. How can we expect a child to learn obedience if a father constantly demonstrates disobedience to God and subjection to every whim of self?

The Benefit: Identity

As Dad the family head, you function as the presenting family figure. You are its major source of identification. It goes by your name. Since you are the family representative, control knob, and face, you provide a symbol or logo of the family. As such, each family member defines personal identity in relation to you. You help each member establish personal identity.

Whereas you tend to identify yourself with your job, your wife tends to identify herself with you. Your children are born with no self-concept, and they begin taking all their cues on self-identity from you. They voraciously read you and interpret you into a new unique expression. Even when they soak up identity from Mom, they still absorb you because so much of your wife's identity is constructed from you.

You help them locate themselves and say, "This is who I am and where I fit. My dad's values, ethics, priorities pour into me and make me who I am." If you provide good leadership, your children build a secure self-identity by the age of six. Don't worry, they will be themselves. If you are not consistent in your leadership, they get confused and struggle to nail themselves down.

One strategic way you help your children locate themselves is in the way they establish their gender roles by their interaction with you. A child develops gender-role identity by copying parents. Moreover, a child's deep security and feelings of beingness are wrapped up in their core understanding of their sexual self. Paul Jewett, in his book, *Man as Male and Female*, claims that gender-role identity is essential:

> Sexuality permeates one's individual being to its very depth; it conditions every facet of one's life as a person. As the self is always aware of itself as an "I", so this "I" is always aware of itself as himself or herself. Our self-knowledge is indissolubly bound up not simply with our human being but with our sexual being (Grand Rapids: William Eerdmans Publishing Co., 1975, 172).

Dr. John Piper, editor of *Recovering Biblical Manhood and Womanhood* (July 1990), addresses this issue in his pamphlet, *What's the Difference?* (Wheaton, Ill.: The Council on Biblical Manhood and Womanhood, 1989, 9):

> The tendency today is to stress the equality of men and women by minimizing the unique significance of our maleness or femaleness. But this depreciation of male and female personhood is a great loss. . . . The con-

sequence of this confusion is not a free and happy harmony among gender-free persons relating on the basis of abstract competencies. The consequence rather is more divorce, more homosexuality, more sexual abuse, more promiscuity, more social awkwardness, and more emotional distress and suicide that come with the loss of God-given identity.

Surprisingly, the father functions as the primary determinant in his child's process of establishing gender-role identity. Fathers are most likely to differentiate their children according to sex. Mothers are usually less concerned with distinctive roles for boys and girls, while dads tend to focus on masculinity for boys and femininity for girls.

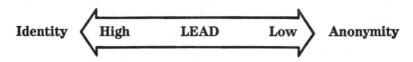

Identity   High   LEAD   Low   Anonymity

Your children need a constant steady supply of positive constructive input from you. Nothing will determine your children's potential in life more than the contribution you make to their identity. What kind of legacy will you inscribe on your children's hearts? Fatherhood expert Dr. Henry Biller writes:

> Fathers more than mothers vary their behavior as a function of the sex of the child, and fathers appear to play an especially significant role in encouraging their daughters' feminine development. The father's acceptance and reinforcement of his daughter's femininity greatly facilitates the development of her self-concept. . . . Comparisons of father-absent and father-present boys suggested that availability of the father is an important factor in the masculine development of young boys. There is evidence that the young father-absent boy is likely to have an unmasculine self-concept (*Paternal Deprivation* [Lexington, Mass.: Lexington Books, 1974], 53, 122).

The Penalty: Anonymity

Children without a strong father in the home grow up with poor ego-strength. The term anonymity, the state of being unknown or obscure, describes how they feel. They feel as if they are irrelevant, superfluous, and expendable. They don't matter. Paternally deprived children feel defective, incompetent, inept, and useless.

These feelings are extremely painful because they run cross-grained to how our human psyche was constructed. God did not create us to be unknown or obscure creatures. He knows each one of us down to the hairs on our heads. We are not nameless microscopic motes of dust. God created us in His image, and we were meant to reflect His stature and dignity.

These people grow up with a loss of identity. They spend their greatest energy trying to establish a sense of being. They fall into the trap of trying to construct feelings of identity from things of the world. They believe these falsehoods:

1. *I am* because I have amassed great wealth.
2. *I am* because I have many possessions.
3. *I am* because I am best at _____.
4. *I am* because I have achieved fame.
5. *I am* because I move with important people.
6. *I am* because I endure intense experiences.
7. *I am* because I alter my mind and moods with drugs.
8. *I am* because I have New Age experiences.

The only hope for establishing your *I am* is to meet God, the great *I Am*, and let Him establish His identity in you. No one can ever establish identity for an eternal creature from the things of the earth.

THE DYNAMICS OF LEADING

In the late sixties, the National Football League underwent a revolution in leadership philosophy. Out went the blood-n-guts, "You're an animal" coaching style and in came the MBA and the "Let's take this approach" style. Tom Landry, Chuck Noll, Don Shula, and Bill Walsh led a new breed of coaches that used more than just muscle and grit to win games. They were masters of football-craft, but they also used their brains and were not afraid to invest their hearts into their teams — they treated the players with dignity.

Leadership in the home must be more dimensional than just spelling out the rules and squeezing kids into conformity. A wise family shepherd uses state-of-the-art skills, his mind, and his heart. He is pleased to impart not only his message but his life. The Bible describes good leadership as a careful blend of skills and heart: "So he shepherded them according to the integrity of his heart, and guided them with his skillful hands" (Ps. 78:72).

The Heart in Leadership

Family management is heart management. A father provides leadership from his heart, and he focuses on the heart of his child. Proverbs 23:26 tells how a boy needs to give his heart to his dad and delight in his manly ways: "Give me your heart, my son, and let your eyes delight in my ways."

Did you notice the responsibility God gives you for your child's heart? Since the Bible says you must watch over your child's heart, you need to know a heart's nature and the rules for its care and feeding.

If the father's heart is not involved in his child-management style, things can go the wrong way: "And he will restore the hearts of the fathers to their children, and the hearts of the children to their fathers, lest I come and smite the land with a curse" (Mal. 4:6).

A person is not a body. A person is a living eternal spirit that temporarily resides in a container that gradually deteriorates to the point where it can no longer serve as a habitat for the spirit. Then, the spirit leaves the body and goes before the presence of God.

A person is not a personality. A personality is merely a collection of behavior tools and defense mechanisms which people use to relate to others. A person lives behind a personality. A person lives in a body and behind a personality. The Bible uses the term *heart* to refer to the essence or center of a person: "Watch over your heart with all diligence, for from it flow the springs of life" (Prov. 4:23).

Heart is translated from the Greek word *kardia,* which comes from a root word that means to quiver or palpitate. It means *the seed of life.* It is the fountain of all thought, passions, desires, appetites, affections, purposes, and endeavors. It is the *anima* (true inner self) by which our body lives. Dr. Paul Kooistra, president of Columbia Seminary, defines the heart as "the center of being where one's personality comes together into an integrated unity" (Class notes from DME 901: New Approaches in Pastoral Counseling, Reformed Theological Seminary, Jackson, Miss., Summer 1983).

The heart of a child acts as a blank screen on which the opinions of others and the lessons of experience keypunch the concept of identity or self-esteem. Dr. Maurice E. Wagner writes in his book, *The Sensation of Being Somebody* (Grand Rapids: Zondervan, 1975), 63:

> As a child's ability to identify grows — and it does as his variety of experiences increases — he regards himself as being a person in about the same degree as others regard him. Either he identifies with their love and develops positive feelings about himself, or he identifies with their disapproval and develops negative feelings about himself.
>
> The infant's first sense of emotional security is associated with being made to feel comfortable. When he is satisfied, he feels contented — he is somebody; when he is hungry, in pain, or miserable and alone, he is threatened by feelings of being nobody.
>
> Thus, identification and love sponsor the development of a mental structure called a self-concept which provides a child with a sense of his own integrity. This structure in the mind takes the place of having to feel contented and comfortable, perhaps pampered, in order to have a sense of being somebody.

These two process charts contrast the formation and results of self-esteem:

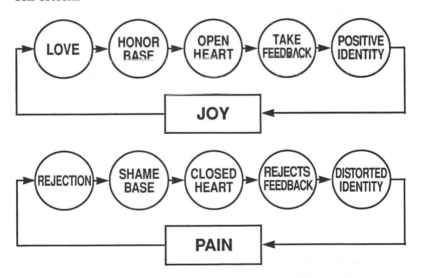

When a child gets love and acceptance, the heart develops an honor-base that gives the child freedom to open up to others and be known. Since others feel comfortable discovering the child, they give essential feedback that allows the child to construct a self-identity. This positive feedback and love helps the child develop an honorable self-esteem.

When a child does not receive the love and acceptance he or she needs, the child feels painful rejection, and the heart develops a shame-base that causes him or her to close up. To numb the pain, the child erects a cluster of defense mechanisms to hide behind. Since others can't discover the child, they give little or no feedback, and the child suffers in silence and fails to secure a healthy accurate identity.

A child's personality derives from a combination of genetic endowment and early environmental influences. Parents constitute, by far, the most powerful early environmental influence. Therefore, the parents lay down the foundational message of self-esteem to a child's heart.

What do you suppose etches the deepest marks on a child's heart? That's right—nothing inscribes a child's heart more deeply and more permanently than the father power of the family shepherd. The dominant male authority figure impacts a child more than any other force. The health of a child's self-esteem is almost directly related to the degree of positive input from the family shepherd.

Not only does a father directly affect his child's heart, but even when the child digests input from the mother, the child indirectly records from the father because so much of the mother's attitude and worldview depends on how her husband shepherds her. If her husband neglects or abuses her, it will affect her ability to give wholesomely to the child. She will struggle with unresolved conflict and be off-center in her dealings with the child.

She may even retaliate against the child because the child bears the father's image, or she may *capture* the child and team up against the father. Either way, the child does not receive natural wholesome input from Mom because of a dysfunctional dad.

The Attitude of Leadership

The 88 Olds incident makes a perfect example of how father power can be matched to a bad command profile to produce tragic results. Dad wanted to be an effective leader and produce a dependable, conscientious, and obedient son. I wanted to reach my full potential as a man. We both failed.

We both received the opposite of what we wanted. Dad felt like a failure as a father and ended up with a son who resented him and did not respect him. I developed into a cheater, liar, and deceiver. I rebelled violently against Major Amos E. Simmons and the authority he represented.

Soon, it was my turn to marry and spawn little crumb gobblers. I applied all the father lore I had picked up from Amos and promptly proceeded to repeat the same cycle by restricting myself to one rigid command profile. In spite of my commitment to excel at fatherhood, I almost ruined my children by commanding them with one style: I treated them like troops.

Major Amos and I learned the same lesson the hard way: Good desires and honest intentions alone do not a family shepherd make. In spite of our shared commitment to be good fathers, we paid a horrible price for not knowing how to properly mix and use father power and command profile.

I wish Dad had been a Christian and I had become one as a small child. Things would have been different, and much pain would have been avoided. Dad would have known about the foundational passages that contrast the negative and positive command profiles and explain the results of each.

Negative Command Profile

These twin passages explain the dynamics behind negative and positive command style:

Children, obey your parents in the Lord, for this is right.
Honor your father and mother (which is the first commandment with a promise),
That it may be well with you, and that you may live long on the earth.
And, fathers, do not provoke your children to anger; but bring them up in the discipline and instruction of the Lord.
—Ephesians 6:1-4

Fathers, do not exasperate your children, that they may not lose heart.
—Colossians 3:21

A closer look at the above passages reveal the negative dynamics of command style. First, this Scripture warns fathers about using destructive methods of child-raising that backfire. In Ephesians 6:4, the words *provoke* and *anger* are the exact same Greek word, *parorgizo* (from the root word orgasm), which means to angrily incite, irritate, or frustrate.

What it means is, if you provoke a child, you will raise a provoker. If you deal with a child in anger, you will produce an angry hostile person. If you incite, irritate, or frustrate a child, the child will become someone who incites, irritates, and frustrates other people.

In Colossians 3:20, *exasperate* means to stir up, excite, or stimulate. *Lose heart* means to break the spirit or dishearten. If you quench and stifle a child to a point of aggravation, you will crush the child's spirit. This can be done by active negative measures or through passive neglect and avoidance.

Combining the thoughts in both verses, we come up with a cause/effect equation that states that certain methods produce predictable results. If you provoke and exasperate children, they will react in one of two ways: They will fly off in screeching rebellion, or they will shrivel up as their hearts rot out.

Positive Command Profile

The above twin passages also explain the dynamics of positive command style and also present us with a positive cause/effect equation. The phrase *to bring up* means to nourish all aspects of the child to maturity. It suggests a process of providing the ingredients from which the child feeds to achieve growth and progress.

The word *discipline* relates to the cultivation of mind and morals by establishing parameters of acceptable behavior, measuring the behavior to the standards, and then making necessary corrections. *Instruction* means verbal training with the aim of modifying behavior to make it acceptable.

Both discipline and instruction imply a predetermined set of child-raising techniques that are quickly located for us by the phrase *of the Lord*. Legitimate effective child-raising techniques have their source in the Lord, that is, the Scripture. Positive Command Style produces a cause/effect equation.

Taking all into consideration, I have paraphrased Ephesians 6:4, the cornerstone passage on paternal command profile:

> Fathers, don't use a command style that frustrates your children and in-
> cites them to rebel automatically against you and your value system and to
> spin out of control. Instead, use God's wisdom, be personally involved,
> and use proper command style to nourish them with biblical principles on
> discipline and motivation.

On the one hand, negative command style can produce sorrow
and tragedy that attacks long chains of family descendants. The
Oldsmobile 88 incident makes a perfect example of its power and
consequences. On the other hand, positive command style can produce light and joy down through the genetic corridors.

The Skills of Leading

My dad, Major Amos E. Simmons, knew troops. He could handle
soldiers. He served in the 3rd Army in World War II on the adjutant
general staff of General George Patton. He received many high
certificates of honor for his service and achievements. Dad knew
troops, but kids *ain't* troops. A lot of men are management geniuses
at work but management dunces at home. It's one thing to excel at
leadership in your career, but it's quite another thing to apply the
principles of command in your homes.

I have talked to some of our nation's most successful business
and military men, who have demonstrated supreme command skills
in their professions. When they are at home, however, even the dog
is out of control. In fact, strong executives have a reputation for
weak fathering.

Brian O'Reilly, writing in *Fortune Magazine* ("Why Grade 'A'
Execs Get an 'F' as Parents," Jan. 1, 1990, 36) confirms this:

> Don't think your brains, money, or success will pave the way to parenting
> glory. In a survey of large corporations providing extensive insurance cov-
> erage, Medstat Systems discovered that some 36% of the children of exec-
> utives undergo outpatient treatment for psychiatric or drug abuse prob-
> lems every year, vs. 15% of the children of nonexecutives in the same
> companies.

The next time you stroll around the hallowed halls of a corporate
castle, pause to ponder that one out of every three men you see has

a child with a serious problem. The executives have twice the number of children in trouble than the other workers' children. They may have many times the money, but which would you rather have?

For some reason, men can manage multinational corporations and direct projects that put men on the moon. When they walk into their homes, however, it seems as if they pass through an invisible molecular force field that sifts out every iota of leadership savvy they possess, tags it, and stores it in a bin for reissue on the way back to work.

Management skills do not automatically follow you home from work. Why not? Why not take the expertise you acquire in the marketplace and utilize it in the pursuit of excellence in your homes?

A manager has several primary functions: He is the custodian of the vision—he is supposed to keep the long-range need and purpose statements in mind; he also gives direction, provides encouragement, keeps the company profitable, and reports to the owners.

A Family Shepherd performs these same functions for the family. He keeps the vision of the family in mind and knows his job description well. He also must master standard management skills like those at work. In addition to all these job skills, however, there is one major difference. At home, he deals with family members, not employees, and he carries a much broader scope of responsibilities.

At home, profit is not the bottom line. Character, convictions, visions, and much more fall under his jurisdiction. These responsibilities require more than just attention to management skills—his heart must be intensively involved with his family leadership.

COME OUT SMELLING SWEET

My dad, Major Amos E. Simmons, knew troops. He could handle soldiers. He accumulated vast experience and knowledge on how to deal with troops, and he passed this sage bit of insight onto me.

I often wonder if he applied this military strategy to fatherhood. Did he plan to work me over in my childhood and make friends after I married and moved away? I don't think that was his plan. But he certainly had his own unique fathering personality. And I have mine. You have yours.

E-TEAM HUDDLE GUIDE
CHAPTER SEVEN: LEADING YOUR CHILDREN

E-TEAM REVIEW
10–15 minutes

Take 10–15 minutes to allow the men to tell about the results of last week's project. This is the accountability part. Be firm with each other and encourage everyone to complete the projects. If anyone encountered difficulty or had a family problem arise, pause to allow the E-Team to address the problem and pray.

E-TEAM DISCUSSION
50–60 minutes

This part allows you to discuss the key concepts in this chapter and relate them to your individual lives. Be sure to leave time to complete the Workout and Encouragement section.

THE PRINCIPLES (Check the text for help.)
1. What is Dave's definition of lead?
2. What does it mean to be Dad in a chain of command?
3. Discuss the chief benefit and penalty of this function.

THE IMPLICATIONS (Why are these ideas significant?)
4. Why is it crucial to consider the heart of the father when talking about leadership in the family? Why should a father focus on the hearts of his wife and children?
5. Read Ephesians 6:1-4 and Colossians 3:21. Think of a real life case study that illustrates the truth of these principles.
6. Why do you think children of executives undergo twice as much outpatient treatment for psychiatric or drug abuse problems than do children of nonexecutives? Do you suppose some men who display excellent leadership skills on the job go home and practice a completely different leadership style? Comment on this.

THE APPLICATION (How do these ideas affect me?)
7. How different is your leadership style at work from your leadership style at home?
8. Describe your dad's leadership style and how you felt about it when you were a child. How do you feel about it now?
9. What would your children like most to change about your leadership style in the home?

E-TEAM WORKOUT
10–15 minutes

Allow each man to choose one of the project options (plays) to perform during the week. If so desired, design your own project. Note: it is essential that each man leave having made a definite commitment to a specific project.

1st PLAY:
Make an appointment with your wife to discuss your dad's leadership style. Then, discuss your leadership style and ask her to give you some honest feedback and suggestions for improvement.

2nd PLAY:
Make an appointment with your wife and study Ephesians 4. Look for the many principles in the 32 verses in this chapter that apply to leadership and chain of command. Discuss how you can apply these principles to improve the effectiveness of your family.

3rd PLAY:
Brainstorm with the E-Team and come up with your own unique project that fits your specific family.

E-TEAM ENCOURAGEMENT
5–10 minutes

Close the meeting in prayer for each other and your families. Request spiritual power to successfully complete your project.

BREAK THE HUDDLE,
GO HOME AND RUN THE PLAY!

Chapter Eight
Equipping Your Children

*"Go home and catch your children doing
something right."*
—*Adapted from* The One Minute Manager

THE BLIND DATE

Sandy met me at the door when I came home from seminary class
and told me: "Dave, I think we have a serious problem with
Helen (twelve years old). She seems depressed and keeps complain-
ing about life being unfair. She says she doesn't want to be a girl."

"That sounds pretty serious," I said. "I don't understand at all.
Where is she coming from? Fill me in. Tell me what you have
observed and what you think."

"Well," Sandy responded, "she doesn't have any girlfriends her
age within walking distance, and she gets lonely and bored. She's
dangling in that awkward age between childhood and young
ladyhood (between toys and boys), where little girls are too old to
play and too young for anything else. She watches you, Dave, out
there playing with Brandon and his horde of friends, and she feels
left out. She thinks boys get all the attention and have all the fun.
But she doesn't want to run with a pack of boys. She doesn't really
know what she wants."

"I don't know what you expect me to do about it," I replied.
"Sounds like a female problem to me. I think she needs a couple of
serious mother/daughter talks to fix her up." I had enough problems to worry about and didn't want to be bothered. Actually, I was
blind to many of the problems in my family because of the pressure
of seminary.

Sandy knew about my blind spot and patiently ignored my callousness and continued to discuss the situation for a while longer. I finally conceded that I would do what I could. We decided that I would ask Helen to go to a nice restaurant with me on a date. Maybe if I could get her to open up and talk to me, I could find out what was really bothering her. After dinner, I asked her out for Saturday night, and she eagerly accepted.

Saturday afternoon, as I watching a football game on TV, Sandy tapped me on the shoulder and said, "Come here and look at this, Dave, you won't believe it." We walked back through the hallway to Helen's room and stood by her door, which was cracked open about four inches. Helen stood by her closet and had three of her best dresses spread out on the bed. She was trying to decide which one Dad would like the best. She had also borrowed some makeup and a pair of panty hose from Sandy (the panty hose were never the same after that.)

I realized that Helen considered this date a big deal. I decided to get serious too. I showered, shaved, put on a coat and tie, and when the time came, I walked outside, got into the car, and drove away so that I could act like a real date driving up to pick up his girl. A few minutes later, I drove up, got out, and rang the doorbell. Men, they learn young. She kept me waiting fifteen minutes.

Finally, she swirled into the living room. I could not believe my eyes. She looked like an eighteen-year-old woman and appeared so beautiful. She exuded great confidence, like she did this sort of thing every day of the week. She announced that she was ready and stood by waiting for me to open the door. A little dazed, I opened the door, said good-bye to Sandy, who sat beaming with pride at her little lady, and I walked Helen to the car.

As we drove away from the house, I asked Helen where she wanted to go for dinner. She chose one of the most expensive steak places in Dallas. I swallowed hard and said, "Sure, Helen, you deserve the very best tonight!"

During dinner, I was stunned by the enchanting conversation she kept up. I had no idea she possessed such cultivated conversational skills. She challenged me and kept me lively entertained. She made an incredible dinner date. I realized I lagged about four years behind in my appraisal of her social development. (And, men, you overestimate your sons by about two years.) It was one of the best evenings I ever had.

After dinner, I took her to do what all women love doing the most—shopping. We went to Town East Mall and puttered around in a few stores. She bought a little gift for Brandon. We stopped in for a little dessert at an ice cream parlor and then headed home.

On the way home, as we turned onto our street, Helen scooted her little bottom across the seat right up against me, put her arm up around my neck, and gave me a giant hug. "Daddy," she said, "this has been the best day of my entire life! I'm so excited. Didn't we have fun, Daddy?"

True. True. But, what made her feel like it was the best day of her life? I asked her why, and she replied, "Well, Daddy, you made me feel like such a woman!"

We never heard anymore out of her about wanting to be a little boy. For the first time in her life, she had a man relate to her as a woman. She experienced the feeling of being with a man who loved her and enjoyed her feminine company. She tasted the rewards of being a woman, and she loved it.

Thanks to Sandy's alertness, I helped Helen get through a difficult time through which all little girls must pass. This process of assisting our children through the developmental phases of childhood on their way to maturity is just part of what equipping them is all about. Fathers, we are responsible to do whatever is required to equip our children to face and master the art and skills of living.

The ANALYSIS OF EQUIPPING

The Fatherhood Function of Equipping	
Function	EQUIP your family.
Role	Be a MENTOR.
Benefit	To give COMPETENCE.
Penalty	DEPENDENCE.

The Fatherhood Function: EQUIPPING
Equipping is the labor that provides children with the right environment and enlightenment required to cope successfully with life.

The Role: Dad The Family Mentor

As Dad the Family Mentor, you do what is required to make each family member successful. This function transfers the skills of competence to them. You help them master the trait of being effective (doing the right things) and efficient (doing things right). Your charges emerge from you able to cope with life successfully. They become achievers.

Ted Engstrom and Norman B. Rohrer say, "Successful people never reach their goals alone." Everyone needs a special equipper, a mentor. They go on to say, "A mentor provides modeling, close supervision on special projects, individualized help in many areas—discipline, encouragement, correction, confrontation, and a calling to accountability. A mentor is genuinely interested in a protégé's growth and development and is willing to commit time and emotional energy to a relationship with an understudy. This goes beyond mere interest and is a commitment that, more often than not, is intense" (*The Fine Art of Mentoring* [Brentwood, Tenn.: Wolgemuth and Hyatt, Publishers, Inc., 1989], 3–4).

I would add that a mentor also provides the environment, tools, and resources required for the transfer of capability. As a father, you need to insure adequate food, shelter, education, recreation, and clothing. You are responsible for providing a healthy spiritual environment. Make sure you are deeply involved in the *body life* by attending a church that worships Jesus Christ, honors the Holy Spirit as Helper, and emphasizes intimate, loving, supportive/confrontive/accountable relationships.

Mentoring is discipleship. This is the function of transferring the claims of Christ down through the following generations. It is disciplining your family members and teaching them to teach others.

The Benefit: Competence

Dad is "He Who Gets It Done." It is he who changes the oil, mows the grass, paints the house, tinkers with large appliances, moves the furniture, and makes repairs. He is the biggest, walks loudly, booms his voice, lifts heavy things, and protects us. Dad has tools and makes things! Dad is the one who "makes it happen."

Research shows a powerful relationship between the involvement of the father and the competence level of the child. Task-oriented

162

fathers push children (boys and girls) to expand boundaries, experiment, take risks, and overcome obstacles to be successful. Relationship-oriented mothers emphasize rapport and sensitivity with people. Moms focus on tranquility and equilibrium.

Children see a strong dad as the primary one who moves the world around. A strong dad, to a child, is the agent of instrumentality. From him, children pick up the zeal to do things rather than be "done unto." Involved dads propel children toward achievement. Dads inspire children to effectiveness (doing the right things) and efficiency (doing things right). Children learn to cope with life much better with an involved child-friendly father.

Without the equipping of an involved dad, the children grow up with a significantly lower level of competence and achievement. The less Dad equips them, the less able they are to cope with life and the more dependent they become. This graph shows the continuum:

Competence   High   EQUIP   Low   Dependence

The Penalty: Dependence
Almost all research shows that paternally deprived children do not compare favorably in any positive area with children with strong fathers. The one word that best characterizes fatherless children is dependence. They do not cope with life well and depend on others to meet their physical, emotional, and psychological needs. They invariably form discordant relationships and dysfunctional families.

They score lower on intelligence tests, have many more health problems, and have trouble making decisions, and delaying gratification. They find it difficult to persevere, concentrate, follow sequences, complete directions, and follow through to attain closure. They end up as the needy people in our society who require others to take care of them.

THE DYNAMICS OF EQUIPPING
This function, to equip your children, is the broadest of the Four Fatherhood Functions and calls for a variety of complex activities.

Basically, it covers the tasks you must do to help your children move healthily through the childhood developmental phases on schedule and mature to the point where you can turn them loose on life.

Someone has said that we are only one generation away from barbarianism. Equipping is the process that transfers civilization down through the generations.

It is the imparting of values, mores, ethics, and behavior patterns. It is the training and discipline aspect of child-raising. It helps kids do right.

The Neglect of Equipping

The past century has seen men almost totally abandon this function. What primarily had been a fatherhood function was passed on to mothers because of neglect and is now delegated to institutions. In the process, children have suffered from a system that is almost criminal in negligence.

Child-raising has deteriorated to the point where Western culture had to invent a "Peter Pan land," called adolescence, to put slow maturing subadults, named teenagers, on hold. Adolescence and teenagers are inventions that never existed in other cultures in other ages and is certainly not biblical. Children historically passed directly from childhood to adulthood in a matter of months and celebrated the occasion with a rite of passage. When they became adults, they put away childish things.

We are now in danger of extending adolescence past the teens into the twenties. In fact, a new term, *Twen-agers,* has been coined to describe young people in their twenties who have not grown up. Twen-agers don't want to accept responsibilities; they postpone marriage and career decisions; and they eschew commitments. They prefer to drift along and let others take care of them.

This slowdown in the maturation process is becoming worse. Research shows that the average nineteen-year-old in 1988 demonstrates the maturity level of a thirteen-year-old in 1955.

Many factors, no doubt, have caused these grim developments, but can anyone doubt that the rise in youth problems has grown directly with the fall of fatherhood involvement with his children. The truth is plain:

Equipping Your Children

Father	Youth
Involvement up	Mature and Independent
Involvement down	Immature and Dependent

Government spokesmen, educators, and social workers have gradually acknowledged that the horrendous problems our public institutions have in trying to equip children are insurmountable. All political and religious research, starting off in different directions, are ending at the same doorstep—all roads lead to Dad. If fathers do not involve themselves with their children and master the art of equipping, their children will have no hope. You can't help an unequippable child.

Fathers, we must rise up and meet the challenge to be Dad the Family Mentor, involve ourselves with our children, and equip them to be competent productive citizens.

The Climate for Equipping

Question: Which answer gives the best picture of a father equipping his child?

A. A father is a sculptor. He sees a beautiful form floating inside the stone and seeks to surface it by chipping, hammering, cutting, and sanding away the parts that don't belong.

B. A father is a gardener. He plants the seed and creates the perfect environment so the plant maximizes its own growth and maturity. He provides the sunlight, humidity, water, and fertilizer for growth and takes pains to keep out the weeds.

In my opinion, B gives the best picture. The father is a gardener, and his family lives in a greenhouse. His responsibility is to make sure the environment is as near perfect as possible for the cultivation of his living plants. Since all plants occasionally need pruning, spraying, and repotting, he needs to be prepared to dish out a little correction and retargeting whenever required.

The process of equipping consists of two areas: the environment and the enlightenment. Each area has two components as shown on page 166.

165

Environment	Enlightenment
You are Dad the Family PROTECTOR	You are Dad the Family MENTOR
You are Dad the Family PROVIDER	You are Dad the Family MINISTER

The Environment
In establishing the proper environment for your family, you are to establish a sanctuary for your family by functioning as the family protector and provider.

1. You are the family protector who builds a *safe zone* for your family.

2. You are the family provider who supplies all necessary resources that your family requires for healthy growth.

The environment responsibility has to do with your role as provider for your family — your business, job, or profession. As shepherd, you earn the resources for a comfortable standard of living for your family.

Warning: Do not abuse your provider role. How silly to bury yourself in your work to earn a thousand arrows and then lose your bow. How smart is it to earn a fortune and lose your family? Your life's mission is with your family; your work merely helps equip the family to accomplish its purpose. Your job is not your purpose.

On my first scuba dive in the Florida Keys, I retrieved a beautiful shell and put it into my bag. The next time I looked at it was three months later when I tracked down an awful smell in my garage. The shell still looked beautiful, but the little creature inside had died and decayed, emitting a horrible stench. That's like a man who escapes into his work to earn the money for a beautiful estate while his family slowly rots away for want of a care-giving family shepherd. Your house is only your habitat: its inhabitants are your life.

The Enlightenment
In establishing enlightenment for the family, you transfer wisdom, culture, and value systems to the next generation by functioning as

166

the family mentor and minister to them.

1. You are the family mentor who dispenses knowledge and skills required to cope with life.

2. You are the family minister who insures spiritual growth and maturity in your family members.

You function as the headmaster of your miniacademy and the priest of your miniflock. You must provide your children with the tools they need to cope with life.

Equipping your children, then, is the process of bringing all necessary resources to bear on getting them as ready as possible to cope with life successfully.

The Objectives of Equipping

"Aim at nothing, and you will surely hit it!" bellowed Professor Howard Hendricks all through my years at seminary. As a result of his pounding, I can't even contemplate a project without immediately conjuring up a picture of what I want it to look like when completed. "Establish the end before you begin!" is a good motto for fathers.

By establishing an end, you can intelligently develop a strategy of fathering and always know what to do next. Carefully defined objectives also tell you when to change course and when to make corrections. "If you don't know where you are going," thundered Prof Hendricks, "any path will take you there!"

My approach to this topic centers on two duties:

1. You must carefully define your long-range objectives for child-raising.

2. You must provide your children with the tools to accomplish these objectives.

These two duties are introduced briefly here and explained in greater detail in Volume III: *Dad the Family Mentor*.

Clearly Defined Objectives

Briefly stated, long-range child-raising objectives fall into three categories:

1. In regard to God: To transfer the truth about God down through the generations.

In Psalm 78:5-7, fathers are commanded to teach the Bible to

their children in such a way that the next four generations will
know God. This command means we are to equip our children to
know God and know how to make Him known.

2. In regard to the child: To help the child achieve maturity in all
areas while maintaining the integrity of the child's particular and
unique design.

With regard to a child's unique design, Proverbs 22:6 commands
us to respect and honor the *bent* or *spin* that God puts on each
Designer Child. Your task is to create an environment that will allow
the child to maximize the development of his or her unique package
of gifts so the child might reach his or her full potential when the
child fills his or her exact slot in the body of Christ, the church.

As far as maturity is concerned, I used to state my maturity
objective for Helen and Brandon as "To take them from a point of
total dependence to a state of strong independence." But, I learned
better. Now, after serious modification, it reads: "To take them from
a point of total dependence through a period of careful independence to a state of healthy interdependence." If they bog down in
the independence stage, they will eventually get off track and end
up co-dependent, which is not a good thing to be. The process looks
like this:

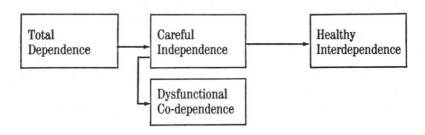

The Three Phases of Maturity

A baby starts out utterly dependent. A baby is like a long tube
with a burp at one end, a mess at the other, and a lot of squeals in
between. They can do nothing for themselves and require constant
attention and care. They progress naturally through the phases of

childhood development until they gain the ability to break the shackles of their dependency by coping with life on their own. They reach a point where they master self-control and *own* themselves.

The independent phase helps a child become *his own person.* This autonomy is essential, but it has a downside: The young person tends to focus on self, resist outside advice, and drift toward isolation. This state is necessary in the "growing up" process, but it is not his or her destination. By the nature of its *meism* and protectionism, it does not allow the making of enriching relationships.

A person must move through independence and, after gaining control of self, channel self into a mutually rewarding community experience. It's in this final stage of healthy interdependence when people experience the deep gratification of relationships and teamwork. It's the synergistic phase of maturity when one becomes part of a whole that has value greater than the sum of its parts.

A person in the interdependence phase possesses all the strengths of the independent phase (like self-reliance and capability) but has a strong character, is in control, and chooses to cooperate with others in a mutually enhancing society. People in the interdependent phase have the ego-strength and confidence to merge with each other in satisfying personal relationships. They can share their sources of inner human wealth and potential without feeling threatened with loss or worried about becoming dependent.

Unfortunately, many young people today get stuck in the independence stage by becoming addicted to the egocentric feelings associated with it. Our culture also encourages them to pursue independence — the rugged American individualistic norm that emphasizes self-assertion and mottoes such as "Do your own thing" and "That's not my bag."

Independence is not a sign of strength, machismo, or maturity as much as it is a signal of arrested growth and lost potential. It is a normal phase that must be worked through by all healthy mature people. If it is not overcome and left behind, the person will fail to get his or her normal social needs for intimacy, love, and respect met in natural ways and will develop unhealthy systems of thought and behavior to compensate for the loss.

They will veer off the maturity process and slip into a state of codependency:

3. In regard to you: To help deepen and strengthen your character. Can anyone doubt that raising children forces a parent to stretch to higher levels of maturity and achievement? Children are God's clever curriculum to help us see ourselves through His eyes. Kids are a training course to get us ready for grandparenthood where we know it all. Sandy has said for years that God should trust children only to grandparents.

Life's Tools for Success

Child-raising takes in much more than those methods used to control behavior. Since behavior stems from character and character from the heart, when approaching the topic of child-raising, you must consider not only behavior but also the child's heart and character.

Furthermore, in keeping with our gardener philosophy, you can't force a child to have a pure heart and a good character. You must set the conditions that enable the child to develop on his or her own. You must equip the child with tools he or she can use to mature for the rest of his or her life. I have listed these tools and broken them into three categories: *Pneuma* (spirit) tools, power tools, and hand tools.

FOR THE HEART

Pneuma Tools: To help know truth.

                           To develop spiritual life.

Faith: Able to believe in God and His Word.
Worship: Able to see and focus on God as He is.
Doctrine: Able to know the truth of God's Word.
Vision: Able to hear and interpret God's call.
Discernment: Able to comprehend eternal values.

FOR CHARACTER

Power Tools: To help be truth.

                                To develop character.

Responsible: Able to obey and be accountable.
Love: Able to consider and serve others.
Trustworthiness: Able to be tested and trusted.
Self-Control: Able to conform behavior to values.
Congruent: Able to match outer person with inner person.

FOR BEHAVIOR

Hand Tools: To help practice truth.

                                To develop skills.

Advancement: Able to master academic and talent skills.
Communication: Able to master relationship skills.
Cooperation: Able to master teamwork skills.
Ministry: Able to master spiritual help skills.
Problem-Solving: Able to master analytical and decision-making skills.

These tools have a direction. They start deep in the heart and work through the character and out to behavior. If a person's heart is right, his character will be sound. If character is sound, behavior will be acceptable.

These thoughts represent an introduction to the objectives of child-raising. Overwhelmed? Don't be. Our great advantage is that God has designed babies to be born grabbing for tools. They will learn them in spite of our performance. But it certainly helps them when we teach them the right tools and how to use them best.

The Process of Equipping
For any project that calls for equipping people to succeed with excellence, I use the Shepherd Equipping Process. It will provide great results when you need to equip children, employees, athletes, soldiers, or anyone.

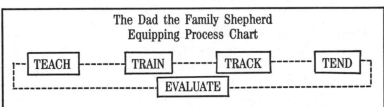

The Dad the Family Shepherd
Equipping Process Chart

TEACH ------- TRAIN ------- TRACK ------- TEND

EVALUATE

Teach: To transfer knowledge (facts and principles), wisdom (applied knowledge), and consequential truth (future results from present behavior).

Train: To merge knowledge, desire, and skills into habits of successful behavior.

Track: To follow growth carefully and encourage positive progress.

Tend: To interrupt, as needed, to help make positive adjustments, corrections, and modifications.

The equipping process, consisting of these steps, is the subject of Volume 3, *Dad the Family Mentor*. Two chapters are devoted to each of these steps.

THE TRUCK

After my wife and I were out for dinner one night with some friends, we drove up in front of our house at about 11 P.M. I looked around and noticed my pickup truck was gone. "Did someone borrow the pickup?" I asked Sandy. "No," she replied. After we went into the house, I saw Helen dart out of the bathroom into her bedroom as if she wanted to avoid us.

I walked back to Brandon's bedroom, and he was missing. He wasn't in the house. We have two house rules for the kids when we are gone. Nobody comes in, and nobody goes out. I realized Helen knew something, but before I could find her, the phone rang. It was a neighbor, about a mile away—we lived on the outskirts of town.

He said what parents dread someone will one day say: "Dave, Brandon is OK. He had a little trouble with the pickup, but don't worry. He's OK."

Naturally, in spite of his disarming words, I panicked. I wanted to know what had happened, but he wouldn't tell me. Finally, he said, "He ought to be there about now. Just let him tell you. I think you should hear it from him."

We broke off, and Sandy and I went to bed. A few minutes later, we heard Brandon approaching the house. We could hear because he was whistling—just as you whistle when you are walking through a graveyard and scared to death. He whistled down the driveway, up the steps, through the front door, down the hallway, and into his room. He never missed a note.

"Brandon," I called. "Son, come in here. We need to talk."

He opened the door as if nothing at all was out of line. "Hi, Dad. Mom," he says.

"Brandon, what in the world is going on around here. Where's the pickup? What have you done? Just tell me the whole story."

He sat down in a chair at the foot of the bed and contemplated his shoes for a while. Now, Brandon is Sandy's son, and so he is very wise. "Well, Dad," he says, "you know how you like me to take good care of equipment and have told me never to leave tools and

173

equipment out overnight in the rain or other bad weather?"

"Yes, I remember," I said, wondering what remote connection, if any, this had with the missing pickup.

"Dad," he continued. "I left my bike over at my buddy's house, and it's supposed to rain tonight. I sat here wondering what I should do. I had to break one rule or another and tried to figure out what you would have done. I figured you would rather have me break the rule about leaving the house when you were gone than letting my bike rust out. One costs you money, the other one doesn't. So, Dad, I made an executive decision to get the bike."

"But what does the pickup truck have to do with it? How does that fit in?"

"Well, Dad, I figured that since you didn't want me to leave the house when you were gone, it would be most honoring to you to leave it for as short a time as possible if I found myself in a situation where I just had to leave. So, I thought I would just scoot over there in the pickup truck, grab the bike, and truck it home. That way, I protected my equipment and was gone as short as possible."

His well-reasoned answer left me mute. Sounded reasonable to me. Maybe he would have gotten off easy in a jury trial, but I wasn't going to let him get by me so easy. He had figured that all he had to do was ease over there in the pickup truck, get the bike back, and ease back home, and Dad would never know. No hurt, no foul.

He had never driven a car before, much less a pickup truck. He had never worked a stick shift standard transmission before. He had never started a car and never pumped a clutch before. Somehow, he had managed all that and got the truck moving. But, he had never driven anything up a steep incline like the hill our house sits on.

He had lurched and belched up the hill to the top and stalled. He had flooded it trying to get it started again. By that time, he was having second thoughts about the whole venture, figuring one rain on the bike wasn't so serious after all. He finally decided just to ease the pickup truck back down the hill and park it where he had gotten it. Dad would never know, and everything would be just fine.

He had never driven a pickup truck in reverse before. Down a steep hill. With a horse trailer hooked onto it! What is the matter with his head? Where do these guys come from?

Of course, he jackknifed the trailer, broke off the hitch, and sent the trailer screaming down the hill. (No horse in it. Surprised?) The truck ended up perpendicular in the road. He ended up hoofing over to his friend's house to see whether his daddy would come get him out of trouble.

As the story unfolded, I could see the distress and anguish in Brandon. He kept looking down at his feet and wringing his hands. I asked him how he felt about all this.

He became still, looked me in the eye, and said with great sincerity, "Dad, I feel terrible. Horrible. I'm never going to do anything like this again!"

I asked him whether he knew the term that described the feelings he was experiencing. He answered, "Guilt?" I said, "Right, Son. Not a lot of fun, is it?"

Then I said, "Brandon, as your father who is responsible for discipline here, what do you think I ought to do about this whole situation?"

Now, Brandon is Sandy's son, so he is very wise. "Gee, Dad," he said, with a studied look in his eye, "I don't know. (Pause) But I do know that whatever you decide, it will be fair."

"I'll tell you what I am going to do. Nothing. It's already all been done. You did wrong. You felt convicted about it. You confessed it. You said you would never do it again. What remains to be done? It's finished. Let's go get the truck."

From a seated position, he launched through the air and landed full length on me. He threw his arms around me and cried out, "Dad, I love you."

Why did he say that? He had come into the room loaded down with real guilt and feeling heavy from the weight of it. Our relationship also suffered from blockage because of his deed standing in the way. Through our discussion, he managed to work his way through the cleansing and forgiveness process. He confessed his guilt, repented, and wanted to restore fellowship with me. It all worked out. I forgave him and took away the barrier that had come between us. He was free, and we were friends. It felt great to get rid of the weight. We were buddies. We got up and went to get the pickup truck.

I think back to the early sixties about a boy who had taken his father's vehicle and done wrong. He abused the Delta 88 Oldsmobile and drove home (backward) with resentment, deceit, and hostility in his heart. He had sinned against his dad, and neither one of them knew the process for dealing with it. The boy didn't recognize guilt and never confessed it. The dad didn't know anything about forgiveness. There wasn't much teaching, training, tracking, or tending happening. There wasn't much love and fellowship in existence. There wasn't much equipping for life taking place.

I think back to the early eighties about a boy who had taken his father's vehicle and done wrong. He abused the pickup truck and guilt was in his heart. But he and his dad knew how to deal with it. They worked through it and restored their fellowship.

The way this incident turned out was not an accident. I had been through many confrontations with Brandon through the years. From the very beginning, we had established this format for dealing with problems. Brandon had been trained to respond this way through games and little things in life. When he was on the spot, he knew what to do and he knew he could talk to me and tell the truth. He felt secure in my love. His behavior was not luck or an accident. It was the result of many years of committed shepherding.

Men, you need to shepherd your children. If you don't, who will?

E-TEAM HUDDLE GUIDE
CHAPTER EIGHT: EQUIPPING YOUR CHILDREN

Dad, the Family Shepherd
E-TEAM

E-TEAM REVIEW
10–15 minutes

Take 10–15 minutes to allow the men to tell about the results of last week's project. This is the accountability part. Be firm with each other and encourage everyone to complete the projects. If anyone encountered difficulty or had a family problem arise, pause to allow the E-Team to address the problem and pray.

E-TEAM DISCUSSION
50–60 minutes

This part allows you to discuss the key concepts in this chapter and relate them to your individual lives. Be sure to leave time to complete the Workout and Encouragement section.

THE PRINCIPLES (Check the text for help.)
1. What is Dave's definition of equip?
2. Discuss what it means to be Dad the Family Mentor. Describe the difference between a sculptor and a gardener.
3. Discuss the chief benefit and penalty of this function.

THE IMPLICATIONS (Why are these ideas significant?)
4. Study the process chart on The Three Phases of Maturity and speculate, in general terms, which step in the process represents best the maturity level of the following broad groups:

Group	Maturity Level
Teenagers of the '60s	
Teenagers of the '70s	
Teenagers of the '80s	
Teenagers of the '90s	

5. To equip a child to reach healthy interdependence with great

success, Dave suggests providing them with the following: *Pneuma Tools, Power Tools,* and *Hand Tools.* How would you rate the general effectiveness of American fathers in this task? If present trends continue, what level of success do you predict for the fathers at the beginning of the twenty-second century?

6. How important do you think it is for you to fulfill Malachi 4:5-6?

THE APPLICATION (How do these ideas affect me?)

7. How do you feel about your children's progress in learning the Pneuma Tools, the Power Tools, and the Hand Tools?

8. How do you feel about the progress you are making in improving your fathering style? Tell the rest of the E-Team what this course has meant to you.

9. Discuss the possibility of taking the next course, *Dad the Family Counselor,* together as an E-Team.

E-TEAM WORKOUT
10–15 minutes

Allow each man to choose one of the project options (plays) to perform during the week. Note: it is essential that each man leave having made a definite commitment to a specific project.

1st PLAY:
Evaluate your effectiveness in transferring the fifteen success tools to your children.

2nd PLAY:
Study Deuteronomy 6 with your wife. Look for principles that apply to equipping your children. Discuss how you can apply these principles to improve the effectiveness of your family.

E-TEAM ENCOURAGEMENT
5–10 minutes

Close the meeting in prayer for each other and your families.

BREAK THE HUDDLE, GO HOME AND RUN THE PLAY!

The Extra Point

Dear Father,

This final point I leave you with: The world needs more long-distance dads — we have enough 100-yard-dash dads. Now that you have seriously begun your fathering enhancement process, go for the long-range system, not the quick fix. Finish what you have begun.

You have just finished Fatherhood 101, *Dad the Family Coach*, which serves as the foundation course for the Dad the Family Shepherd Fatherhood Institute. This course provides a base for all the other courses in the curriculum because it presents the basic biblical philosophy of fatherhood and includes a brief conceptual survey of the Four Fatherhood Functions.

The next course, Fatherhood 102 — *Dad the Family Counselor*, covers, in great detail, three of the Four Fatherhood Functions: To Love, To Bond, and To Lead. The third course, Fatherhood 103 — *Dad the Family Mentor*, covers the function, To Equip.

These next two courses get into the real nitty-gritty of fathercraft. The actual coaching tips and refined techniques of these functions are spelled out in a style that helps you easily grasp and use them in your fathering style. If this course puts you in the classroom to study the game plan, the next two courses take you out on the practice field and let you knock a little.

Take encouragement that we will not be denied: Those of us who want to master fatherhood will have the heart and master the skills to do so. We have the assurance of Malachi 4:5-6 —

"Behold, I am going to send you Elijah the prophet before the coming of the great and terrible Day of the Lord.

"And he will restore the hearts of the fathers to their children, and the hearts of the children to their fathers, lest I come and smite the land with a curse."

So, go for it. Continue your E-Team and perfect your fathering style.

Sincerely,

Dave Simmons

Appendix A

Dad, the Family Shepherd

E-TEAM

E-TEAM Captain's Guide

This E-TEAM **Captain's Guide** is the comprehensive resource which fully equips a man to be a successful E-TEAM leader. This material will help you understand how to lead and direct an E-TEAM correctly and successfully. Please familiarize yourself thoroughly with the following information if you intend to direct an E-TEAM.

An **E-TEAM** is a group of four to five men who meet weekly for eight weeks to encourage each other to convert biblical, family-life principles into family behavioral patterns and practices.

An **E-TEAM Captain** is a man who leads a group of men through an E-TEAM course for the purpose of building unity, providing encouragement, and improving the family shepherding skills of the men in the group.

E-TEAM PHILOSOPHY

E-TEAM courses are based on the belief that a few good men who share the common desire to improve their family shepherding skills can and will benefit far more by interacting with each other through such courses, than if they individually attended a conference, paid a counselor for private counselling, or read the hottest new book about this subject. The basis for this conviction is found in the Scripture:

Hebrews 10:23-25: "Let us hold fast the confession of our hope without wavering, for He who promised is faithful; and let us consider how to stimulate one another to love and good deeds, not forsaking our own assembling together, as is the habit of some, but encouraging one another; and all the more, as you see the day drawing near."

Men need to assemble together to stimulate and encourage each other. It is important that men meet together on a weekly basis to examine biblical family principles, to share and discuss common problems, to challenge and confront one another, and to hold each other accountable. Men need to help each other make progress in becoming better family shepherds. Men need the encouragement and the synergism that comes from being in a small team of individuals who are committed to each other.

Proverbs 27:17: "Iron sharpens iron, so one man sharpens another."

Ecclesiastes 4:9-10: "Two are better than one because they have a good return

Appendix A

for their labor. For if either of them falls, the one will lift up his companion. But woe to the one who falls when there is not another to lift him up."

An E-TEAM provides the form and the format for bringing men together for edification. Progress is achieved in small but definite increments as men meet together to digest a single, dynamic, biblical principle and weave it into their family lifestyle. Such progress multiplies the effectiveness of building family relationships.

USES OF E-TEAM COURSES

This E-TEAM course can be adapted easily to almost any men's class or assembly program, small group or large. The course is especially suitable for a small team of four to five men, directed by an E-TEAM captain.

In larger groups, make general announcements to all the men then for the discussion and workshop sessions, the men should divide into smaller, four-to-five-man teams for personal interaction and involvement with each other. This facilitates the discovery process.

This course makes an excellent change of pace for Christian educational programs already in progress. It would be profitable and refreshing for a church or a men's Bible study to inject this course, with its principles about men and the family, right along with a series of doctrinal studies, or possibly between two book studies.

Moreover, E-TEAM courses make perfect one-day or two-day programs for men's retreats. Such an activity is easy to plan and to administer because it provides a good balance between lecture and small-group discussion. Of course, the strength of these E-TEAM courses is the format for weekly application projects. Therefore, it would be important to plan the projects in such a way as to allow for a system of accountability and encouragement; men must follow through with the projects after the retreat is history.

Each participant will come away from the courses with a different perspective about his own responsibilities within the family. Each man will make renewed, stronger commitments to improve the process of shepherding his own family.

SCHEDULE OF AN E-TEAM LESSON

Try to arrive early, and encourage E-TEAMmates to be on time. If your E-TEAM decides to meet early in the morning, meet in a restaurant for breakfast together, and if possible, try to meet in a smaller, separate room or wing of the establishment where you can meet personally and undisturbed. Otherwise, try to meet in a quiet place (i.e., a teammate's home, an office, a room in the church, etc.), and arrange to have coffee and donuts on hand. Small men's groups always appreciate this kind of gesture.

If your E-TEAM elects to meet together in the early evening, try to arrange for some lighter refreshments. If your team meets over lunch, try to insure that each team member has plenty of time to arrive and eat.

The following suggestions may be helpful for scheduling your E-TEAM Huddles:

1. E-TEAM Review	10–15 minutes
2. E-TEAM Discussion	50–60 minutes
3. E-TEAM Workout	10–15 minutes
4. E-TEAM Encouragement	5–10 minutes

Time limits should be established at the discretion of each team. Some teams will have more time to meet together than others. Select a time frame which best fits the needs of your team, and stick to it. End your meetings on time, and always close the meeting with prayer for each other. Make sure the men commit themselves to do a weekly project and to prepare for the next E-TEAM Huddle.

THE PARTICULARS OF AN E-TEAM HUDDLE

1. *Frequence of an E-TEAM Huddle:* Try to meet weekly for 60 to 90 minutes.

2. *Size of an E-TEAM:* Try to maintain team size to four or five men; this is the ideal size. Smaller or larger teams adversely affect the quality of interaction and personal involvement. If a congregation or a large assembly of men pursue an E-TEAM course together, a pastor or an appointed leader should give direction. Individual teams of four or five men should be formed and maintained for the duration of the course. Each separate team should have its own team captain, who leads the team through the Huddle. The pastor/leader opens the meeting. Then the teams separate and interact among themselves for the rest of the meeting.

3. *Environment:* Location and time are important factors for success. Perhaps the best situation is a teammate's home, an office, or a boardroom. 6:30 A.M. to 7:45 or possibly 8 A.M. is always an excellent time to meet together. Meeting early before work insures that the E-TEAM Huddle will conclude promptly and on time. It's a good idea to provide or to meet where there is access to coffee, juice, donuts, or other light breakfast items.

Some E-TEAMs like to meet during lunch hour. If yours does, make sure that this time frame is not too constricting for your team. All teammates must be able to meet together comfortably at the lunch hour and agree on it BEFORE setting the E-TEAM Huddle in a lunch hour time period.

Evening meetings are also possible, but remember that meetings in the evening would take men away from their families at a time when they need to be at home the most. Some men already may have too many evening meetings scheduled. Research by Dad the Family Shepherd has found that early Saturday mornings prove to be one of the best times for the E-TEAM Huddle.

Church meetings are also ideal, but be sure that such an environment is by official agreement (i.e., you may need to clear such meetings with your pastor, the elders, or the deacons first). Of course, the church should have a small, comfortable meeting room. Some churches schedule regular meetings for their men (i.e., Sunday School, evening training classes, etc.), and these meetings are perfect for incorporating E-TEAM courses for the men of the church.

DESIGNATED ROLES IN AN E-TEAM

1. *The E-TEAM Captain:* The E-TEAM Captain is the responsible individual who plans, organizes, and conducts the direction of the E-TEAM Huddle. The Captain must secure the E-TEAM playbooks and the meeting place. The E-TEAM Captain should appoint a time keeper and a refreshment chairman. Moreover, the Captain should insure that the meetings conform to the schedule agreed on, he prompts the discussion, and he makes sure that each team member has an opportunity to share his thoughts and feelings.

The E-TEAM Captain does not have to teach, nor must he have special experience in leading small groups. He only needs to follow the instructions in this curriculum. Because an E-TEAM is essentially a discussion group, there should be

Appendix A

as much natural interaction and personal involvement between team members as possible. This is the key to success. Allow the group to run itself, but keep things moving.

2. *The Time Keeper:* An E-TEAM Time Keeper should keep the Captain informed about the amount of time left in the meeting; the meeting should stay on schedule. It is especially important to reserve some time at the end of the meeting for a short discussion about the weekly projects, for personal commitment, and for prayer.

3. *The Refreshment Chairman:* The Refreshment Chairman should make sure that team members take turns providing refreshments. This man should not have to provide the snacks each week, but he should attempt to inform team members when it is their turn to supply them. Of course, should your team meet in a restaurant for breakfast or even for lunch, each teammate becomes responsible for his own meal, and no Refreshment Chairman is needed.

The E-TEAMmates have four basic responsibilities:

a. To complete the reading assignment before the meeting.

b. To participate in the E-Team discussion.

c. To encourage the other E-Teammates.

d. To complete the weekly project.

4. *E-TEAMmates:* Participation by all members of an E-TEAM determines the overall success and effectiveness of the E-TEAM learning experience. The more all team members participate, the more team members will benefit. Teammates on any team should make every effort to work together and contribute to the overall success of the team. Just so, the E-TEAMmates on an E-TEAM are actually their own greatest resource. As men get to know each other better, they soon discover that the best counsel, advice, and wisdom come from other men who share similar experiences and concerns.

HOW TO START AN E-TEAM COURSE

1. Pray about starting an E-TEAM course. This is your first and foremost step.

2. Contact your pastor. Invite his participation—either on your own E-TEAM, or encourage him to start his own E-TEAM. Discuss this matter, and get his ideas. Avoid any competition with his ministry. Try to complement his work.

3. Challenge four other men to meet together with you for just eight weeks to complete an E-TEAM course. Explain that there is a short reading assignment for each lesson. Mention that the meetings involve fellowship together and a few discussion questions based on Dave's book. Explain that the project which follows is probably something each man would like to accomplish anyway.

4. Obtain and distribute the E-TEAM course. Make sure that the men receive their playbooks well in advance of the first E-TEAM Huddle. Men need to familiarize themselves with the materials BEFORE the first E-TEAM Huddle. Encourage the men to complete the first assignment BEFORE they arrive for the first Huddle. They should read the scouting report and session one: Father Power before the first meeting.

5. If it is absolutely impossible to distribute materials before the first E-TEAM Huddle, then schedule your E-TEAM course for a nine-week duration. Use the first meeting to distribute the playbooks to each man, to get to know each other, to look over the introductory material together, and to complete the first assignment as a team. At the second meeting, begin with Dave's first cassette lecture, and then complete the first lesson. In this way, your E-TEAM will finish the last seven lessons on schedule.

6. Remind the men always to bring their E-TEAM playbooks, Bibles, and pens or pencils.

7. Call each E-TEAM member the night before the E-TEAM Huddle. Remind each man of the meeting, its time and location, and to do the assignment.

8. Try to arrive early and make sure that plenty of refreshments are on hand. Make sure the room is neat and in order.

HOW TO DIRECT THE E-TEAM HUDDLE

1. *Arrival of E-TEAMmates:* Be sure to extend each E-TEAMmate a hearty welcome, and try to encourage fellowship among the men.

2. *Start of the E-TEAM Huddle:* Begin promptly. Announce the official start of the meeting, and notify the Time Keeper that the E-TEAM Huddle is coming to order. Sitting in a circle or around a table, the men will be more likely to open up and share their ideas freely and naturally. Keep the discussion moving, but focus on the topic and maintain the schedule. Men may continue to enjoy the refreshments throughout the E-TEAM Huddle.

3. *E-TEAM Review:* Explain the purpose and the procedure of this part of the meeting. Men should feel relaxed and open to sharing their opinions and ideas. Keep the atmosphere nonthreatening. Prompt the team with the first question, and then withdraw. Allow the discussion to unfold naturally. Sharing should be voluntary and without pressure. Keep this part of the meeting within the 10 or 15 minutes of allotted time.

4. *E-TEAM Discussion:* Ask the men to share their ideas, comments, and opinions. Some of them may raise questions. Discussion should begin naturally, but if there seems to be some delay, prompt the men by reading the first question presented in this section of the playbook. Most men will participate. Try to pace the discussion, but allow the men to share their thoughts and ideas fully. Be sure to allow time for reading over the projects and closing in prayer. If special needs pop up in the discussion, don't be afraid to depart from the discussion guide and stay with the needs of the men.

E-TEAM Workout: This section involves personal application through the commitment and completion of suggested projects. In most cases, these projects require only a small amount of time to do, and usually they involve activities that most men actually intend to do at some point in their lives. Few men do not desire to improve their lives; the great majority are either too busy to do so, or they lack the motivation to begin. It is in this area of life where E-TEAM courses provide the necessary motivation and the encouragement for applying biblical truth without overwhelming a man's personal schedule or abilities. Most of these projects are uncomplicated and interesting to do.

Occasionally, some of the suggested projects may, for one reason or another, be inappropriate for one or more of the men on your particular E-TEAM. This should present no special problem because E-TEAM courses are entirely flexible.

Individuals and E-TEAMs are free to create their own projects to fit particular needs. The important thing to remember is that E-TEAM members do a meaningful project which should fit and follow-up its respective lesson. This is the area where men keep each other accountable. Remember: the key to application is DOING a project. You may want to call your E-TEAMmates after several days to see what progress they are making, but be very low-keyed.

If you follow these simple guidelines, directing an E-TEAM should prove to be successful and completely rewarding. In addition to making progress in your own life and family shepherding skills, you will witness and participate in the growth and development of the other men on your E-TEAM, and all of you will improve your understanding of the role of a family shepherd.

6. *E-TEAM Encouragement:* The last part of the E-Team huddle should be spent in encouragement. This is done best by prayer. Have the men pray for each other and for each other's families. Pray for God to encourage each man to follow through on his commitment to complete the project.

HOW TO TERMINATE THE E-TEAM COURSE

One of the distinctive values of an E-TEAM course is its specific, short duration. E-TEAM courses do not require men to make long, drawn-out commitments. To maintain this value, the course should be terminated promptly.

1. At the close of the last lesson, state officially that the E-TEAM course is completed. Allow your TEAMmates to suggest the possibility of continued E-TEAM Huddles or additional E-TEAM courses. Discuss this issue only if they bring it up. If this happens, see instruction #3.

2. Thank each man for attending, contributing, and participating. End the course with prayer, after making sure that you have definitely terminated the course.

3. If your team expresses interest in pursuing another E-TEAM course, find out what they would like to do next. Then close the meeting in prayer. Later in the week, call each man personally, and get his ideas or preference from among the following:

a. Start another E-TEAM course with the same E-TEAMmates.

b. Become an E-TEAM Captain, and start your own E-TEAM course with four new men.

c. Start or join another men's group to pursue other materials or Bible study (ask your pastor for his advice).

d. Continue to work on your shepherding skills and meet informally with other men.

If your E-TEAM wants to continue together, suggest that they appoint a new E-TEAM Captain to give others the experience of leading an E-TEAM. If they are quite happy with your leadership, and you feel comfortable as Captain, feel free to continue to serve in this capacity. Dad the Family Shepherd will be happy to continue assisting you to help reach families by building men.

Appendix B

The Dad the Family Shepherd Video Conference

The three volumes in the Dad the Family Shepherd Series originated out of the live conference that Dave Simmons has been teaching since 1984. The conference, entitled *Build Your House on the Rock*, covers not only fatherhood but other critical issues that men must face. The eight-hour conference contains these messages:

FATHER POWER:	How to harness father power. How to build a dynamic heritage.
LOVE UNCHAINED:	How to love beyond normal limits. How to put love into action.
THE MASTER PLAN:	How to take charge of your family. How to develop family teamwork.
HONOR THY WIFE:	How to understand your wife. How to develop family teamwork.
3-D SEX:	How to communicate in three dimensions. How to maximize your wife's love.
MISSION CONTROL:	How to keep your priorities balanced. How to manage your resources.
CHILD SECURITY:	How to build child security. How to prepare children for the teens.
CHILD MANAGEMENT:	How to increase child confidence. How to equip children to solve problems.

This conference is now available on video. The video package is designed to be used for conferences and is not for sale. You or your church must schedule a conference and use the video for the presentation.

VIDEO — THE CONVENIENT CONFERENCE

The Video Conference Is a Flexible Conference
Schedule one anytime, anyplace for any number. There is no minimum attendance required as in the live conference.

The Video Conference Is a Proven Conference
Men are conditioned to respond to video from years of watching TV. The video conference has state-of-the-art technology and computer-generated graphics. It contains the exact same content as Dave's live conferences.

The Video Conference Is a Personal Conference
This ministry tool allows you to establish your own personal fatherhood ministry. This is a way you can begin to reach out and help the men you know in a strategic way. When you help a man with his family, you gain a friend for life.

HOW TO SCHEDULE THE VIDEO CONFERENCE
1. Evaluate the state of fatherhood in your community and pray about getting involved to do something about it.

2. Contact the Dad the Family Shepherd office for more information and ask for the 14 minute video promo clip.

Contact:

Dad, the Family Shepherd
P.O. Box 21445
Little Rock, AR 72221
(501) 221-1102

3. Take the material to your pastor and start the process.

Appendix C

The Fatherhood Institute

A MINISTRY OF DAD THE FAMILY SHEPHERD

In light of the deterioration of the family caused by the decline in performance of fatherhood, ask yourself these questions. Does my church have:

A fatherhood basic training process?

A fatherhood wellness and enhancement process?

A fatherhood diagnostic and remedial training process?

A fatherhood crisis center and an intensive care unit?

Many churches are keenly aware of the need to help fathers but fatherhood enhancement has been a neglected discipline. It has been difficult to ascertain where fathers really are, what are their specific needs, where do they need to be, and what needs to be done to get them moving.

After years of research and interaction with fathers and pastors, Dad the Family Shepherd has pioneered a fatherhood equipping process that can enable your church to tackle the fatherhood issue head on. DFS has developed a comprehensive fatherhood equipping process that can easily be adapted to your church with relatively minor cost and energy. It is called the Fatherhood Institute.

THE REASON FOR A FATHERHOOD INSTITUTE

The Fatherhood Institute receives its mandate directly from the Bible:

"And he will restore the hearts of the fathers to their children, and the hearts of the children to their fathers, lest I come and smite the land with a curse" (Mal. 4:6).

"He must be one who manages his own household well, keeping his children under control with all dignity (but if a man does not know how to manage his own household, how will he take care of the church of God?)" (1 Tim. 3:4-5).

THE NEED FOR A FATHERHOOD INSTITUTE

As you cut through all the surface symptoms that plague the American family, you eventually strike the heart of the crisis: lack of competent male leadership in the home. We live in an age in which fathers fail in the role for which God created them. As a direct result, too many children grow up in dysfunctional homes which will handicap future leadership for the church. Faulty fathers produce flimsy families and when families suffer, the church weeps and the nation groans.

THE PURPOSE OF A FATHERHOOD INSTITUTE

The present trends of family deterioration can only be reversed by returning to God's plan for fatherhood and the family. The church must act in obedience to Scripture by calling men to fathering excellence so that leadership for Jesus Christ might be extended to future generations. The Fatherhood Institute exists to enable a church to enhance the paternal commitment and performance of fathers. We reach families by building men.

THE DESCRIPTION OF THE FATHERHOOD INSTITUTE

The Fatherhood Institute is a comprehensive fatherhood training process. It is designed and packaged so a church can easily adopt it and adapt it to their unique situation and equip their men to become more effective family shepherds.

It features a curriculum of eight-week courses and is formatted for small groups of men called Encouragement Teams (E-Teams). Fathers make a commitment for one course at a time and the courses are offered on a tri-semester basis—fall, winter and spring.

There are many components and systems in the total Fatherhood Institute package but the outstanding feature of the process is that it is adaptable to each individual local church with its own personality, character, appearance, and flavor. Each church has its own way of doing things, and programs that do well in one may not fly in another. No program perfectly fits all churches. The Fatherhood Institute furnishes you the principles of fatherhood ministry and a menu of fatherhood training components from which you develop your own strategy and curriculum.

THE FEATURES OF A FATHERHOOD INSTITUTE

1. It is pastor friendly: It can be implemented by laymen, thereby spreading and developing male leadership throughout the church.

2. It draws on the experience and resources of Dad the Family Shepherd, the National Center for Fathering and international spokesmen dedicated to the cause of fatherhood.

3. It brings men together in small groups for personal interaction and accountability and enables fathers to cross train fathers.

4. It is learner- and application-oriented using multimedia elements (video and audio segments), textbooks, questionnaires, group dynamics, case studies, and projects.

5. It is comprehensive in that it contains core courses, electives, and special fatherhood remedial, recovery, and crisis programs.

THE COMPONENTS OF THE FATHERHOOD INSTITUTE

The Fatherhood Institute consists of a variety of components that fit together to form a comprehensive learner-oriented training process. The primary components are:

1. A churchwide fatherhood survey
2. The E-Team Captain Clinic

3. A Dad the Family Shepherd Conference
4. The Personal Fathering Profile (PFP)
5. The E-Team Courses
6. Gathering of Men

A Churchwide Fatherhood Survey
This project will provide the church with an accurate realistic picture of the state of fatherhood in the church and the specific needs of the men and their families.

The E-Team Captain's Clinic
This Saturday morning clinic trains the E-Team Captains on how to facilitate small groups and certifies them in the explanation and use of the PFP.

The Dad the Family Shepherd Conference
An eight-hour weekend conference that covers the basic significance and responsibilities of fatherhood and challenges the men to commitment to excellence in fathering.

The Personal Fathering Profile
This psychometric instrument, developed by the National Center for Fathering, provides a man with a picture of his fathering style in terms of the four fathering dimensions, the twelve factors of strong fathers, and the five fatherhood satisfactions.

The E-Team Courses
These are the small group meetings where men develop trust, intimacy, vulnerability and accountability. Here, they study the biblical principles of fatherhood and learn to implement them. They support and encourage each other and help solve one another's problems.

The Gathering of Men
This is a banquet at the end of the year when all E-Team members and their wives get together to celebrate the accomplishments of the men and praise God for the changes He has made in all the families.

For a consulting appointment to discuss how your church can establish a Fatherhood Institute, contact:

Dad, the Family Shepherd
P.O. Box 21445
Little Rock, AR 72221

Appendix D

Dad the Family Shepherd Resources

To order: Add 10 percent for shipping and handling to your payment and send it to: Dad the Family Shepherd, P.O. Box 21445, Little Rock, AR 72221 (501) 221-1102

Build Your House on the Rock $40.00 This is an audio recording of the complete eight-hour Dad the Family Shepherd live conference by Dave Simmons. The eight tapes are edited for maximum time efficiency and shipped in a handsome bookshelf binder.

Build Your House on the Rock Conference Manual $9.00 This 125-page book contains the notes, charts, pictures, Scripture references, and outlines for the eight hours of instruction described above.

The Home Run Course Book $4.00 A four-week E-Team Course features the highlights of the conference. This booklet also contains E-Team Captain instructions and tells you everything you need to know to conduct a successful E-Team. It requires the use of the Home Run Course tape.

The Home Run Course Cassette $6.00 This tape provides the audio portion for the four meetings of the Home Run Course.

The Friendship Course Book $4.00 A four-week E-Team Course that covers the principles that help men establish better male friendships. It explains how to generate and sustain close friendships, how to mend broken friendships, and how to screen out unproductive friendships.

The Friendship Course Cassette $6.00 These personal comments from Dave will provide helpful insights to encourage E-Team members in their friendships and is essential to the Friendship E-Team course.

Quiet Time $3.00 This booklet excels in profound insight into improving your personal relationship with God.

Quiet Time Cassette $5.00 This audio version of Quiet Time increases your learning curve.

God's Power for Fathers $15.00 This book provides a treasure of Scriptures for fathers.

Getting Away to Get It Together $6.00 This planning manual tells you everything you need to know to conduct your own marriage enrichment weekend with your wife. It guides a couple through a marriage evaluation process and helps you establish a strategy for improving your marriage.

Personal Fathering Profile Certification Packet $65.00 This mini-course allows you to become officially certified to administer the Personal Fathering Profile (PFP) as well as providing you with your own PFP computerized printout.

Taking Men Alive $7.00 Charles G. Turnbull provides incredible insights into the process of helping others trust Christ.

The Fatherhood Institute Manual $15.00 This packet tells you how to establish an effective Fatherhood Institute in your church. It presents the reasons that make a fatherhood ministry mandatory, the top twenty principles for working with men and a comprehensive strategy to help you adapt the principles to your own unique church.

This Is Where I Came In:
Black America in the 1960s

Gerald L. Early

University of Nebraska Press I Lincoln and London

The lectures on which this book is based were
sponsored by the University of Nebraska Press,
the College of Arts and Sciences, the African
American and African Studies Program,
and the Department of History at the
University of Nebraska–Lincoln.

© 2003 by the University of Nebraska Press
Manufactured in the United States of America

♾

Library of Congress Cataloging-in-Publication Data
Early, Gerald Lyn.
This is where I came in: Black America in the 1960s /
Gerald L. Early.
    p. cm. — (Abraham Lincoln lecture series)
Includes bibliographical references and index.
ISBN 0-8032-1823-0 (cloth: alk. paper)—
ISBN 0-8032-6749-5 (pbk.: alk. paper)
1. African Americans—Civil rights—History—20th
century.   2. African Americans—Social conditions—
1964–1975.   3. United States—History—1961–1969.
4. United States—Race relations.   5. Moore, Cecil B.
(Cecil Bassett), 1915–1979.   6. Ali, Muhammad, 1942- .
7. Davis, Sammy, 1925- .   8. African Americans—
Biography.   I. Title.   II. Series.
E185.615.E16 2003
323.1'196073'009046–dc21
2003047302

Contents

Introduction

The following three essays, which were originally delivered as the 2000 Abraham Lincoln Lectures, are about the 1960s, a strange decade in American history but perhaps not as uniquely so as some may think. Or perhaps we think about the era's uniqueness in the wrong way. Typically, the tremendous social and political turbulence generated by the civil rights and the anti–Vietnam War movements, two of the more strident and dramatic social reformations this country has ever experienced, are seen as a series of watershed events: the striking number of political assassinations—from the president of the United States to several African American political figures and agitators[1] to right-wing leaders like George Lincoln Rockwell; the incredible instances of violent summer urban race riots, usually propelled by an instance, real or imagined, of police brutality; the rapid changes in sexual mores, undoubtedly intensified by the introduction of the birth control pill; the astonishing acceptance of the recreational use of illegal drugs; the unexpectedly dramatic transformation of the national African American character from seeking the acceptance of whites to a militant, nationalistic rejection of all things "white"; the cultural and political construction of a youth culture that was both populist in its urge to be unfettered and consumer-driven in the rage of its superficial appetites.

But were there not other equally unsettled and disruptive decades in American life? What about the 1850s, with the secession crisis, the Dred Scott decision, John Brown at Harper's Ferry, Bloody Kansas, and the savage beating of Charles Sumner in the Senate chambers? What about the era of Reconstruction, which gave us the transformation of blacks from slaves to citizens, the emergence of black elected officials in the south, and the most long-lived and feared of all American terrorist, vigilante organizations, the Ku Klux Klan? What about the anarchist uprisings and violent labor disputes of the 1890s and the assassination of President William McKinley (1901)? Surely, after 1951, the Korean War had become as unpopular and, for the nation's leaders, as intractable and unwinnable a war as Vietnam was more than a decade and a half later. Were not the race riots after World War I, instigated by whites, as violent as, if not more so than, the riots of the 1960s? All of this is probably true, but the 1960s cannot be dismissed as déjà vu or part of an inescapable pattern in American life (although I think it is safe to say that societies and civilizations do go through cycles). The New Left certainly has had an effect on the cultural expression of American life that far outreaches anything like the influence it exercised as the Old Left (and all our politics became something like cultural struggles of expression, of creative temperament and identity therapy as realpolitik). It was during these days that the New Left, in unwitting conjunction with the conservative Right, thoroughly discredited liberalism. (Remember Phil Ochs's 1966 satirical tune "Love Me, I'm a Liberal" or the fact that blacks in the later part of the 1960s began to use *liberal* as if it were synonymous with *hypocrite*.) The 1960s provoked a crisis in liberal democracy, and liberalism— New Deal liberalism—certainly did not survive unscathed, having to apologize for itself in some measure. Nineteenth-century classical liberalism, albeit with a new anticommunist twist, became largely the preserve of the conservatives.

We are all cursed to live in interesting times, uniquely interesting times, as it happens. No person lives in the age of his grandparents or even an age that his grandparents are likely to understand fully. (This is why we should not try to fight our grandparents' fights, or, as military people put it, never refight the last war.) What made the 1960s different is that, as Stanley Crouch has so perceptively pointed out, it was an age of redefinition. But, I might add, it was an age of self-conscious redefinition on a scale that was quite beyond anything we had ever experienced in American life, both narcissistic and populist. The sweeping influence of technology was partly responsible for this. The fact that so many people thought a certain level of power was within their reach, was achievable, that liberalism could be superseded by something called liberation, was also responsible. The 1960s was a time when democracy had never seemed more promising, and it was a time when it had never been more threatened. It was a time when everyone believed in democracy more fervently than ever and it was a time when no one believed in it at all. Perhaps what was most frightening about the 1960s was the totalitarian passions of both the Left and Right: on the one hand, class hatred and anarchy disguised as a form of heroic romanticism, on the other, racial hatred and class provincialism disguised as an expression of order and tradition.

I came of age during the 1960s: that is to say, I lived most of my teen years during that decade, but these lectures are not autobiographical in any telling way. In fact, I can only say that the risk I felt in talking about the 1960s was the possibility that I might get in the way of what I wanted to say and do. My level of detachment about the subjects I speak of might surprise some readers. I am not nostalgic about the 1960s. I cannot even say that I liked the 1960s, in large measure because at the time I was a maladjusted teenager who hardly liked himself. On the whole, while I was living during those days, I thought it was a pretty lousy time to be alive. I felt everything intensely and ignorantly, in a way that might have been funny had I not been such a distinctly uninteresting kid whose innocence was more a defect than a virtue. As a teenager, one cannot help but think two entirely irreconcilable thoughts: that the world is an extension of one's own conceit and that the one is an utter cipher in the world. What the era can reveal about me is not important, but it might be instructive for the reader to see what I can reveal about the age through a detached consideration of some people and events that were, in some instances oddly and in others predictably, important to my understanding of the times as I remember living them.

These lectures have been revised, in part because at the time I gave them they were essays in progress and not, by any means, in a final form. So much more research and commentary about Muhammad Ali has appeared since my lecture about him was delivered that it would have been remiss of me not to make adjustments in light of it. In its original form, the essay on Philadelphia NAACP president Cecil Moore did not have an ending in its own right: I borrowed one from another essay I wrote on Philadelphia. Now it has the ending it should have had when it was delivered. I think that, taken together, these essays—on Muhammad Ali, Sammy Davis Jr., and Cecil Moore and black Philadelphia—provide an informed view of the 1960s from a particular angle: on some of the varieties of dissent and their contradictions. I had originally intended to call this book "Princes Kept the

View," a line from Bob Dylan's "All Along the Watchtower," a song that brilliantly sums up the 1960s as both a mood and an idea. But my wife and daughters loathed that title, and so I thought of another.

The title of this volume is an expression likely to be unfamiliar to the young, if my daughters are an apt example. During my boyhood in the fifties and sixties, when my mother or my older sisters took me to the neighborhood movie house, we didn't worry about getting there at the time the film started. Usually, two films were on the bill (the A film and the B film), as well as a short subject and probably a cartoon, and since they were shown continuously, people stayed in the theater for as long as they wished to go through the entire cycle of offerings. If you arrived in the middle of a film, you simply watched it until the end, then sat through everything else. When the film you'd seen part of when you entered was shown again, you watched it until you came to the part you had seen; then you would say, "This is where I came in," gather your belongings, and leave. The 1960s was where I came in. That is to say, the 1960s was the first decade in which I had some awareness of what was going on in the world and that what was going on in the world mattered to other people—and the fact that it mattered to other people also made it matter to me.

My wife and daughter like this title better, and I must admit that I do, too. It is my one blatant concession to autobiography.

This Is Where I Came In

Muhammad Ali as Third World Hero

> *All that is solid melts into air,*
> *all that is holy is profaned . . .*

> Marx and Engels,
> *Manifesto of the Communist Party*

King of the World, 1975

In his November 1975 *Playboy Magazine* interview, Muhammad Ali, still flush from having regained the heavyweight title in October 1974 in a stunning upset of the heavily favored George Foreman, exclaimed, "You can go to Japan, China, all the European, African, Arab and South American countries and, man, they know me. I can't name a country where they *don't* know me. If another fighter's goin' to be that big, he's goin' to have to be a Muslim, or else he won't get to nations like Indonesia, Lebanon, Iran, Saudi Arabia, Pakistan, Syria, Egypt, and Turkey—those are all countries that don't usually follow boxing. He might even have to be named Muhammad because Muhammad is the most common name in the world" (emphasis in original). No other athlete, American or foreign, and certainly no other boxer in history, could claim such broad international popularity as Ali did during the height of his fame in the 1960s and 1970s, particularly in many of the countries that make up what is known as the Third World. Indeed, every nation Ali named in this interview was represented at the 1955 Bandung or Afro-Asian Unity Conference, an event that intensified the already prominent twentieth-century idea of a "colored" consciousness or a unity of purpose among colonized, dark-skinned peoples in the face of the European or white world. And, of course, nearly all the countries he named have large Muslim populations. For a time, Muhammad Ali was not only the most famous American Muslim but arguably the most famous Muslim in the world.

It might be said that herein lies the tale, in part, of American liberalism's confrontation with Islam, but it is unclear what type of Muslim Ali was supposed to be in the 1960s or which precise doctrine he believed. We know only that he vigorously protested the idea of being American or Christian (while arguing that his choice of religious beliefs was his right as an American), that he thought whites were devils; God, named Allah, was black; and that divine retribution would redeem black-skinned people after they had shown themselves worthy through their own efforts. While these beliefs might be packaged for the believer as something "Islamic," there is little to distinguish them from garden-variety black messianic nationalism. The fact may be that "Islam" may have served to revitalize and modernize black nationalism for a black messianic citizenry that had come to suspect the West instead of being in awe of it.

In the light of the terrorist attack of September 11, 2001, it would be a mistake to say that the United States historically has been anti-Islam or that whites have been anti-Islamic. It would be equally wrong to say that some African Americans have been attracted to Islam because they see it as a "black" religion. (The overwhelming majority of African Americans who have become Muslims did so because they thought of Islam as a truly multiracial religion, not a black one.) What the confrontation between Ali's orthodox racial reactionism and American liberalism demonstrated was liberalism's abhorrence of racialized religion and liberalism's discomfort at having exposed its own invisible, universalist racialized assumptions.

. Ali, I suggest, was the biggest hero of the entire colored world in the post–World War II era, a person who combined protest and action and exhibited fierce racial pride and extraordinary egotism about his own powers. (No black public figure in history seemed more blatantly in love with his own being and his own possibilities than Ali, and for peoples denigrated because of their color and their supposed inferiority, Ali's ego had no small significance.) Ali displayed both a racialized and universalist spirituality much in keeping with the sort of Orientalism or quest for eastern spiritual purity that characterized a number of black American conversions to Islam in the 1960s and even earlier and that characterized an important aspect of black cultural nationalism generally at this time, as it possessed not only a very strong religious impulse but a very strong tendency toward aesthetics and self-help psychology. This point about black nationalism in the 1960s as both religion and aesthetics is important. Ali's emergence as a virtuous hero of color for both black America and the world is of a psychological piece with the emergence of the 1960s avant-garde jazz of John Coltrane, Archie Shepp, Max Roach, Pharaoh Sanders, and the Art Ensemble of Chicago, which tried to blend black nationalism and black entrepreneurialism with a black aesthetic and thus promote the "healing" power of a so-called pure "black" music as therapy. Ali's emergence is also of a piece with Maulani Ron Karenga's Kawaida philosophy, conceived in 1966, whose seven principles became the basis for the African American holiday Kwanzaa, a celebration designed to make black nationalism an aesthetic, entrepreneurial, and religious expression and an act of therapy as well. Ali evidenced no pretension or sense of privilege in feeling that people owed him homage for being champion. He saw his public role as the colored, Islamic heavyweight champion as a series of duties, not indulgences.[1] He was the egotistical hero as selfless padrone and patriarch, as faithful brother.

An example of this last point: in the 1975 *Playboy Magazine* interview, Ali explained why he added former welterweight champion Kid Gavilan[2] to his entourage: "See, once you become a Muslim, you want for your brother what you want for yourself. For instance, Kid Gavilan was a black boxing champion who had trouble in Cuba after he retired and he wound up in Miami working in a park. Newspaper reporters used to write stories about it that would embarrass Kid Gavilan and when I heard what he was doing, I thought, 'Kid Gavilan ain't gonna work in no *park*.' So I found Kid Gavilan and now he works for me, and I pay him a lot better than what he made in the park" (emphasis in original). It is clear from Ali's explanation that he saw in his duties a remarkable conflation of the religious and the racial. What Ali did, in truth, is not unusual at all in the sport of boxing: ex-champions, aged, broke, and broken, are often made members of a new champion's circle, a reflection of how tradition and respect, condescension and honor, are passed down and preserved in this profession. Ali here interprets this practice as religious (a Muslim does these sorts of things even for non-Muslims like Gavilan) and racial (although Gavilan is a Cuban, he is a black man, and blackness transcends nations; thus, in aiding him, Ali symbolically fulfills his own vision of ministering aid to the colored or Pan-African world). Ali sees his entourage not just as a form of patronage (many boxers and celebrities see their circle of cronies and flunkies in this way), but as a kind of symbolic diasporic in-gathering. Ali was, during his active days as a boxer, nearly as mythical a figure of a unified colored world as Gandhi.

Malcolm X tried very hard to be a sort of black American ambassador to the Third World. The Marxist-Leninist and black arts advocate Amiri Baraka called Malcolm "a statesman,"[3] a striking and not entirely inappropriate hyperbole since it was surely Malcolm's outsized ambition to be the head of a black American state. This was Malcolm's goal particularly after his departure from the Nation of Islam in 1964, when he tried to use Islam to create a world community of color and his race to create a form of Pan-Africanism. He never achieved Ali's level of hero worship or popularity, although Malcolm, to be sure, was a highly influential figure. One has only to examine Ali's 1964 African tour for proof of this mass acceptance. Before doing so, however, it is necessary to look briefly at the relationship between Malcolm X and Muhammad Ali.[4]

Muhammad Ali and the Nation of Islam

Muhammad Ali fought for the heavyweight title against Sonny Liston on February 25, 1964. Malcolm X had become friendly with the young fighter before this; in fact Malcolm and his family were present at Ali's Miami Beach training camp before the fight, much to the chagrin of the fight's promoters. Malcolm fired up Ali with the idea that the fight was a crusade, a religious war between the crescent and the cross. (Admittedly, Liston, a poor, uneducated black man who grew up a sharecropper's son in an intensely racist Arkansas, went to prison for armed robbery, and had been a thumb crusher for organized crime, made an unusually inappropriate symbol for either Christianity or the West, unless one were to argue that Liston himself was a victim of both, but Malcolm's idea certainly inspired Ali, and he used it in subsequent fights against black "infidels".) Malcolm had a ringside seat at the fight, and he was probably the only member of the Nation of Islam (NOI), or perhaps one of a handful, who actually thought Ali would beat the heavily favored Liston. Even before Ali formally announced his conversion to the NOI, immediately *after* the Liston fight, rumors about it had been circulating for weeks in the press. Although Malcolm had been suspended from the NOI in November 1963 by its leader, Elijah Muhammad, for making insensitive (actually, imprudent) remarks about the assassination of President Kennedy, he was still the most well-known so-called Black Muslim of the time. Wherever he went, the press followed, particularly to the camp of the handsome, loud-mouthed, agitated, energetic heavyweight fighter known then as Cassius Marcellus Clay.

But Malcolm X did not convert Ali. When the two first met in Detroit in 1962, Ali was already a fellow traveler, if not a member of the NOI. The Louisville fighter had been attending meetings for about three years before he announced his membership. "I'd sneak into Nation of Islam meetings through the back door. I didn't want people to know I was there. I was afraid if they knew, I wouldn't be allowed to fight for the title. Later on, I learned to stand up for my beliefs," Ali said.[5] Ali first learned of the organization at a Golden Glove tournament in Chicago in 1959. His early teachers were Abdul Rahaman, Ishmael Sabakhan, and Jeremiah Shabazz. Malcolm X came in a little later and thoroughly mesmerized young Clay with his pride, his rhetoric, and his logic. Clay probably would have become a Muslim even had he not met Malcolm X, but Malcolm provided compelling affirmation for the young boxer. He particularly needed Malcolm X at the first Liston fight in 1964 because so few people thought he would win and the NOI, on the whole, officially gave him very little support. At the time, young Clay did not know that even Elijah Muhammad thought he would lose and had told Malcolm not to associate himself with the fighter for fear that his inevitable defeat would reflect poorly on the NOI. Moreover, Elijah Muhammad despised the sport of prizefighting and was not especially keen about having Clay as a member of the NOI when he first joined. John Ali, the national secretary of the group, condemned Jeremiah Shabazz when he learned that Clay was being lured into the organization. Shabazz said: "The Messenger [Elijah Muhammad] told me I'd been sent to the south to make converts, not to fool around with fighters."[6] The NOI's inner sanctum thought Clay was a clown, and he was kept rather at arm's length until after he won the championship. He was completely loyal to the Honorable Elijah Muhammad, and some aspects of his life were completely controlled by the NOI. In many respects, Ali was an obedient, submissive member of the NOI, and the organization took considerable advantage of it, but Ali was also something of an exception because he became, after all, the goose that was producing golden eggs. Certainly, no one expected *him* to be out on street corners hawking bean pies and copies of *Muhammad Speaks*, the sect's newspaper. Where would the NOI have been after the assassination of Malcolm X had the charismatic, stylish boxer not been in the fold?

After Ali won the title in 1964, the internal rift in the NOI worsened: Malcolm X, by far the most intelligent and the most famous of all the organization's ministers, left to form his own group after reportedly having made several efforts to patch things up with Elijah Muhammad. He was dissatisfied with the political passivity of the group and with the group's incorrect practice of Islam; this latter concern was causing a rift between Elijah Muhammad and two of his sons as well. Ali was, initially, unsure whom to follow, and both Malcolm X and Elijah Muhammad, realizing what a magnet his fame and youth would be, desperately wanted him. Elijah Muhammad lured the young fighter with a name, Muhammad Ali. Normally, most Black Muslims are given an X to stand in for their slave names, as the group referred to the natal names of their believers. (Clay was known in the group as Cassius X.) The believer was not to get his true, "original" name until the second coming of Master Wallace D. Fard Muhammad, the mysterious founder of the NOI. This amounted to having one's identity completed at the time of apocalypse or judgment, quite in keeping with the millennialist nature of the organization's beliefs. Elijah Muhammad announced Clay's new name, Muhammad Ali, at the organization's annual Savior's Day Rally, almost immediately after the Liston fight. Ali was both embarrassed and honored at being singled out: "Changing my name was one of the most important things that happened to me in my life. It freed me from the identity given to my family by slavemasters," he said in retrospect.[7] This name change turned out to be one of the most startling and contentious symbolic acts in American race relations in the 1960s. Never had so many been so annoyed by something so seemingly minor. As Ali said at the time, celebrities change their names and reinvent themselves every day: why single him out for doing it?

On March 6, less than two weeks after Ali won the title, Elijah Muhammad met with Ali to tell him to break off his relationship with Malcolm, since Malcolm was not returning to the fold. Ali did so immediately. Ali was deeply impressed by this slight, fatherly, asthmatic man who, though poorly educated, was also clever and determined. Elijah Muhammad was now Ali's spiritual leader, but the fighter was also deeply intimidated by him and by the power of the NOI. Ali respected and liked Malcolm X, but he respected and feared Elijah Muhammad. The wily Elijah Muhammad had not endured years of government surveillance, a prison term during World War II for sedition and draft dodging, rival cults that meant to cut him down, jealousy, bickering, envy, and a wife who hated him for his uncontrollable infidelity to be undone by a slick-talking, ex-con street hustler formerly called Detroit Red whom he had lifted from the gutter and made what he was. By the time Ali fought Liston again, in Lewiston, Maine, in May 1965, Malcolm X had been murdered by members of the NOI, and Ali thoroughly repudiated any friendship he had with Malcolm. Ali's response to Elijah Muhammad's edict was precisely what the old man expected. He knew that the major reason people join cults is to be sheltered from the outside world and to be sheltered from the dilemma of thinking through how to make a choice. The three most famous men associated with the NOI were Malcolm X, Muhammad Ali, and Louis Farrakhan: it is a small irony that Malcolm X played a pivotal role in the recruitment of both Ali and Farrakhan and that both of them turned against him in the end. It is another small irony that the excessiveness of Malcolm's own ambition to be a statesman of something like the black diaspora or Third World made it possible for Ali to fulfill aspects of that role far better than Malcolm ever could.

Ali in Africa

Osman Karriem, who arranged Ali's spring 1964 African tour, had actually discussed the idea with Malcolm X, who encouraged him to take Ali abroad. Karriem believed that Ali would be well received abroad, for the champion had been a powerful draw for Third World diplomats and ambassadors when he visited the United Nations with Malcolm X a few days after winning the championship. "I arranged the trip," Karriem said. "To me, it was necessary to give the kid some breathing room. There was so much going on in his life, and this was a way to take him out of the line of fire."[8] Ali left for Africa on May 14, 1964, with his brother, Rahaman, also a member of the NOI, Howard Bingham, Karriem, and Herbert Muhammad, one of Elijah Muhammad's eight legitimate children.

It was while in Ghana that Ali made public his rift with Malcolm X. The men's paths crossed at the Hotel Ambassador. Malcolm was leaving Ghana, having just finished a stay that had included a meeting with the colony of expatriate black Americans who were living there (including Maya Angelou and Julian Mayfield), a session with Kwame Nkrumah, and a lecture at the University of Ghana.[9] Before arriving in Ghana, Malcolm had completed the hajj, the holy journey every devout Muslim is required to make once in this lifetime. Since the followers of Elijah Muhammad did not practice the hajj, this signified Malcolm's spiritual break from Elijah Muhammad and the NOI. When Malcolm made an overture to greet Ali, the fighter snubbed him. Ali's visit to Ghana was covered daily in the Ghanaian papers; although Malcolm was also given press coverage, it was not nearly so extensive. Indeed, on Monday, May 18th, and Tuesday, May 19th, the *Evening News*, the paper founded by Kwame Nkrumah, Ghana's first premier since the country had gained independence, ran huge front-page photos of the boxer. In the paper's May 19th edition, he was photographed wearing traditional African robes and was accompanied by Nkrumah himself. This was not the only time Ali was photographed wearing traditional African clothing while he was in Africa, and so it comes as something of a surprise that when he saw Malcolm in Ghana, dressed as a devout Muslim in white, Ali said to reporters: "Did you get a look at Malcolm? Dressed in that funny white robe and wearing a beard and walking with that cane that looked like a prophet's stick? Man, he's gone. He's gone so far out, he's out completely." Either Ali was being hypocritical or he was not aware of traditional Muslim attire for penitents who have taken the hajj. Ali fought some exhibitions in Ghana and made several public appearances, all of which were very well attended.

The May 18th sports section of the *Evening News* described the crowd that greeted Ali at the airport in Accra as follows: "A large enthusiastic crowd, carrying placards, some of which read 'YOU ARE WELCOME HOME, KING OF THE WORLD,' 'CASSIUS CLAY YOU ARE ON YOUR LAND,' 'GHANA IS YOUR MOTHERLAND CASSIUS CLAY,' all added to the glamour of the occasion." It was reported in the Ghana papers that Ali's trip would include visits to Nigeria, the Ivory Coast, Guinea, Mali, the United Arab Republic, and Algeria. (A tour such as this would have taken two months; in fact, Ali's trip lasted only about a month and covered only Ghana, Nigeria, and Egypt, or the United Arab Republic, as it was called at that time.) The more elaborate itinerary as reported in the Ghanaian papers may have stemmed from Ali or someone in his circle exaggerating the extent and length of the tour, or it might have been the original intention for the tour to be far longer than it was. In any case, it seems fairly clear that the tour was in something of a state of flux even from the beginning.

On May 20, Ali was quoted in the Ghana press about his visit with Nkrumah[10]: "When the two of us met last Monday at Flagstaff House, I humbled myself before him, a thing I rarely do, because I saw in him a dedicated man who is anxious to free Africa and bring about unity." The fact that Ali was nearly insufferably proud did not offend his African audience: instead, it seemed to thrill them. He also expressed a wish to defend his title in Africa, which further excited his audience, as no heavyweight boxing championship match had ever been held in sub-Saharan Africa, including South Africa. Ali was precisely the larger-than-life figure that his audience expected and wanted; the fact that he was a black American "coming home" made him even more mythical and appealing.

Ali's trip to Nigeria was cut short from a week to three days. In Mark Kram's *Ghosts of Manila: The Fateful Blood Feud between Muhammad Ali and Joe Frazier* (2001), which is without question, along with Nick Tosches's recent biography of Sonny Liston, one of the most bitterly critical books on Ali ever written, Ali's trip to Nigeria is described in this way: "Ali stayed long enough to insult the looks of Nigerian women and, saying it was just a little place, he beat it to Egypt, the fortress of mighty Islam and home to the women he had remembered from Cecil B. DeMille epics."[11]

What actually happened in Nigeria is a bit more complicated than Kram's quick assessment would indicate, although Ali's view of Africa and Egypt probably had been influenced, to some degree, by the Hollywood biblical epics that were popular in the 1950s and 1960s. Ali cut short the trip in part because he wanted to go to Egypt, and Egypt particularly wanted to have him. But it is unclear when this was decided. In the June 2, 1964, edition of the *Daily Times*, one of Nigeria's major papers, there was a considerable spread on Ali's arrival at Lagos airport, and it was reported then that his stay would last only three days. So, even before Ali made any remarks about the looks of Nigerian women, even before he arrived in Nigeria, the week-long visit had been cut short. It is not likely that the visit was abbreviated as a result of anything that happened to him in Nigeria: huge crowds there greeted him holding signs that read "HAPPY BACK HOME MOHAMMAD ALI KING OF THE WORLD," and when Ali alighted from his plane, he cried to the crowd, "I Am King of the World!" The crowd shouted its assent. (During his African visit, Ali was commonly referred to in the press and among the crowds as the King of the World. Unlike in the press in Ghana, the Nigerian press commonly referred to Ali by his Islamic name. He met local dignitaries and appeared publicly in African traditional dress.[12])

The controversy about Ali's truncated visit to Nigeria (he did not box any exhibitions there) was discussed fully in a column in the June 8, 1964, *Daily Times* by Cee-Kay, who had covered Ali's entire visit. The writer blamed the National Sports Council, a government agency, for its poor organizing and planning of the event, and the article argues convincingly that Nigeria was actually a late addition to Ali's schedule after he had already made arrangements to go to Egypt. In discussing the poor planning, Cee-Kay pointed out that there was no convertible at the airport to take Ali on his motorcade journey. The photos in the papers show Ali sitting on top of a small car with a sun roof. Ali actually had to take a taxi, at his own expense, when he departed for the airport three days later. Also, there were problems when he was taken to his hotel from the airport and then hastily taken to a dignitary's house for lunch. Ali apparently did make remarks about Nigerian women, although precisely what he said is unclear (they may very well have been disparaging), and about how much more significant Egypt was for him as a Muslim. His preference for Egypt was clearly because he saw it as the center of Islamic culture and, like many Afrocentrist-minded blacks, was impressed by the fact that the country has monuments, unrelated, of course, to its Islamic heritage but rather to a "glorious" African past of empire and conquest that also happens to impress white folk. The Nation of Islam was never focused upon sub-Saharan Africa and built its myths largely on connections between black Americans and the Middle East. It was not for nothing that Elijah Muhammad constantly spoke of "the Asiatic black man."[13]

Ali's visit to Egypt, which lasted two weeks, was covered extensively by the Egyptian press, nearly every day, including a front-page story in the *Egyptian Gazette* on June 4, 1964, to announce his arrival. While in Egypt, Ali made his most blatantly political statement to the press after having watched a film about the battle of Port Said; on June 10, the *Egyptian Gazette* gave this account of it: "Commenting on the film he saw on the Suez battle, Clay said that during this battle the U.S. Press tried to make it appear as an Arab aggression against Israel and an attempt by Israel to defend itself against this aggression. 'I have now understood the truth about the battle. I now know that it was an aggression against you. I wish such an aggression would take place now and I should have been pleased to fight on your side and under your flag,' he stressed." That remark is, of course, interesting in light of Ali's subsequent battle with the United States Selective Service Act and his refusal to fight in Vietnam. Would fighting for Egypt against Israel be considered religious or political? Was the intense Arab nationalism of the moment a proxy for a Pan-Islamic world or a proxy for a "colored" world? Exactly what kind of conscientious objector was Ali? How can one tease apart his religion from his politics when his religious conversion seemed nothing more than the militantly mystical reinscription of a racialized political commitment? Ali and his brother were photographed with Egyptian president Nasser, with whom Ali had an audience, in the June 18th and 20th editions of the *Egyptian Gazette*. He and his brother were photographed leaving Egypt on June 23rd, appearing in the *Gazette* on June 24th.

On the whole, despite the problems in Nigeria, the African tour was an enormous success for Ali; it certainly had to buoy his spirits as he now knew he had an incredibly large following in African and Muslim countries. There was an alternative home for him if things did not work out in the United States owing to the intensely hostile reaction to his Islamic conversion. Also, the trip established him as the new star of the NOI. Granted, the NOI's own outreach to the Middle East helped, in some measure, to make this trip possible, but Ali received press coverage and attracted crowds that far exceeded the reception Malcolm X or Elijah Muhammad had received on their visits to the Third World Muslim nations a few years earlier, or Malcolm's far more extensive spring 1964 trip that had included stops in Saudi Arabia, Lebanon, Egypt, Nigeria, Ghana, and Algeria, where he met with several diplomats and heads of state.[14] Malcolm was an exciting political figure and rhetorician, but Ali was something heroic, glamorous: a knight, a prince, a star. He was, ultimately, more useful for politicians because he was an athlete and less of a threat to the interests of those who promoted his heroism or admired his skill. Ali was right: he was, in a way that no other American boxer or athlete had been before, truly, the strange king of a changing world.

Malcolm X and the Racialization of Islam

Ali succeeded despite his own racialist, sometimes blatantly racist, beliefs. His hatred of interracial marriage, for instance, which he condemns at some length in his 1975 *Playboy Magazine* interview, or his self-praise for not having sexual relations with white women, sound a bit odd today, but at the time, it was the general perception among many blacks that successful blacks viewed interracial marriage as a sign of success. Remember, Ali was a contemporary of Sammy Davis Jr., who had one of the most publicized interracial weddings in American cultural history. That Ali succeeded in tying racial solidarity to his religion, making it virtually a tenet of faith that to marry outside of one's religion was like marrying outside of one's race, was possible only because group loyalty as a form of heroic self-determination is always appreciated by the persecuted.

Ali was never accused by his legion of fans in the Third World of racializing his religion, although he clearly did so. The same was not true of Malcolm X, who was dogged, much to his detriment, by that charge. The racialization of Islam in the United States as both a political and spiritual act is important to think about. Even black jazz musicians of the 1950s, such as the drummer Art Blakey, the singer Dakota Staton, the pianist Ahmad Jamal, and the sax players Yusef Lateef and Shahib Shihab, all of whom converted to Middle Eastern or orthodox Islam, were partly and self-consciously driven by racial reasons to do so, feeling that it was a truer, more appropriate religion for black people than Christianity and that Islam was a religion where all were treated as equals.[15] There were also no images of God in Islam, meaning that black Muslims did not feel oppressed, as black Christians did, by the force of an iconography that depicted God, Jesus, Mary, the apostles, the saints, and every other major figure in the religion as Europeans.

In some sense, it is impossible to avoid the subject of the racialization of religion for the black believer. Is Islam in America, because of the country's racial history, an unavoidably "colored" ideology? The Nation of Islam strongly emphasized a simple idea: black people needed a religion that addressed and interpreted their experience in a way that was completely independent of whites. In 1964 Ali described his conversion to Islam in this way: "one day this Muslim minister came to meet me and he asked me wouldn't I like to come to his mosque and hear about the history of my forefathers. I never had heard no black man talking about no forefathers, except that they were slaves, so I went to a meeting. And this minister started teaching, and the things he said really shook me up. Things like that we twenty million black people in America didn't know our true identities, or even our true family names. And we were direct descendants of black men and women stolen from a rich black continent and brought here and stripped of all knowledge of themselves and taught to hate themselves and their kind."[10] It is clear why Malcolm X could not separate race from Islam: for him, religion had no political force or meaning unless it was an explicit ideological challenge to white Christianity, which, for Malcolm, was nothing more than a white ideology that Europeans had used to make whiteness holy and to profane all people of color.

The first organization Malcolm X created after he left the NOI was the Muslim Mosque Inc. He announced its formation at a press conference on March 8, 1964, just two days after Muhammad Ali had been told to shun him. It was an attempt to advance Islam as a means of ending racism. The paradox here, of course, is that Malcolm pitched Islam to black Americans as a religion that unified black people with the nonwhite peoples of the world, which was certainly racializing a nonracialist religion, and for which he was criticized by other Muslims in both the United States and abroad. In some sense, Malcolm was used to this criticism, as the NOI had been criticized since the late 1950s by various Muslims both here and abroad for its insistence on racializing the religion. Malcolm had gone to Egypt and other Arab countries in 1960 and so was very aware of the existence of "white" Muslims and the nonracialist character of Islam long before his hajj of 1964 during which, he claims in his *Autobiography*, he first became aware of the nonracialism of Islam.[17] Indeed, at many of his lectures and public speeches in the United States, he was often challenged by Middle Eastern Muslims. He deflected some of these challenges very well but he was, nonetheless, bothered by them. Malcolm had been invited to take the hajj when he visited Egypt and the Middle East in 1959, but he refused because he felt he was not prepared to undertake such an expression of devotion at the time. When he confronted Middle Eastern Muslims, Malcolm felt extremely ignorant about his religion, as the NOI observed very little that was proper Islamic practice, and he was embarrassed by this ignorance. Nasser may have made the offer to Malcolm to take the hajj for political reasons, as Nasser, at the time, was interested in outreach to sub-Saharan African nations. He may have thought it politically expedient to try to heal the breach between Middle Eastern Muslims and the NOI. Middle Eastern Muslims were exasperated by but tried to be tolerant of the NOI. I spoke to a few Islamic scholars who worked for the State Department in the 1950s and 1960s; they said that Muslim countries were nonplussed by the NOI and were unsure how to treat the group. Indeed, in 1959, when immigrant Muslim organizations in North America criticized the NOI for being racist, Malcolm accused "blue-eyed" Muslims of being slave masters. So, there was considerable tension surrounding the subject of racialism and Islam once the NOI emerged as a potent force in American racial politics in 1959, and Malcolm seemed never to have lost his belief in a kind of racialized Islam as an instrument for Pan-Africanism and for Third World anticolonialism.

Another reason for the creation of The Muslim Mosque Inc. was that Malcolm was convinced it would uplift black people morally. The NOI had always had a reputation for being able to do this, especially because of its success in converting black men in prison. Until accusations began swirling in the 1960s, even before Malcolm was murdered, that some mosques were involved in criminal activities, the NOI, for a time, enjoyed a greater reputation for morally uplifting poor blacks than black Christian churches did. There were several obvious reasons for this success: the stringent, cloistered, cultlike nature of the group, which resembled hard-core Calvinism more than anything else; the power of the Muslim conversion as a form of political and spiritual regeneration; and, finally, the NOI's insistence, like that of Father Divine's Peace Mission Movement, on a present-centered God with heaven and hell as earthly, not otherworldly, experiences. It made God both palpable and historic, immediate and all-powerful—a God who does distribute His goods according to who deserves them.

The power of being uplifted attracted Ali to the NOI: "Elijah Muhammad was trying to lift us up and get our people out of the gutter," Ali said many years after 1964. "He made people dress properly, so they weren't on the street looking like prostitutes and pimps. He taught good eating habits, and was against alcohol and drugs. I think he was wrong when he talked about white devils, but part of what he did was make people feel it was good to be black."[18] Of course, this preoccupation with moral uplift gave the Black Muslims' form of black nationalism characteristics similar to those of earlier forms of black nationalism, or, to use another term, race preservation. One finds moral uplift jeremiads also in such early works of W. E. B. Du Bois as "The Conservation of the Races" in 1897, or in the works of Alexander Crummell, the

Pan-Africanist Episcopal minister Du Bois admired, and indeed in most of the writings of most black leaders, from Frederick Douglass to Marcus Garvey. As Malcolm X said at the 1964 press conference for Muslim Mosque Inc., "This will give us a religious base and the spiritual force necessary to rid our people of the vices that destroy the moral fiber of our community."[19]

The Muslim Mosque Inc. failed. About eight months before his death in February 1965, Malcolm X invented another organization called the Organization of Afro-American Unity, modeled after the Organization of African Unity, created in 1963 in Addis Ababa, Ethiopia, and meant to bind together the independent African nations that started it. The Organization of Afro-American Unity held its first rally on June 28, 1964, announcing a more secular, Black Power–oriented charter than that of the Moslem Mosque Inc. The Pan-African influence here is obvious. Less obvious but clearly stated was the concern with making the black American struggle a human rights issue on the international stage. What Malcolm hoped for, in part, was a kind of standing Bandung Conference, where all black American political factions could come together as did all the independent colored nations of the world in 1955, an event so significant for the Black Muslims that Elijah Muhammad said it signified "the fall of the white man."[20] (Something like this kind of organization was finally realized in the United States in

1970 with the formation of the Congress of Afrikan Peoples.) Another obvious goal of the Organization of Afro-American Unity was the attempt to lessen the Muslim character of his groups, because, after all, African Americans were and still are overwhelmingly Christian. Ironically, Malcolm's attempt to politicize and racialize what was, in essence, a foreign religion so that it could be used as a tool in the formation of an international, anti-imperialist community of coloreds had gotten in the way of his ability to form and maintain a political organization that would, ideally, free American blacks from their western-ness, from their American-ness, from, in Malcolm's view, the prison of their own deformation. Malcolm insisted that black Americans had to make their struggle international in scope and to unite with other black nations. He desired for some African member-states to present a petition of black American grievances to the United Nations. When he broached this at a meeting of the Organization of African Unity in July 1964 (which he attended as an observer) in the form of a memorandum, he was gently but plainly rebuffed. Thus, the Organization of Afro-American Unity failed too, even though some of Malcolm's followers tried to keep it going after his death. Ali was, in a sense, right in 1964 when he snubbed Malcolm in Ghana and said to the press: "Nobody listens to Malcolm anymore." Ironically, Malcolm's influence as an icon and martyr was enormous after he died.

What is important to distinguish here is that Muhammad Ali's success as an international figure obviated any need for him to be identified with a protest or militant black American organization. Indeed, his 1964 African tour already demonstrated that. He was attractive to some because he was a Muslim, but few knew or cared that he belonged to the NOI or that he spoke on its behalf. To be sure, Ali had far less ability than Malcolm X to found an organization or to lead one. Ali, in fact, never had such ambitions. He was a remarkable political figure because he transcended politics even as he embodied something political.

What explains, in part, the intensity of Ali's acceptance was that he was a champion sportsman, flamboyant to boot, which, by the very nature of sports, was bound to make him a charismatic figure. Also, as a fighter, Ali participated in a sport that dramatically and even crudely represents the nature of struggle and adversity and can easily be interpreted racially and politically. It seems no accident that prizefighting rose as a major spectator sport in the United States during the age of industrialism in the 1880s, which was also the age of social Darwinism and the reinscription of racism as the major social and political ideology with the end of Reconstruction. What sport could better romanticize the ideas of social Darwinism than boxing? What sport better brought together the gentleman amateur and the roughneck lower-class professional in a bond of masculine ritual that glorified punishment, cruelty, endurance, and sacrifice? Professional boxing, with its strict color line in the heavyweight division in the latter part of the nineteenth century, was seen simply as a demonstration of white male supremacy; it evolved into a sport that dramatized white ethnic particularism in its golden age from the 1920s to the 1940s as a white working-class sport in the United States. Prizefighting also represented class crossover or slumming of a very specialized sort for the rich men who often supported boxers, controlled amateur boxing and most athletic clubs in the United States, and who bet on the outcome of fights. Throughout its history, boxing represented upward mobility for poor males, if they were lucky enough to become champions and make money. Finally, prizefighting has symbolized black male revolt from the earliest days of integrated competition in the sport. Whites were always uneasy about blacks beating whites in the ring. And blacks attached far more significance to it than it deserved.

The fact that he was a boxer was fortunate for Ali in his quest for a new context for African American hero worship, as he participated in a sport that was popular in the United States and had cultural resonance throughout the world. Boxing has always been popular in much of Europe (modern boxing originated in seventeenth-century England), in Asia (from where most small boxers hail), and in Latin America and Africa as well. Indeed, one can find amateur or professional boxing virtually anywhere in the world where there are poor young men who live in brutal, impoverished neighborhoods where physical prowess of the type boxing represents is highly respected and plays both a practical and honorific role in the creation of manhood.

As brilliant as Malcolm X was and as much as he resonated with downtrodden, colonized "colored" masculinity because of the years he spent in prison and in the hustler's underworld, he did not possess the charismatic range of elements of a downtrodden, colored, colonized masculinity that Ali did in being a great boxer. The mere fact that Ali was a fighter certified his manhood in an era when black nationalism and color consciousness was intricately connected to masculinity. Malcolm X was obsessed with the politics of manhood, which may explain why he was attracted to Ali the prizefighter, the ultimate symbol of manhood of some fantastic sort. There were also other great black boxing heroes upon whose legacies Ali built his own myth: particularly, Jack Johnson, the first black heavyweight champion, who was prosecuted under the Mann Act in 1913 because he flaunted his white girlfriends and wives; Joe Louis, the great heavyweight champion and beloved American symbol of democracy during the late 1930s; and Sugar Ray Robinson, probably the most stylish and the most cool of all black boxing champions, and the one Ali most admired.

What is even more significant about Ali, reflecting the startling hybridity of a colonized and a post-colonial consciousness, was that he both purposefully and inadvertently created himself as a Third World hero of a colored world that needed protection against the hostile, indifferent, corrupt, or uncomprehending white corporate world that largely financed the professional fight game and controlled the sports media. He also envisioned the colored world as a site for revolt against the white world controlling sports and entertainment, and Ali used this conception against the demand that he please this white world and be controlled by it if he expected to make his way in his profession. This urge for independence on Ali's part is vital in considering his importance as a racialized political hero: fighters exist in a highly individualistic, nonunionized, nearly laissez-faire sport where strong management personalities (trainers, managers, promoters, corporate executives) and social Darwinism (eat or be eaten) rule. Ali's cultivation of a colored image and ideology became a new, individualistic exhibition, by turns petulant, sincere, immature, contradictory, and incisive, childlike yet manly, self-mocking yet zealous, making explicit what many on the Left and the Right felt was the political nature of all sports. It must be remembered that Ali was a very naïve young man, and fairly unworldly, as one might expect the average black boy from a segregated southern town to be. This is why he was attracted to a homemade cult like the NOI. One way, of course, to comprehend the rise of Muhammad Ali as a black anti-establishment hero is to understand this paradox: Ali sought independence, but he also wanted an authority to approve of that quest. Like most young people, Ali ultimately desired the approval and the symbolism granted by authority.

To those on the Left, Ali humanized his sport by making it and himself explicitly political through his own set of definitions. In essence, he refused to be a mere "mortal engine," to use John Hoberman's expression. He forced the public to take his whole being, the full range of his humanity, into account in judging him as an athlete, and not just his performances in the ring. He also gave his performances in the ring a great deal more drama and effect than they would have possessed without the political overlay he forced on them. His fights became the most rousing, pulsating sort of theater imaginable. And, for the Left, after he joined the Nation of Islam (despite the fact that from a leftist perspective, the NOI was a counterrevolutionary organization that basically endorsed a militantly expressed, racially coded, bourgeois fantasy of regeneration through respectability), and especially after he refused to be drafted, Ali became not only a kind of symbolic rebel against the tyranny and racism of the American state but also a perfect victim of it.

For the Right, Ali was suspect because he seemed to lack sportsmanship, refused to honor the code of ethics that governed behavior in high-pressure athletic competition. He bragged about his abilities and saw his opponents as mere pawns, often openly disrespecting them. He also created political dramas with his opponents in an opportunistic fashion. The Right viewed Ali's conscientious objection to the Vietnam War as illegitimate because he belonged to a cult organization, largely run by thugs and con men, that espoused a lot of fantasy racialist claptrap. The Right's final objection to Ali was that his opposition to the state was wrongheaded. Far from being a victim of a tyrannical, racist America, the argument went, Ali was the beneficiary of a fluid and open American democracy.[21] Without it, he could not have existed.

Both the Left and the Right got Ali partly but significantly wrong. What the Left got wrong was, first, the idea that Ali transcended being a "mortal engine" and that he humanized sports. Indeed, Ali, like most great boxers, fought far past his prime, suffered severe physical damage because of it, and seemed to have been controlled by the princes of boxing, namely, promoters and television, as much as any other boxer. And although he suffered for his stance against the draft by being denied a license to box in the United States for nearly four years and, further, being denied the right to fight abroad, he actually paid less of a price than many athletes who engaged in military service during wartime, who sacrificed years of their careers, and, in the cases of athletes like Ted Williams and Bob Feller, put themselves in harm's way, engaging in combat. Ali was extraordinarily self-absorbed; he never cared about the sport of boxing as a whole and did very little, even with the enormous popularity he had, to help his fellow boxers or to improve the sport. Had Ali, at the height of his popularity in the 1970s, called for a union for boxers, the issue might have gotten the public traction it needed to actually become a popular debate.

The Right got Ali wrong as well. Ali's denigration of his opponents was something of a tradition in boxing; certainly, boxing had a complex history of ritual male insult between the opponents. This behavior was probably meant to instill anger in the combatants and thus give them a reason to fight related to a defense of honor, which seemed equally important to boxing's audiences throughout the existence of the modern version of this sport. Also, Ali was not the first athlete to brag about his abilities. The baseball pitcher Dizzy Dean, for instance, did the same and got the same results as Ali: enormous adulation coupled with intense dislike. Babe Ruth did this as well.

Ali created political dramas with his opponents largely because he was an opportunist who realized that to make the outcome of a fight between two black men relevant to whites, it was necessary to create a certain sort of gate appeal. He decided to exploit the times he lived in by making, unfairly and counterproductively, his opponents Uncle Toms. In politicizing his opponents in this fashion, Ali was highlighting large issues surrounding boxing at the time: if fights are about symbolism, he seemed to be asking his opponents, whose symbol are you? This seems to me a fair question to have asked. Ali became a representative and symbolic political figure in much the same way as did Jack Dempsey, the slacker who avoided the draft, and Gene Tunney, the fighting marine, when they fought in 1927 and 1928. The cost of all of this for Ali was what every black man pays when he speaks his mind: whites will chop you down. What his admirers respected about Ali was that, in the end, with all the pressure he faced, he did not sell out, he did not recant, he did not repudiate what he said or what he was.

How much Ali was controlled by the NOI is difficult to say. This raises the question that Mark Kram, I suppose, really wanted to investigate in *Ghosts of Manila*: did Ali actually believe what he said when he opposed the draft? What happened to Ali would have been the same whether or not he knew what he was doing. Why should it matter whether it was inadvertence or design that drove him? What Ali and the NOI clearly understood was that to declare being black something like being holy was to profane America, or, according to the press, to profane Ali's own American-ness. Ali, Malcolm X, Elijah Muhammad, and the entire Nation of Islam posed an interesting response to this claim, one that no one, certainly not the mainstream civil rights organizations of the day, was ever able to answer persuasively: Well, if it is true that we profane America in our assertion of ourselves, well, what's wrong with that? Or, put another way, from their perspective: What's so great about America that it oughtn't to be profaned by a group whom America has already thoroughly and shamelessly profaned for hundreds of years? The Right was correct in saying that Ali was made possible by a fluid democracy, but Ali, just as important, was the product of fixed, highly racialized, caste-arranged society that most whites did not wish to acknowledge. "I just spoke my mind; that's all," Ali reflected a decade ago, "I said things black people thought, but were afraid to say."[22]

Sammy Davis Jr., Establishment Rebel

In the winter of 1999, *Entertainment Weekly* listed, in this our list-crazed age, the 100 greatest entertainers of the last fifty years (1950–2000). Sammy Davis Jr., a man who was called during his own time the world's greatest entertainer, was not among the chosen. This is strange not only because Davis was a far better and far more significant entertainer than some of the people who did make the list—Tom Cruise, Jerry Seinfeld, Janis Joplin, Cher, and Julia Roberts, to name a few—but because few performers have ever reflected the glory of their times more fully or carried the burdens of their times with greater anxiety or gut-wrenching honesty than did Davis. He was not merely a talented, seminal entertainer but also an important man. He represented something far more in our society than success, or, put another way, his success had more weight because of who he was, when he accomplished it, and how he did so.

Here is one small example of Davis's significance:

as part of his act, Davis did fast-draw and twirling tricks with prop guns. He parlayed this into some roles on television westerns, most notably when in February 1962 he was featured as a feared gunslinger on an episode of *The Rifleman* called "Two Ounces of Tin." He was not the first black to appear on a television western—that honor would go to Joel Fluellen— but he was the first black to appear as a gunslinger on a television western. It was such a noteworthy event that George Lincoln Rockwell, head of the American Nazi Party, commented on it as a sign of the degeneration of American culture in his 1967 book *White Power*. Whatever the quality of Davis's acting, his appearance on this show was historically important as well as entertaining—if one found television westerns entertaining, which they actually were in their heyday. And in the 1960s westerns did more to liberalize white racial attitudes than they are commonly given credit for.

In today's world, a performer who tried to do as many things as Davis—sing, dance, act, do comic bits, play a few musical instruments—would probably not be successful, simply because the era of the multipurpose entertainer and the variety show, vaudeville-type performer is gone. There are performers today who are capable of doing such a number of things as Davis did in his prime—Madonna, for instance—but there are no performers today who want to be known for doing all of them or who want to be known as someone whose act is built around the idea that he or she could or would do them. Perhaps it is because Davis left no legacy (in the sense that no one has followed in his footsteps in trying to be precisely the same type of entertainer and crossover presence he was) that he is rather on the verge of being both forgotten and dismissed.

Because of the kind of entertainer he was, Davis is not likely to attract a great deal of interest from academics, either, who tend to gravitate toward the people in popular culture whom they can claim as geniuses. Not even the most ardent of Davis's admirers would make that claim on his behalf. Davis made very little art that was of lasting importance or permanent availability: he was primarily a dancer and stage performer, and dance and stage acts are difficult to archive as artifacts or unearth archeologically. Davis appeared as a guest on a number of television shows over the years, probably more times than any black person in the history of television, but none of these shows acquired lasting stature, and his most important movies—*Anna Lucasta*, *Porgy and Bess*, and *A Man Called Adam*—are rarely televised. (Two of them are not even available on video.) Davis lived a mythic life, but there is little material around now upon which to base the mythology.

In 1962 the great soul and pop singer Sam Cooke explained the difference between himself and Sammy Davis Jr.: "When the whites are through with Sammy Davis Jr., he won't have anywhere to play. I'll always be able to go back to my people 'cause I'm never gonna stop singing to them. No matter how big I get . . . I'm not gonna leave my base."[1] The whites were never "through" with Davis during his life—until his very last concerts he remained a major draw anywhere he played, especially in Las Vegas. Yet Davis always had a considerable black following as well: some forget that two of his biggest selling singles, "I've Got to be Me" (1969) and "The Candy Man" (1974), were routinely played on black radio stations and that *Ebony, Jet,* and most black newspapers wrote extensively about him throughout his life. In thinking about the *Entertainment Weekly* list, one wonders if, after his death, the whites have finally abandoned Sammy Davis Jr. and whether there is now no one around to acknowledge his accomplishments. Is Davis now a man without a fan base? Perhaps he always was such a man. Perhaps his story is a complex parable about crossover success, racial self-hatred, and the early days of racial integration.

The absence of Davis from the *Entertainment Weekly* list says a great deal about the extent to which the current generation has lost touch with the legacy of the black entertainer and with what that legacy says about American social and political history and black entertainers themselves, who worked under terribly constrained conditions as a force for good art and for social change. Before Davis died in May 1990, he was among the last men standing who had endured the awful, degrading days of the 1930s and 1940s black vaudeville, where entertainers worked for less pay under strictly segregated conditions, and with an act that often had to accommodate racial stereotypes to please white audiences. Show business is a precarious profession for anyone, but it was especially so for black performers, who were the first to be fired when times got hard and whose choice of material was tightly restricted by the racial mores of the day.

Davis's last film, *Tap* (1989), although clearly a vehicle for its star, the dancer Gregory Hines, was also a touching tribute to the black hoofers of the 1930s and 1940s, and a special elegy to Davis, who had the biggest role of any of them in the film (as Little Mo, the man with the dream who never lost faith in either Hines's character or in the power of tap dance). Though Davis looked frail in the film, aged and vulnerable, there was still something of the sly hipster about him. He looked finally like a man who had lived in his life, who had come to an appreciation of it for better and for worse, and not like a hedonistic tourist or callow sensationalist.

No one really knew it at the time of the film's release, but when *Tap* was being filmed, Davis was dying—this perhaps lent poignancy to his characterization. His health had been deteriorating since 1983, when a damaged liver, the result of years of drinking, sickened him. He had had two hip replacement surgeries—in 1985 and 1987—the result of years of dancing. After filming *Tap*, he was diagnosed with throat cancer, the result of years of smoking cigarettes. It was as if, in a rush, in a moment, all his excesses had come pounding on the door demanding payment for long-overdue bills. Davis was never good at controlling his excesses. And seeing him in *Tap*, where the ravages of his life had so marked him on the brow and in the soul, one felt a great sorrow that Davis had never been better used as an actor in his career. Because the maturity he had gained at such a great price seemed to enrich him as a performer only after he had lost much of his ability to perform, one almost wished that in *Tap*, Davis's career were really just beginning. But in fact it was over; Davis would live less than a year.

It was a supreme disadvantage that Davis grew up as a child performer during the Depression, not only because the racism of the day prevented him from becoming the huge star that he deserved to be—he had as much talent and appeal as Shirley Temple, as his role in *Rufus Jones for President* (1933) can attest—but because becoming a professional performer at such a young age prevented him from getting any sort of formal education. He almost never set foot in a classroom, and Davis felt this inadequacy all his life. As he said in a 1966 *Playboy* interview: "People hearing me today don't think I have no education. I've worked—*hard*, man, to be able to give this impression. Blood, sweat, and tears went into every combination of words that I use now." Davis learned, in his way, to become an articulate man, even a man who read a lot, although as he said, he was not well read.

Davis educated himself in part because of pressure: he wanted to fit in with the show-business people around him, and many of those people were sophisticated and probably better educated than he was. The fact that many of these people were also white intensified the pressure Davis felt. Like most blacks, especially black people during the early days of integration in the 1950s, when he became a major star, and the 1960s, when he enjoyed his peak period of stardom, Davis did not wish to look ignorant around whites. He felt self-conscious, as many blacks do around whites, about the sort of things that would typecast him as a Negro. As a result, he fought hard to get out of the black vaudeville circuit, and while he brought important aspects of that portion of the entertainment world to the mainstream, he also fought hard against aspects of the black entertainment world that had nurtured him.

"I studied the acts and saw that most Negro performers work in a cubicle," he wrote in his best-selling autobiography, *Yes I Can*. "They'd run on, sing twelve songs, dance, and do jokes—but not to the people. The jokes weren't done like Milton Berle was doing them, to the audience, they were done between the men on-stage, as if they didn't have the right to communicate with the people out front. It was totally the reverse of the way Mickey [Rooney] played, directly to the people, talking to them, kidding them, communicating with them." So abhorrent did he find the Jim Crow nature of black stage entertainment, so uneasy was he with the taint and stigma of his min-strel past, that Davis rebelled by thoroughly assimi-lating in his own act. When he began doing comic impressions of famous white entertainers like Jerry Lewis, Frank Sinatra, James Cagney, Cary Grant, and others in the late 1940s, Davis was doing something no black performer had ever done before: he became the first black performer to make his admiration for, his emulation and imitation of, his friendship and cronyism with, white performers an essential com-ponent of his stage persona.

For this, he was to attract a larger crossover audi-ence than any black performer in history. For this, he was to become not only a bitterly misunderstood man but an intensely hated figure by many, both black and white, for in becoming both Yiddish and a WASP Davis committed, according to some, an even worse act of betrayal and degradation than the be-trayal and degradation that his crossover was meant to combat. He was, in large measure, a paradoxical person who made his contradictions very public: this was the source of much of the distress he was to experience in his life with the black public whom he wanted both to live down and to live up to. It is not quite right to say that Davis lived a life of self-indulgence and hard work. This, of course, he did, and with a vengeance, but the self-indulgence seemed an expression of something else. What Davis actually seemed to be doing was living a life, through self-indulgence and hard work, whose goal was compensation. He always seemed to be making up for something.

If most people with any literary background were asked to name the best-selling black autobiography of the 1960s, they would probably be inclined to say *The Autobiography of Malcolm X* or Claude Brown's *Manchild in the Promised Land.* No one is likely to mention Sammy Davis's *Yes I Can,* published in 1965, which sold as well as either of the other books, and, in some circles, better than both combined. *Yes I Can* sold so many copies that it kept Farrar, Straus, Giroux in business when many thought the company would go under. Of all the black autobiographies of the 1960s, Davis's book may yet reemerge if more academics and intellectuals read it and actually begin to appreciate its importance.

That is to say, I think a very plausible case can be made that in the 1960s Sammy Davis Jr. was a more influential and important person than either Malcolm X or Muhammad Ali, the two blacks, outside of Martin Luther King Jr., usually seen as the most seminal black personalities of the time.

By the mid-1960s, Davis was the biggest black star in American show business, his face and name more recognizable than those of any other black performer. He was then starring in a Broadway musical called *Golden Boy* (his second time on Broadway as a star—he was the lead in *Mr. Wonderful* from 1956 to 1957); he was a host of his own television show; he was a popular recording artist with hits like "The Birth of the Blues," "What Kind of Fool Am I?" and "Who Can I Turn To (When Nobody Needs Me)?"; he had major roles in such movies as *Porgy and Bess*, *Ocean's Eleven*, *Sergeants Three*, and he was the dramatic lead in *A Man Called Adam*. He had done so many benefits that he had to be hospitalized for exhaustion, and he had raised more money for civil rights than virtually anyone else. Indeed, Davis got his fellow Rat-Packers to give a benefit for the Southern Christian Leadership Conference (SCLC) at Carnegie Hall in January 1961 that raised 12 percent of SCLC's budget for the year. He was one of the organizers of the "Broadway Answers Selma" show at the Majestic Theater in New York in 1965. What black man's image had more permeated popular culture than Davis's up to this point? What black man in entertainment was able to get more white establishment dollars transferred to civil rights coffers? He was probably the best fundraiser of the civil rights movement outside of King himself. Davis's ability to raise money through his benefits, coupled with his own charitable contributions—which in the mid-1960s amounted to more than a hundred thousand dollars a year—made him a curious one-man band of wealth redistribution in the United States. He did this without possessing a single leftist bone in his body. He was driven mostly by guilt, a sincere need to be helpful, and a deep patriotic and fairly simplistic belief in his country. For Davis, all politics were personal and psychological. His politics were all about his particular brand of self-consciousness, and they were all about his being something of a romantic.

This world of black vaudeville (the professional black *entertainer*) and the world of the black jazz musician (the professional black *artist*) certainly converged during the years before World War II, but they were not ever really the same world. Certain figures like Louis Armstrong bridged them, even, in his genius, contained them, but the two worlds diverged, especially after 1945. For a defined period, Davis was an important link between these two worlds. And his service in this capacity, particularly at the time he did so, was enormously important for both jazz and black American variety entertainment. In this regard, Davis's 1966 film *A Man Called Adam* (the other major film of his career besides *Tap* and the only drama in which Davis ever had the lead role) is significant. The story of a tragic, fallen black jazz genius bedeviled by personal demons and trapped in an emasculating web of white corporate racism, *A Man Called Adam* brought together the worlds of jazz and variety entertainment. It would be wrong to dismiss this film as just a black version of *Young Man with a Horn*, the famous 1950 film starring Kirk Douglas as a tragic trumpeter and based on Dorothy Baker's 1938 novel of the same name (which was in turn inspired by Otis Ferguson's essays on the cornetist Bix Beiderbecke). To be sure, the two films share many features: the cultural prototype of the jazz musician as romantic hero has made this unavoidable, even inevitable. But one must be reminded that *A Man Called Adam* was a serious attempt, if, for many who have seen the film, a deeply flawed one, to examine the life of a black person trying to devote himself to art and artistic creation. It was by no means the first dramatic Hollywood film in the post–World War II era to look at the life of the black jazz musician—Sidney Poitier played a jazzman in *Paris Blues*, released in 1961; Harry Belafonte played a jazz vibraphonist in *Odds Against Tomorrow*, released in 1959; and Nat Cole portrayed W. C. Handy in the 1958 film *St. Louis Blues*. But *A Man Called Adam* explores the theme of the jazz musician as disturbing, even disruptive creative presence, with greater melodramatic intensity than any of the previous films.

When he made *A Man Called Adam* in 1966, Davis was almost certainly the highest-paid black entertainer in America. When Davis appeared on Broadway in *Golden Boy* in 1964, his salary of $10,000 a week was the highest in American theatrical history. *Life* magazine, in reviewing the show, said: "He's worth it." This figure was actually a significant pay cut for Davis, who was earning somewhere between five to ten times that amount per week working Las Vegas and the supper club circuit. Davis's financial contributions and overall commitment to civil rights were such that he was awarded the prestigious NAACP Spingarn Medal in 1968. Perhaps it was some small satisfaction to Davis to win it after the black columnist Evelyn Cunningham, who was sometimes critical of Davis, had suggested in the September 28, 1957, issue of the *Pittsburgh Courier* that Louis Armstrong be awarded the Spingarn Medal for his sharp criticism of President Eisenhower and his handling of the integration of Central High School in Little Rock. Davis achieved a certain notoriety during these events because he criticized Armstrong's remarks. Whatever rift this may have caused between the two performers apparently was breached or healed sufficiently when they played together in *A Man Called Adam*. In any case, Armstrong never won a Spingarn Medal. The only jazz musician who has is Duke Ellington in 1959. In fact, more operatic singers have won the Spingarn—Roland Hayes in 1924, Marian Anderson in 1939, and Leontyne Price in 1965—than have jazz musicians. Davis was no opera singer, but why shouldn't he have won the award if the measure was financial support of the civil rights? In a 1980 interview in *Ebony*, Davis estimated the amount of the money he gave to black causes—"legitimate bread and also rip-off bread"—at "seven figures or more." This is more money than any major mainstream jazz figure ever contributed to the civil rights movement and more than probably all of them did in aggregate.

Between October 1955, when he appeared on the cover of *Downbeat*, the major American jazz magazine, and 1966, when *A Man Called Adam* was released, Davis made a number of jazz-oriented records with Carmen McRae, Quincy Jones, Count Basie, Laurindo Almeida, Marty Paich, and Buddy Rich. For a man who was not a jazz singer and who was considered apolitical at best and an Uncle Tom at worst, Davis linked jazz and civil rights, two decidedly non-commercial, non-middle-American pursuits, in an extraordinary way.

At the time of its publication, *Yes I Can* was clearly the most complex, the longest, and the most candid autobiography of any black person in show business, probably one of the most intricate, confessional autobiographies of any show business person, period. It remains so today. The story Davis tells tracks his life from his birth in 1925 in Harlem to his 1960 marriage to the Swedish actress May Britt, combining the rags-to-riches success story that Americans love with a kind of subversive epithalamium at the end in tribute to the white woman he married against the wishes of many. Davis's marriage to Britt was the most famous interracial marriage in American social history, outweighing even the black heavyweight champion Jack Johnson's December 1912 marriage to Lucille Cameron, whom federal authorities had wanted to testify against the fighter in a Mann Act indictment they were preparing. (Naturally, the marriage threw a bit of a monkey wrench into that plan. The government found another witness with which to build its case against Johnson.)

Davis tells of beginning his career as a child of

four, traveling with his father, Sammy Davis Sr., and Will Mastin, a man he referred to as his uncle although they were not related. Both Mastin and Davis Sr. were dancers who took the little Davis with them all over the black vaudeville circuit. With the aid of his father's mother, Davis was able to skip school. Interestingly, two years after Sammy was born, Davis Sr. had another child, a girl, with Sammy's mother, Elvera Sanchez, a dancer. The marriage soon broke up, and the daughter lived with the mother's parents. There were years of grinding poverty during the 1930s. Then, from 1943 to 1945, the army intervened. Davis suffered greatly while in the army. He was a very small man, only 5'3" and around 120 pounds. This, plus the fact that he was in an integrated unit station in Wyoming, made him the prey of racist bullies. His nose was broken twice in fights with racist soldiers. He was captured by a group of them once and had a racist slur painted on his chest, supposedly for making eyes at a white WAC captain who wanted him to perform in some shows. Years later, he said in a *People Magazine* interview that he had had some sort of homosexual encounter in the army. It was unclear whether he was saying he had been raped, although he did say his size played a major factor in the encounter. That he might have been preyed upon sexually because of his size was never mentioned in *Yes I Can*, but it would not be surprising for a man of that size to be sexually victimized in an all-male, warrior-oriented institution like the army.

But the army years were not all bad. Even the brutality of the racist soldiers was useful in giving Davis an idea of the intensity of the racism in the society in which he lived, something that his father and Will Mastin had generally sheltered him from. Also, it was in the army that a sympathetic sergeant taught Davis to read. Davis admitted that before joining the army he read nothing but comic books. (Apparently, he continued the habit of comic book reading even after his stretch in the service. Eartha Kitt chided him for it when they first met in the early 1950s in San Francisco, at a time when she was a bigger star than he was.) But in the army he read Wilde's *The Picture of Dorian Gray*, the complete works of Shakespeare, *Cyrano de Bergerac*, "Carl Sandburg's books about Lincoln, books by Dickens, Poe, Mark Twain, and a history of the United States." So, the army was a form of education for Davis in several ways, as prison was for Malcolm X in his own self-mythology. Davis certainly became aware in the army of the difficulty of the pursuit of integration and what it might cost him or any black person to be a pioneer on that frontier. The experience did not seem to shake him. After the army, he seemed all the more determined that he was going to be a crossover act. "My talent was the weapon, the power, the way for me to fight," he writes in *Yes I Can* about the shows he did during his army years. "It was the one way I might hope to affect a man's thinking." He adds a few paragraphs later:

I'd learned a lot in the army and I knew that above all things in the world I had to become so big, so strong, so important, that those people and their hatred could never touch me. My talent was the only thing that made me a little different from everybody else, and it was all that I could hope would shield me because I was different.

I'd weighed it all, over and over again: What have I got? No looks, no money, no education. Just talent. Where do I want to go? I wanted to be treated well. I want people to like me, and be decent to me. How do I get there? There's only one way I can do it with what I have to work with. I've got to be a star! I have to be a star like another man has to breathe.

In the mythology of show business, of course, adversity makes the star, and what could be a bigger adversity in Davis's mind than being black, especially an uneducated black who was ugly?

After the army, Davis describes his life in *Yes I Can* through five major events: reacquainting himself with Frank Sinatra in 1947 and eventually being taken under the wing of the great singer; the automobile accident in 1954 that cost him his left eye; his conversion to Judaism a few years later; the disastrous love affair with the white actress Kim Novak that led to his 1958 marriage to and divorce from (in a matter of months) the black dancer Loray White; and his courtship of and marriage to May Britt in 1960 and the birth of their daughter a year later. Through describing these events Davis unfolds the narrative of his rise as a huge crossover star, the man whose face was to become as familiar as that of any white performer in the relatively new world of television, the black man whose name was to become synonymous with Las Vegas, the great playground of the post–World War II American West. But also part of this story is the account of a man who spent money like a maniac (Davis's whole adult life was an effort to get out of debt despite earning fantastic sums of money), a man who gambled foolishly, who drank heavily, and who was frustrated by the limitations race placed upon him, especially on his ability to exploit television to develop his skills as an actor. By the end of his career, Davis felt that he had lost the ability to communicate with his audience despite the fact that his performing schedule resembled a marathon. It is a story of cringing desperation and miraculous triumph.

Albert Goldman, who wrote highly controversial biographies of John Lennon and Elvis Presley, reviewed *Yes I Can* for the *New York Review of Books* in January 1966. He despised Davis. Goldman wrote:

> *[Davis's] singing is non-descript, a mixture of the styles of at least a half a dozen other performers, including his hero, Frank Sinatra, and Billy Eckstein [sic], Billy Daniels, Tony Bennett, and Anthony Newley. His dancing combines familiar routines from vaudeville and musicals; his comedy derives from Jerry Lewis . . .*

and even his "impressions," the strongest part of his act, are for the most past borrowed from a handful of relatively obscure Broadway comics. Only his versatility, his energy, his fanatical desire to please, are wholly Davis's own.

In another performer this all-inclusive embrace of the going thing might simply indicate a lack of talent, but in Sammy Davis, Jr., it means something more. One notes, for example, that in all his work there is not a single expression of that racial identity . . . that has traditionally given the Negro entertainer his power. Thus Davis seems to be refusing the label "Negro entertainer"; he is taking his "color" from his professional milieu rather than his ethnic origin. He might even be called the first "colorless" Negro performer; for like Diahann Carroll and Bill Cosby, later embodiments of the same idea, what Sammy Davis, Jr. offers his audience above everything else is the opportunity to "prove" that they can respond to a Negro without consciousness of his race . . .

Always an idolator of the stars, a brash Broadway "hippie," constantly "on," constantly doing the "bits," he identified with white America—or that part of it "the Business" represents. Even his conversion to Judaism can be understood as an act of conformity to his professional world.

I have felt something like this at times when thinking about Davis. And a certain feeling like it came upon me again when I saw *Entertainment Weekly*'s list. Having grown up seeing Sammy Davis Jr. on television in a number of different venues—variety shows, talk shows, dramas, westerns, situation comedies, musicals—having heard his records on the radio, having seen him in the movies, I suppose that what I most depressingly realized about his absence from the *Entertainment Weekly* list is that it is very possible that Davis was ephemeral. Maybe he is not being forgotten so much as he is simply evaporating. Perhaps Davis's work, in sum, was broader than it was deep. Perhaps, despite his ubiquitous presence during his heyday, he made no truly lasting presence. He did everything well enough to assert his will but nothing well enough to make these assertions worth remembering beyond the moment. He was a complex performer in his way but not always a pleasing one, because he was so transparently superficial, so desperately sincere. He may have been egotistical about his talents and his ability to grab an audience, but he never took either for granted. In the end, the engine of desperation that drove him, that, after all, drives all artists who want to survive on their art, took him with it when it broke down, and he was nothing more than the personification of his desperation to succeed.

But lots of people are remembered vividly in America for being important simply because of their own desperate need to be important. Perhaps this is what attracted Richard Nixon and Sammy Davis Jr. to each other. Davis was not a conservative, in any respect, by temperament, and for ideological reasons, he never endorsed Nixon, though he did support Nixon in 1972 because Nixon took him seriously, listened to him, liked him, had him spend the night at the White House. Jack Kennedy wouldn't let Davis come to his inauguration in 1961, despite the fact that Davis had campaigned tirelessly for him, because Davis had just married May Britt the previous November and inviting an interracial couple to the White House might have made some of Kennedy's other guests and supporters uncomfortable. Davis never forgot that humiliation. For him, all politics were personal—as, I suppose, they truly are for everyone. Everyone really only cares about his own slights, his own ass, his own dreams.

Goldman didn't hate Davis for the same reasons African American nationalists and militants hated him in the 1960s: for being a sellout and an Uncle Tom because he married a white woman (the fact that several noted black militants and nationalists were also married to whites only indicates that hypocrisy is at the core of political consciousness) and because he hung around with whites like Sinatra, Dean Martin, Shirley MacLaine, and other Rat Packers. Goodman's hatred is also different from the way blacks hated Davis in the 1970s: because he endorsed Richard Nixon for re-election in 1972. (I think the famous photo of him embracing Nixon at the Republican National Convention hurt Davis more with blacks than did the actual endorsement.) No black, no matter how much he or she may have hated Davis, would ever have said that he was a mediocre, fraudulent *performer*, although they may have said he was a fraudulent, second-rate *personality*.

Goldman hated Davis for two reasons: first, Davis was not a real black person, and second, and just as important, Davis was, in essence, a fake Jew. There was something about Davis's aspiration to be a show business Jew (rather than a Jew in show business) that Goldman found disgusting, unseemly, unbecoming of a black person. But there is something more: Goldman was unnerved by Davis's use of an ersatz Jewishness to assimilate, probably because it brought into an uncomfortable light white Jews' own identity and their own need to assimilate, and, of course, the undeniable fact that on some level in America the white Jew could assimilate in a way that left the African American no alternative but the charismatic expression of his racial identity that Goldman so admired. In essence, Goldman admired the fact that blacks were trapped in a way white Jews were not and thought that through this entrapment blacks remained authentic. In this way, blacks became a source of both envy and relief for the white liberal imagination, and particularly for the Jew. But what does *authentic* mean, especially in the realm of art and popular culture representation where all is meant to be artifice?

Davis himself was familiar with this sense of being trapped. As he said in his 1966 *Playboy* interview: "I remember so well the first book I ever read about my own people, and the effect it had on me. It did something to me. That was *Native Son*, by Richard Wright. Then, later, I read *Black Boy*. They made me feel something about being black that I had never felt before. It made me uncomfortable, made me feel trapped in black, you know, in a white society that had created you the way it wanted, and still hated you."

In criticizing Davis's lack of originality, Goldman does no more than acknowledge Davis's own insecurities about his own talent, which he freely confessed in a number of interviews and in his two autobiographies (the last, *Why Me?* was published in 1989, a year before his death). Davis was not interested in being an original—he was far more interested in being an individual. He explained what individuality meant to him in a conversation with May Britt he recounts in *Yes I Can*: "Look, I make a lot of money and I'm big in the business because of three things: I've got talent, I've worked hard, and every bit as important, I have let myself remain an individual . . . We are all born as individuals and in a million and one little ways I've managed to remain Sammy Davis, Jr. . . . Whether the people know it or not, my individuality is part of what they're buying when they come to see me. What I'm saying is, I know I'm not perfect but whatever I am in sum total, my faults and my virtues have combined to make one-of-a-kind, and it works for me."

To understand Davis's quest for individuality, it is necessary to place him in several contexts. One that might be useful is Davis's connection with other black singers. Davis was actually one of several black male singers who came along between 1940 and 1960 as romantic balladeers. These include Billy Eckstine, Johnny Hartman, Herb Jeffries (most famous as the movie character the Bronze Buckaroo), Nat King Cole, Billy Daniels, and, finally, Johnny Mathis, who was also for a time a teen idol, rather like Ricky Nelson or Frankie Avalon, although he always sang middle-of-the-road pop material. In some measure, Harry Belafonte might be included here as well, but he relied greatly on his appeal as a folk singer or a singer of quasi-folk material. I would not argue that Davis was the best of this lot of singers. He was also not the most original, not by any means; and as Goldman pointed out, he imitated some of his contemporaries when he was doing impressions. But when he was singing in his own voice, Davis would not have been mistaken for any of them.

And Davis, as I pointed out earlier, had signature tunes: some, like "Gonna Climb Me a Mountain," "I've Got Be Me," or "EE-OO Eleven," the theme song of *Ocean's Eleven*, were so stamped with Davis's personality that one could hardly imagine another person doing them. Despite whatever limitations he had as a singer, Davis's was certainly an individual voice. He was not a jazz singer, though sometimes he was a jazzy singer, in the bad sense of the word *jazzy*: over-brassy, overly hip, overly cocky. But he had many of the best qualities of a good pop singer: good intonation, the ability to stay on pitch, good enunciation, a strong sense of swing, and an ability to read the lyrics of a song with conviction. More important, Davis was part of a movement in which black male singers became known for singing love songs, something that had been denied them before because the entertainment industry did not want black men to become sex symbols. Davis helped break down that taboo, and because of his highly publicized sex life, particularly his romances with white women, which were even more publicized than the white loves of Billy Daniels, he lent a frightening and vivid reality both to the songs and to himself as a sex symbol despite the fact that he had neither the looks nor the physical stature of a typical male hunk. Davis first made the tabloid press for his interracial liaisons in March 1955 when *Confidential* did a story on him and Ava Gardner, suggesting they were an item. Emmet Till was murdered in Mississippi for whistling at a white woman in August of the same year. Davis was, in many respects, daring the very public he wanted so desperately to court: in this way, he was an anti-establishment rebel with establishment material and an establishment audience.

From World War II on, American popular culture reflects the ever intensifying need of the black male for self-assertion, particularly since this desire had been artificially and cruelly repressed before.

Jackie Robinson represented this new urge in one realm; trumpeter Miles Davis represented it in another realm.[2] Like the others in this coterie of black male entertainers, Sammy Davis was both Mr. Inside and Mr. Outside, but he was even more different and even more daring.

"Certainly those who live on the margin of society," wrote Daniel Bell in his essay "America as a Mass Society: A Critique,"

the Upper Bohemians, whose manners soon become the style for the culture—seek frantically to find different ways of emphasizing their non-conformity. In Hollywood, where Pickfair society in the twenties counterfeited a European monarchy (and whose homes crossed Louis XIV with Barnum & Bailey), "non-conformity," according to Life *magazine (in its jumbo Entertainment issue of December 1958—readership twenty-five million), "is now the key to social importance and that Angry Middle-Aged man, Frank Sinatra, is its prophet and reigning monarch." The Sinatra set,* Life *points out, deliberately mocks the old Hollywood taboos and is imitated by a host of other sets that eagerly want to be non-conformist as well. Significantly—a fact that* Life *failed to mention—the reigning social set and its leaders, Sinatra, Dean Martin, Sammy Davis, Jr., are all from minority groups and from the wrong side of the tracks. Sinatra and Martin are Italians, Davis a Negro. In earlier times in American life, a minority group, having bullied its way to the top, would usually ape*

the style and manners of the established status com-
munity. In Hollywood, the old status hierarchies have
been fragmented, the new sets celebrate their triumph
by jeering at the pompous ways of the old. "[3]

Davis, unlike Muhammad Ali or Malcolm X, the leading black iconoclast figures of the 1960s, both of
whom exemplified a nonconformity that was profoundly to change the way black Americans saw
themselves, found a way to become a nonconformist
within a completely white context. Davis's nonconformity was itself an expression of rebellion, but it
operated completely within the confines of established white American middle-of-the-road popular
taste. The Rat Pack rebelled not by challenging or de-
fying popular taste but by mocking it with their own
excesses and lived-out *Playboy* fantasies. The Rat Pack
gave Davis a frame of reference, an image, a way to
break through completely to a white audience after
he left the Will Mastin Trio in the late 1950s. But it
did not consume his entire life. He spent a great deal
less time with Sinatra than many people think, and
for several years in the late 1970s and early 1980s, the
two men did not speak at all because Sinatra was upset that Davis was sniffing cocaine. But in the 1960s,
the Rat Pack defined Davis, and in an unprecedented
fashion: no black public figure had ever been so totally characterized by a voluntary professional and
social association with whites.

Davis was the youngest member of the Rat Pack. He was ten years younger than Sinatra, eight years younger than Martin, seven years younger than the comic Joey Bishop, and two years younger than Peter Lawford. Goldman rather snidely referred to Davis being "an idolator of the stars," but he failed to mention that Davis first met Sinatra in 1941 in Detroit when he was only fifteen years old. Sinatra was twenty-five and a big star with Tommy Dorsey. Why shouldn't Davis, a struggling black kid in an act that was on the verge of not making it, have idolized him? Sinatra arranged for the Will Mastin Trio to open for him in 1947; he continued to provide major assistance to Davis for a number of years, getting him good film deals and a lucrative record contract with Reprise Records, Sinatra's company. It must also be remembered that, in 1960, when Davis became indelibly identified with the Rat Pack because of his role in *Ocean's Eleven*, he did not have nearly the record of accomplishment that his fellow actors did, despite his long years in show business. Sinatra and Martin were long established film stars, recording stars, and nightclub acts. Even Lawford and Shirley MacLaine had accomplished a great deal more in film (Lawford also in television) than Davis had come close to doing. It is little wonder that he would have looked up to these people. They were accomplishing what he hoped one day to do himself. But he felt that he couldn't do it if the only thing people, especially white people, were going to see when they looked at him was his race. He felt as if he were distinguishing himself through his association with white performers and by separating himself from other blacks. In this way, Davis thought that he would no longer be judged as one of a group of black entertainers or as someone representing blacks; he would be judged purely and solely as an individual since his audiences could no longer situate him in a black context.

Davis was also physically smaller than any of the Rat Packers. This may have had as much to do with how he was sometimes treated in their stage routines as his race. Davis made three movies with the Rat Pack: *Ocean's Eleven*, *Sergeants Three*, and *Robin and the Seven Hoods*. He made three more movies with Peter Lawford: *A Man Called Adam*, *Salt and Pepper*, and *One More Time*. This was all by 1970. Davis was to appear in only three more movies from 1970 until his death twenty years later. When the Rat Pack unraveled, so did Davis's hope of a movie-acting career. He did, however, continue to appear on television with great frequency, and he remained a huge name in Las Vegas for his entire life, though he never quite had the presence, was never quite the cultural force he had once been. What Sammy Davis Jr. was, as a national phenomenon, was intricately connected with the 1950s and 1960s, between Korea and Vietnam, the Cold War at its most intense and at its craziest, the height of the sexual revolution that not only gave us the image of the playboy and the Cosmopolitan woman liberated by the birth control pill, but also of interracial and homosexual sex released in American society, not as forms of protest, but virtually as forms of expressive, nonconformist energy. Sammy Davis Jr. was somehow at the heart of this; somehow in this era, he mirrored America's own emancipation, its own confusion, its own self-destructiveness. But if Davis was the personification of the crisis of liberalism in the United States during the Cold War, of the Jew who desired color-blind merit and the black who was rather taken with the romance and the adventure and the anger of protest, he was also nothing if not the personification of old-fashioned will. He was, further, the pure embodiment of self-consciousness in an age that moved rapidly from the idea of identity to the idea of the self, from being inner directed and Puritan to being an outer-directed personality in need of periodic adjustments. If, as Dostoyevsky wrote in *Notes From the Underground*, "any sort of consciousness is a disease," then Davis was a particularly afflicted man. Davis might be remembered, in some complex and important ways, aside from his achievements as an entertainer, which I think are considerable; despite one's own doubting tendency to think that perhaps they are a bit overblown, they actually stand up very well to the legacies of other performers. He made racial self-hatred a major national mythology and drama, and he made the need to redeem himself because of that self-hatred equally a national mythology and drama. So, blackness became his curse and his salvation. It was during the

1950s and particularly the 1960s that many blacks may have felt uneasy, even angry, about such ambiguity: after all, he was acting out as an individual aspects of their own collective psyche. But Davis gave us an incredibly rich and strange embodiment of something Ralph Ellison had one of his characters say in the prologue of his novel *Invisible Man*: "Black is . . . and Black ain't."

Cecil B. Moore and the
Rise of Black Philadelphia, 1964–1968

Police and the Board

On August 8, 1964, the noted African American lawyer, court of common pleas judge, and former city councilman Raymond Pace Alexander was quoted in the *Philadelphia Tribune* as saying that he did not think that Philadelphia "was on the borderline of explosion." Alexander was disagreeing with Andrew G. Freeman, the head of the Philadelphia branch of the Urban League, who had called the city "a racial tinderbox." Complaints about police brutality ran high in the black community of Philadelphia, but Alexander pointed out that the Police Advisory Board, a civilian watchdog group formed in 1958 to review complaints of brutality, seemed to have done much to ease the tension around that issue. At the time, Philadelphia was one of the few cities to have such a review board.

The board was made up of eight distinguished local citizens and was started by Mayor Richardson Dilworth. Liberals thought such review boards were helpful in creating better relations between the police and the communities in which they worked, particularly, it was thought, in racial minority communities where the residents viewed the police, who were often white, as an occupation force. It is difficult to gauge how helpful the review boards really were. The vast majority of all complaints of police brutality brought before the board were dismissed upon review, usually for lack of corroboration, or simply because the incidents were minor to begin with.

By June 1964 the board had received 510 complaints over the period of the six years of its existence. The complainants had withdrawn more than half of the complaints before a hearing was held. One hundred and fifty-six complaints were resolved in favor of the police. Forty-one cases involved a minor police infraction or impropriety. Only eighteen cases of the 510 were judged serious enough for recommendations of suspensions or reprimands. The police might have looked at this as a general vindication of their performance. They didn't. Some African Americans may not have felt justly served by the existence of the board, probably thinking it sided with the police more times than not, but the black community, on the whole, of course, supported the existence of the board simply as a place where their complaints could at least be heard and where some cops were found guilty of having acted improperly, which is more than would have happened had there been no police board. Conservatives and the police themselves, by and large, hated police review boards, seeing them as unwarranted, unprofessional intrusions into matters that should be judged solely by the police and the prosecutor's office. Problems with police conduct, conservatives and police felt, were personnel matters to be dealt with internally by the police department. If there was evidence of criminal misconduct, the matter would be forwarded to the prosecutor's office, which could request a grand jury investigation. According to this view, the main achievement of the Police Advisory Board was to enable people who didn't know anything about police procedures to police the police. (No other government employees are subject to such scrutiny.) To liberals, a Police Advisory Board was necessary because citizens of any community had a right to police the police, to oversee the people whom they paid with their taxes and who had such sensitive and important jobs.

When Democratic mayor James Tate appointed Howard R. Leary—an Irishman with bookish inclinations—as police commissioner in 1963, Philadelphia had one of the most liberal-thinking top cops in the country. Leary had always supported the idea of a police review board made up of civilians. He was the son of a bricklayer and had grown up in North Central Philadelphia when that area of the city was largely Irish Catholic. He put himself through Temple University Law School at night. The most visible person on the police force who most vehemently disagreed with Leary was Frank Rizzo.

In 1963 Frank Rizzo had just become one of four deputy police commissioners. Rizzo was placed in charge of six thousand uniformed police officers. He was famous not only in Philadelphia but across the country for being a tough-talking, no-nonsense cop who didn't mind busting a few heads to clear up a crime-infested area. Rizzo was a firm believer in the "broken window" theory of crime prevention: in other words, he thought, as do many political scientists and criminologists, that to rid an area of crime, the police must roust and harass minor criminals— petty thieves, prostitutes, small-time drug pushers, gamblers, and the like—while rigidly enforcing minor statutes. By ridding an area of minor criminals, the theory goes, the police prevent major crime from taking place. Rizzo had success with this tactic in the north, south, and west Philadelphia police districts where he worked during the early years of his career. However, when he was policing the Rittenhouse Square area, his results were mixed, largely because he was using the tactics in a politically liberal district that didn't like cops who didn't take civil liberties seriously. To those who liked Rizzo's methods, he was a tough, strict cop. To those who didn't, he was a blowhard, a bully, and a bigot. Rizzo's politics were conservative: he blamed the liberals, the leftists, softhearted judges, and the ACLU for the wildly spiraling increase in violent crime plaguing America in the 1950s and 1960s.

Rizzo's father had been a policeman, and young Frank grew up mostly on his beat in South Philadelphia. Rizzo attended, but did not graduate from, South Philadelphia High School. Although Rizzo would never live in South Philadelphia again after his father moved the family to Germantown in 1940, he used the Italians—his own ethnic group—as a populist base from which to achieve political power. Rizzo spent a year in the navy before being discharged for medical reasons in 1938. He became a police officer on October 6, 1943, at the age of twenty-two. He had three things his father, Ralph, had lacked: a huge ego, a flair for dramatic bravado, and incredible ambition. When Rizzo became Police Commissioner in May 1967, one of his first acts was to get rid of the Police Advisory Board. Both Leary and especially Rizzo are important actors in the tale I am about to tell.

What Was in the Air

Raymond Pace Alexander continued in the August 8, 1964, *Tribune* article to say that not only was the Police Advisory Board important in easing racial tensions, but so also were the Human Relations Commission (of which his wife, Sadie, was a member), Heritage House, and the North City Congress. The *Philadelphia Inquirer*, in an editorial that appeared later that month, agreed with Alexander, saying: "Philadelphia has enjoyed a good reputation in this 'long hot summer' we were promised. The great majority of both Negroes and whites have made extraordinary efforts to keep relations fair and decent. Delegations from other troubled cities have come here to learn how it's done and often have benefited." But Alexander was fearful of the possibility of the outbreak of violence. In the *Tribune* article he made a special plea for a halt to all racial demonstrations. He wrote an open letter to Martin Luther King stating this. At this time, King was struggling with his campaign to integrate St. Augustine, Florida, which had become a bloody struggle and near carnival of violence. King and his followers, as one commentator put it, "found St. Augustine unique among the sites of racial conflict in the South: in contrast even with Birmingham, where Bull Connor had at least succeeded in persuading the Klan to hold at bay for a while to let him operate, St. Augustine had by the summer reeled into a dizzy limbo of all law, with its police acting not so much to avert as to supervise and abet its popular sprees of violence."[1]

There was a certain sense of the apocalypse in the air in the summer of 1964: on August 6, members of the Mississippi Freedom Democratic Party met in Jackson, Mississippi. They would not succeed in replacing the all-white Mississippi delegation to the Democratic convention to be held at the end of August in Atlantic City (where Lyndon Johnson would be easily nominated as his party's candidate for the presidency). The archconservative and anti–civil rights Arizona senator Barry Goldwater had been chosen as the GOP's standard-bearer in San Francisco just one month earlier. To the liberals, to the civil rights marchers and leaders, and to African Americans, generally, he seemed the most horrible manifestation of white reaction short of Alabama governor George Wallace. "Extremism in defense of liberty is no vice" is probably Goldwater's most famous statement, certainly the most quoted. By the middle 1960s, when the Student Nonviolent Coordinating Committee (SNCC) would abandon both nonviolence as a tactic and integration as a goal, and when riots were afflicting big cities around the country during the summer, it could be said that blacks, particularly young blacks, had adopted Goldwater's adage with a slight change: Extremism in cause of liberation is no vice. But old guard black civil rights leaders in the south like Charles Evers, brother of the assassinated Medgar Evers and now working for the NAACP himself, would not recognize the Mississippi Freedom Democratic Party's convention even though his office was in the same building where the convention was taking place. There was a growing generational strife in the black leadership of the civil rights movement and growing concern over how militant blacks should be in pressing their claims for full citizenship. SNCC's Freedom Summer, which had started out so hopefully, descended in despair over the supercharged intransigent racism of the white south, one powerful example of which was revealed when the bodies of three civil rights workers were finally unearthed on the sweltering afternoon of August 4 in Philadelphia, Mississippi, after a search that had consumed virtually the entire summer. Young blacks in SNCC were also troubled by the fact that the white press focused on SNCC's white members that summer despite the fact that whites made up only 20 percent of SNCC's staff and had nothing to do with the founding of the organization.[2]

Perhaps Alexander, who was himself an old guard black leader, was dismayed by both the insistence of black insurgency during this civil disobedience phase of the civil rights movement and the terrible violence with which whites often responded to the demonstrations. The United States in 1964 seemed at times to have the apocalyptic air of an impending race war. But the idea of not having any more demonstrations was certainly not anything that Cecil Moore, the pugnacious head of Philadelphia's NAACP, wanted to hear. When Cecil Moore was installed as president of the Philadelphia branch of the NAACP on January 3, 1963, after winning a lopsided vote in October 1962, he said: "We are serving notice that no longer will the plantation system of white men appointing our leaders exist in Philadelphia. We will expect to be consulted on all community issues which affect our people."[3] Moore was saying, in effect, that a new black leadership had emerged, one selected by black people themselves to press their interests, not one chosen by the white power structure or white government or corporate interests desiring to contain blacks. Moore certainly didn't listen to Alexander, and the men butted heads several times during the middle 1960s. Alexander was wrong about whether Philadelphia was going to explode with racial violence. Bad things were to happen in Philadelphia later in the month of August 1964.

The Philadelphia Phillies baseball team, for the first time in years, was in a pennant race in 1964, thanks to the pitching of Jim Bunning, who had thrown a perfect game against the Mets on Father's Day, and lefthander Chris Short; and thanks in no small part to the arrival of their muscular, moody, slugging third baseman Dick Allen, who would go on to be the National League's Rookie of the Year. He was the first real superstar black athlete to play for the Phillies. Allen had a very tough time trying to get the local sportswriters to stop calling him Richie. He thought Richie made him sound like he was ten years old.

The Riot and the Careers It Made

On Friday, August 28, 1964, police officers Robert Wells, black, and John Hoff, white, drove to Twenty-second and Columbia to answer a complaint about a car blocking the intersection. When they arrived they found Mrs. Odessa Bradford, thirty-four, quarreling with her husband, Rush, also thirty-four.[4] They had been married for fifteen years. Both had been drinking. He was on the passenger side of the car, and she was on the driver side. The couple was on their way to visit Mrs. Bradford's mother, who lived at 1721 North Twenty-sixth Street. Mrs. Bradford would not or could not move her car when the policemen asked her to do so. The officers then tried to remove Mrs. Bradford bodily from the car. At this point, a bystander named James Mettles, forty-one, attacked the police. "You wouldn't manhandle a white woman like you did this lady," one of the bystanders yelled at the officers.[5] When police reinforcements came to the scene, the crowd grew larger, and a barrage of bricks and bottles began to rain down from the rooftops of nearby buildings, smashing the windshield of a police car. But the police succeeded in clearing the scene, and everything seemed well in hand. The incident with the Bradfords happened at 9:35 P.M.

By 11:00 P.M. things were not so well. First, rumors began to spread in the neighborhood that Mrs. Bradford was pregnant and had been shot and killed by the police. None of this was true, but the tension over police brutality, an issue that still had not been addressed to the satisfaction of most African Americans despite the existence of the Police Advisory Board, fueled the story. Oddly, despite her rough handling by the police, Mrs. Bradford had not been injured, but both the officers who initiated the arrest had to be treated at Philadelphia General Hospital for cuts and bruises. A North Philadelphia black political activist named Raymond Hall started the rumor that Mrs. Bradford was pregnant and had been murdered. Crowds of people began milling around on the street, especially in the area where Mrs. Bradford had been arrested. More bricks and bottles began to fly, more broken windows. By 2:30 A.M. rioting and looting had spread all the way down to fifteenth Street. Mobs of black folk were smashing stores on Ridge Avenue all the way to Norris Street and south to Jefferson Street. Street corner orators whipped the crowds into a frenzy, urging people to drive all white policemen, merchants, and citizens from North Philadelphia. Among those accused of inciting black North Philadelphians to riot was Florence Mobley. She denied the charges but there is a photo of her in the September 19, 1964, *Philadelphia Tribune*, taken during the riot, showing her standing on top of a refrigerator clearly exhorting a crowd of people around her to do something. Whether it was to riot is, of course, unclear from the photo, but Florence Mobley, like Raymond Hall, was a known militant activist in the area. Another militant, Shaykl Muhammad Hassan, who operated the African-Asian Cultural Center, which was located at 2336 W. Columbia Ave. and seemed to have been a hotbed of black militant political activity in North Philadelphia, was arrested and beaten by police. He claims that his arrest and beating caused the riot and that he had made a deal with

Rizzo to try to calm people down but was arrested for, in fact, inciting them to riot.[6] Muhammad Hassan was charged with inciting to riot, and several black ministers testified against him at his trial, although a white merchant offered a different view, saying that Muhammad Hassan was urging people to go home. An all-white jury convicted Muhammad Hassan. He had also been clearly injured by the beating he endured.

Whether Muhammad Hassan had a deal with Rizzo cannot be verified, but Rizzo was trying very hard throughout the riot, under orders from Commissioner Leary, to find leaders who could help disperse the vandals and looters. Moreover, Muhammad Hassan never blamed the police for what happened. The *Tribune* reported this account: "Muhammad said he strongly believes that the real trouble came when Commissioner Rizzo ordered police to take him to the hospital. 'The mob thought the police had beaten me intentionally and that they were hauling me off to jail,' explained Muhammad. 'THIS IS WHAT REALLY TRIGGERED THE BLOODY RIOTING IN NORTH PHILADELPHIA,' Muhammad stated. 'The people thought I was another victim of police brutality.'"[7] Muhammad Hassan's account could be correct, for he felt the mood for the riot had developed when police had starting searching homes in the area looking for a drug dealer. It could also have been just some egotistical ranting on his part. In the official report on the riot issued by the Human Relations Commission,

Muhammad Hassan is mentioned, but his story is given no credence.

Despite the fact that Rizzo clearly spent part of his time running around trying to find peacemakers, what he wanted to do was to rush in immediately with a strong show of police and quell the riot before it got started. Commissioner Leary had formulated a strategy in 1963 to deal with a civil disturbance of this sort, but it did not include such a tactic. Leary wanted to keep physical violence and human casualties to a minimum. There were to be no pitch battles between the police and the rioters, even if that meant greater property damage and more looting. Jack Franklin, a photographer for the *Tribune*, gave this eyewitness account: "Patrolmen stood around in small groups of four or five and watched the looting but made no effort to stop anyone. I asked one officer why he didn't attempt to make an arrest. 'We're under orders not to interfere!' he told me. 'We are too outnumbered. If we tried to step in, there would be real bloodshed.' "[8]

It is impossible to say which tactic would have been better. Less property destruction and perhaps just a little loss of life would have occurred had the police made a strong show of force early on. Perhaps, because of the strong antipolice feelings in the community, a strong show of force might have produced a bloodbath. A year later, in 1965, in Watts, one of the worst riots in American history, a strong police response intensified the riot, inducing a frenzy in the black Los Angeles community. However, a lack of a strong police response in Detroit in 1968 allowed rioters to get the upper hand early in a riot that destroyed vast portions of that city. How strong were the antipolice feelings of the rioters? The *Tribune* photographer Jack Franklin gives this account: "I walked west on Columbia Ave. in the same direction which I had heard sirens. At 23rd St., I saw several red cars and patrol wagons. A large group of people, mostly women and teenage boys, had congregated on the corner and was shouting insults at the small knot of police officials conferring in the middle of the street. I heard one boy, who appeared to be about 17, shouting: 'Kill those dirty bastards. Those rotten cop bastards ought to be dead.' A young woman shrieked: 'Let's run them out of North Philadelphia. Those white cops have no business up here.'"[9]

When the riot ended on Monday, August 31, 2 persons had been killed and 339 injured, including 239 black residents and 100 police officers. Three hundred and eight people had been arrested, slightly more than a third of these from outside the riot area. The majority were charged with burglary. Property damage, mostly to businesses, was estimated at 3 million in 1964 dollars. Compared to other big city riots of the 1960s, the Philadelphia riot was fairly sedate, not nearly as bad as those in Newark, Detroit, or Watts. No other major race riot took place in Philadelphia in the 1960s.

The handling of the riot was helpful politically to Rizzo in the long run and the short run, although at the time he was terribly angry with Leary's strategy and later called him "a gutless bastard."[10] Whites were growing more and more fearful of black crime and urban unrest. Rizzo made it very plain and very public how he would have preferred to have handled the riot, and whites generally and even some blacks agreed with him. Both the black and white newspapers of the city described the riot in the same way: the *Philadelphia Inquirer*, in an editorial on August 30, 1964, wrote: "[The riot] was simply a case of a disorderly welter of thugs, hoodlums, and morons taking advantage of any incident to set off an orgy of violence and thievery." The *Tribune*, in a front page editorial dated September 1, 1964, wrote: "Thugs, thieves, and hoodlums, in open defiance of police and other law enforcement officers, smashed windows, removed merchandise and carted it away with reckless abandonment."

By 1960, the black population of Philadelphia was 535,000 or about 27 percent of the total population of the city. In ten years, the black population had increased by over 150,000. Nearly a third or about 175,000 blacks lived in North Central Philadelphia along with about 22,000 whites. (The *Philadelphia Inquirer*, in its August 30th edition, put the number of black residents in North Central Philadelphia at 225,000.) There had to be a growing sense among many of the city's whites that blacks seemed to be taking over the city. Remember that until World War II, North Central Philadelphia had been largely white with strong ethnic mixtures of Jews and Irish Catholics. Most of the businesses that were destroyed on Columbia and Ridge Avenues during the 1964 riot were owned by Jews; this exacerbated tensions between blacks and Jews and certainly encouraged at least some Jews to be supportive of a political figure like Rizzo as his career as a public figure blossomed. The fact that the civil rights movement itself seemed to be generating so much violence and such potent disorder in the streets made many whites fearful. Rizzo certainly offered himself as someone who could stem the tide of lawlessness and sheer menace that seemed to be erupting in Philadelphia. It must be remembered that even the whites at this time who were supportive of civil rights thought blacks wanted too much too quickly. Some greatly feared that the civil rights movement was going too far and that blacks were determined to push themselves into places where they were not wanted. This sort of thinking had a lot to do with white opposition to the integration of Girard College, which I shall discuss momentarily.

The blacks of Philadelphia were herded in ghettos, suffered from the worst medical care (and, consequently, the worst health), and were the least educated of Philadelphia's population, the most likely to be unemployed, and the most poorly housed. In the history of Philadelphia, blacks had been denied not only power but also any access to it. The presence of blacks in Philadelphia as a community goes back to the eighteenth century. When W. E. B. Du Bois did his famous study *The Philadelphia Negro* for the University of Pennsylvania in 1898, he found a vibrant but highly impoverished and harshly oppressed black population with many of the same problems that faced the black residents of North Philadelphia in 1964. Indeed, virtually nothing had changed for the black population of the city from the time Du Bois's book was published, in 1899, to 1951, when Richardson Dilworth and Joseph Clark led the Democratic reform movement that ousted the Republican machine from power. Philadelphia was an extraordinarily racist city when it was controlled by the Republican machine for the first half of the twentieth century. Fighting that entrenched racism in the 1950s and 1960s proved difficult, even though there were more liberal city administrations in power. Generally, local politicians ignored blacks except at election time. But blacks made progress, and not only in improving their economic status in the city. As the sociologist Digby Baltzell has pointed out, the black middle class began to expand in the 1950s in Philadelphia because the city began to open more white collar, professional jobs to blacks.[11] Blacks also began to organize themselves better politically in the 1950s. The level of frustration and anger in the black community in the early 1960s was high, especially because the civil rights movement had heightened the political consciousness of ordinary blacks and because slowly improving economic conditions had heightened people's expectations. One might say that conditions reached a certain climax in 1964 with the riot and that, in the words of the Chamber Brothers, time had come for black Philadelphia.

Commissioner Leary had called the Uptown Theater when the rioting started, almost literally pulling the emcee Georgie Woods off the stage to explain the situation to him. Woods, a vice president in the NAACP, was hosting a show at the North Philadelphia theater that included B. B. King, Ben E. King, Garnet Mims, Gladys Knight and the Fabulous Pips, The Tams, the Soul Sisters, and Inez and Charlie Foxx. Leary wanted Woods to use his influence to get people off the streets. Woods tried but was unsuccessful. Judge Raymond Pace Alexander, wearing a large blue helmet, tried to disperse crowds. "You're making things bad for yourselves and for this community," he said. The crowd jeered him. "Go home, you Uncle Tom," he was told, "We don't need any handkerchief-head judges around here."[12] Alexander lived in the middle-class, highly integrated Mount Airy and was not considered by many blacks to be a member of this community but rather just another sellout to the white establishment. Alexander may have been dismayed that what he had done for black Philadelphia was so quickly forgotten. He was a man of considerable accomplishments.

Cecil Moore, too, tried to calm the crowds and get people to go home. When he first addressed a crowd he was hit by a brick. The tough ex-marine grimaced but bravely remained on his feet although the brick nearly knocked him unconscious. He grabbed a bullhorn and pleaded with the crowd. They jeered him again. Moore even drove around the riot area on Saturday, August 29, with Mrs. Bradford sitting beside him, shouting through a bullhorn that Mrs. Bradford was alive and well, was not pregnant, and had not been beaten or harmed by the police. No one listened. Though Moore, unlike Alexander, lived in the neighborhood and spoke the gruff, plain language of these folk, they still wouldn't listen to him. I think Moore learned two lessons from this riot, both of which helped him enormously as a black leader through 1968. First, Moore now knew that most black leaders, with few exceptions, didn't have the full trust and support of the black masses because the black masses didn't feel that these people truly represented their interests. He knew that one of the reasons they weren't trusted was because most blacks thought those leaders put their class interests ahead of the interests of the group. This observation has been made by such diverse commentators on race as Carter G. Woodson in *The Mis-Education of the Negro*, E. Franklin Frazier in *Black Bourgeoisie*, James Baldwin in the essays he wrote on Martin Luther King and on Harlem, Malcolm X in various speeches he made against the civil rights establishment, and Gunnar Myrdal in *An American Dilemma*. As Moore himself said of black middle-class leadership, "It is from their lofty perch midway between the integration they long for and the segregation from which they have profited that every principle of Negro progress has been sacrificed."[13] This is a virtual paraphrase of Woodson, Frazier, and the others I mentioned. During the riot, Moore found himself being treated like any other establishment black leader, despite the fact that he lived in the neighborhood, despite the fact that he had led demonstrations, despite his militancy. Moore's ineffectiveness during the riot intensified his desire for independence. Through the powerful years of his leadership, Moore distanced himself not only from the white political and corporate establishment but from the black political establishment as well. He did not answer to the local or to the national officials of the NAACP. He did not answer to the black ministers of the city (and even defeated a prominent black minister, Henry Nichols, when he ran for re-election as Philadelphia NAACP president in 1965). He did not answer to the black professional establishment represented by people like the Alexanders or J. Leon Higginbotham. He answered to absolutely no one about his actions. To the black leadership of the city, Moore at times seemed like an egotistical rogue agent, publicly denouncing them and refusing to enter any settlement unless he was personally a part of it. This proved to the grassroots contingent that he did not have any other interests in mind or any other interests to protect but their own, or at least this was how many interpreted Moore's actions and attitude. This gave him more authority than any other black leader had ever had in the city, because after the riot, he was the only black leader who was absolutely trusted by the masses, the only one who had the faith of several hundred thousand black folk. His leadership was never at odds with the people he represented, as was the case with many other black leaders. The course he followed as an independent was risky, and a lesser man would probably have been destroyed by it, undermined by other black leaders and discredited by the white establishment, but Moore was a brilliant strategist and had an uncanny understanding of the times he was living in, of the mood of his historical era.

One reason Moore succeeded in the way he did was that unlike, say, Malcolm X, he was a black anti-establishment figure with the authority of a black establishment organization, the NAACP, behind him. This authority helped to legitimize him not only because the organization was held in high regard by most African Americans—even if they weren't members of it, and even at times when they complained about it—but also because it gave him a secular base of operations. After all, despite its shortcomings, an organization that could boast the names of W. E. B. Du Bois, Thurgood Marshall, Charles Houston, James Weldon Johnson, and Walter White was bound to have cachet among black Americans in the 1960s. Moore's style actually helped to relegitimize the organization for many blacks who thought the NAACP was too conservative, too middle class, too out of touch with the day-to-day lives of working-class black folk. Moore's accomplishment was to take a black middle-class, integrationist organization that sought change through legal action and to reshape it, on the local level, into a militant, populist organization that engaged in direct action protest. He was one of the first black leaders on a local level to use effectively the new political ideas of Black Power. He combined black nationalist rhetoric, such as his creation of "a black agenda" and his insistence that everything in the black community should be under that community's control, with integrationist aims, such as the integration of Girard College.

The campaign to integrate Girard College was a brilliant stroke because it enabled Moore to combine nationalist rhetoric—how can black people allow a lily-white institution to exist in their community?—with the integrationist aim of getting the school to admit black students. Frank Rizzo has always been given credit for the fact that no other major race riot happened in Philadelphia during the 1960s, and perhaps he was something of a deterrent. But I think a good portion of the credit should go to Moore and his Girard College campaign in particular. Those demonstrations served as a safety valve for black political expression in Philadelphia. In concentrating on Girard College, Moore gave blacks what Martin Luther King would have called a form of creative political engagement: it required discipline, courage, and organization, and it diverted their minds from destructive and undisciplined acts like rioting.

The Marine and the Making of a Racial Leader

Cecil Bassett Moore was born in Yokon, West Virginia, on April 2, 1915, to Dr. Alexander Moore, a physician, and Beulah, a teacher. He was, in short, the child of an affluent, middle-class, professional black family. He graduated from Bluefield College in Bluefield, West Virginia, and earned a law degree at night from Temple University, graduating in 1951, the same year that Raymond Pace Alexander became Philadelphia's first black city councilman. Moore spent nine years in the Marine Corps, two and half of which were overseas, leading a group into combat against the Japanese. This was at a time when few blacks were in the Marine Corps, considered to be the elite of our country's combat soldiers, so Moore's entire history was actually that of Du Bois's Talented Tenth. Moore's background gave him discipline, training in organizing people to achieve a goal, and, most important, a sense of how to command. Moore learned much about the social problems of African Americans in the city when he became a whiskey salesman while attending Temple Law School and visited many of the bars and taprooms in the black community. He learned about the underhand political dealings that kept those taprooms open and how little say black people had about what went on in their communities. He learned that no one believed in the political system as a set of values: people simply wished to use it to get from it what they could.

Moore's first run-in with Frank Rizzo occurred when Rizzo was working out of the Sixteenth District in West Philadelphia back in 1952. Rizzo was cracking down on all the speakeasies in the area, including private homes and the Elks Lodges. Moore led a group of young black lawyers who fielded the black complaints that began pouring in when Rizzo came to the Sixteenth District. Moore and the lawyers met with Rizzo, who was polite but very firm about his intentions to enforce the law against speakeasies. The lawyers formed the Young Independent Political Action Committee to pressure the Democratic Party to open up leadership opportunities for blacks. They thought they had worked out a deal with the party to have the raids stopped or curtailed, but after Rizzo left the area, the raids became even worse than before. It was in West Philadelphia that Rizzo earned the name of the Cisco Kid, and it was through this encounter that Cecil Moore learned a great deal about how big city politics and race work. He also learned that blacks who tried to work the system the way white ethnics did had very little power and very little success.

At times, Moore expressed himself as a cynic, but he seemed to be more of a realist than anything else, particularly about the exercise of group power and in his insistence that the black middle class was powerless without the strength of the black working class and poor behind them. In this way, Moore, although a Democrat, was free from association with either the Democrats or the Republicans. This was very important, because he freed himself from being patronized or bought out by these political machines or becoming merely one of their clients. Moore knew that simply delivering black votes for the big city political machine on election day would get blacks virtually nothing in return. It had already been tried. In effect, Moore believed what A. Philip Randolph believed: that pressure politics was essential for blacks to gain anything from whites, and that in order for pressure politics to work, blacks had to demand, not ask, for things: if they wished to control their own destiny, they had to be organized and disciplined, and they had to insist on a seat at the table of power. It isn't that other black leaders in Philadelphia did not believe in these principles, or at least some of them, but that no one before Moore and no one during the height of his influence had so effectively put them into practice to make pressure politics work.

Moore made himself an independent almost as soon as he became the president of the local NAACP. On taking the job, he immediately protested the fact that the Ford Foundation, about to launch a major study of North Central Philadelphia, had not considered the NAACP to run the program. Blacks had not been consulted in a study that would be, in essence, about themselves. The Ford Foundation ignored Moore's protest. Moore then said that he would organize a black boycott of Ford Motor Company products. The Ford Foundation chose not to ignore Moore when he made this threat. The reason for this was because in 1959 four hundred black Philadelphia ministers organized a "Selective Patronage Program" to force companies to open up their doors to black employees. The most successful boycott organized by these ministers was against the Tastykake Baking Company. The ministers demanded that the company hire at least two black drivers, two black office workers, and four blacks at management level, and blacks virtually ceased buying Tastykake products in Philadelphia. The company yielded to the ministers' demands. In April 1962, the *Philadelphia Bulletin*, the evening daily, had been targeted with the same results, so the Ford Foundation was aware that a boycott was not an idle threat, and Moore knew that the Foundation knew this. The black leadership in Philadelphia did not feel at all comfortable with Moore's tactic, and Raymond Pace Alexander wrote Moore a letter, signed as well by fifteen other well-known black leaders, telling him that while they agreed with his aim, they found his methods unnecessary. Alexander wrote that the goal of getting a black to be part of the team for this study could be achieved "without bombast, silly threats, and ineffective antics, which are more consistent with the Black Muslims' approach than the methods of the NAACP." Moore responded by saying, "Today Philadelphia has again witnessed the spectacle of a form of 'chestnut removal' by people they have long since given up any hope of providing effective leadership for the Negro populace."[14] The Ford Foundation decided to appoint a black associate director to the North Central Philadelphia study project. Moore took credit for the success of his pressure politics tactic.

Already by early 1963, just a few months into his job as NAACP president, Moore was serving notice that he was, indeed, a lone wolf. Immediately after the riot, several community leaders formed a committee to find ways to prevent another riot from occurring. Moore was not invited to be part of this group. In an interview with *Time Magazine*, he said, "So now the ministers, the liberals, the part-time professional, part-time Negroes want to form an emergency committee to stop riots. What the hell do they know about it? Do you know that not one of those bastards asked me to attend the meeting? I invited myself, so I could walk out if it didn't go my way." Over the next several years, he proved right in many ways what he said about himself in that interview: "I'm the goddamn boss."[15]

The Mummers Day Parade and Blackface Makeup

I would like to conclude by looking briefly at two of Moore's major accomplishments during the years 1964 to 1968: first, the ban on the use of blackface makeup by the Mummers during the Mummers Parade, a Philadelphia tradition involving colorfully costumed groups who parade down Broad Street (Philadelphia's main thoroughfare) each New Year's Day, and, second, the modification of Stephen Girard's will, which resulted in the racial integration of Girard College. In both instances, I think it would be instructive to compare Moore's methods in the 1960s with the methods used by Raymond Pace Alexander in the 1950s when he tackled these same issues.

The first attempt to get a ban on the use of blackface makeup and racially denigrating behavior on the part of the Mummers was in 1954, when Dr. Frank Burse, after watching the antics of some of the Mummers on television, decided some sort of protest was in order. Black ministers sided with Dr. Burse and protested the use of taxpayers' money as the basis of the prize money awarded to the best of the Mummers every year. When the problem reached the Human Relations Commission, which had been formed only a few years earlier under the reform administration of Clark and Dilworth, Raymond Pace Alexander, then a member of the city council, proposed that the city government should take a stand against the use of blackface makeup. Councilman Alexander's resolution asked for an end to the mimicking, ridiculing, or satirical stereotyping of any race of people and argued that if such practices continued, the prize money should be withheld. The resolution was passed, but the Mummers refused to meet with the

Human Relations Commission to discuss it. Indeed, the Mummers' leadership threatened to take the parade to New York. Finally, a compromise was reached where the Mummers promised not to "intentionally mimic, mock, or portray any race, creed, or religion." There was no ban against blackface. There was no withholding of prize money. Parade judges were simply "requested not to reward any marcher or group who use[ed] ridicule of a racial or religious group as its theme."[16] It was a fairly hollow victory for Burse and Alexander because they had no leverage within the political or legal structure to make a better deal or to force the Mummers to heel through extralegal means such as pressure politics. Clearly, the free speech implications of the case meant that there was only so far any court or legislative body could go before crossing the line and violating the constitutional rights of the Mummers. In part, the limitations of this victory were simply a reflection of the times. Alexander did not have behind him the force and revolutionary energy of the civil rights movement and the more activist black population that Moore was to enjoy ten years later. Alexander obtained his resolution even before the Supreme Court handed down the *Brown* decision, which was not to come for another few months.

The idea that blacks might be offended by something was becoming more visible in public cultural discourse: an NAACP protest had succeeded in taking *Amos and Andy* off television just shortly before the fight with the Mummers. But that show had black actors; the Mummers were white men donning blackface, an old tradition in western European culture. At this time in history whites were less likely to accommodate blacks on an issue in which they felt blacks were telling them how to act.

Part of Alexander's lack of success on this issue is attributable to temperament and background. Alexander, and men and women like him, were part of the old guard black middle class, which was the very class of blacks that Moore despised, that E. Franklin Frazier, Carter G. Woodson, and others harshly criticized, and that the civil rights movement tended to overturn. I do not in any way wish to sound pejorative in describing Alexander in this way. He was an extraordinary man and just as important to the history of race in Philadelphia as Cecil Moore. Alexander, a lifelong Philadelphian, was born in 1897 to a poor family. He attended Central High School, where his superior academic achievements earned him the right to be class's commencement speaker. He earned a scholarship to the University of Pennsylvania, from which he graduated with honors. He then attended Harvard Law School—this from a boy who started out shining shoes on Thirteenth and Green streets.

Alexander was part of new black middle class when he came of age during the 1920s, overturning the black elite that existed before. In becoming a member of the Boule[17], an organization that deeply shaped Alexander's values when he was a young man, Alexander was part of a new generation of professional black men who gained their status through economic and educational achievements and not through skin color, the approval of whites, or family background as the old black elite, coming out of slavery, had done. Alexander's was the first black law firm to locate its offices in downtown Philadelphia at a time when there were few black lawyers in the city at all and when many blacks went to Jewish lawyers because they felt the Jews were better trained (and, that being white, they would have more influence in the legal system). Alexander's firm handled hundreds of civil rights cases for which he never took any money. It was Alexander who, in 1925, through the courts, de-segregated Philadelphia's downtown movie theaters. He also led the fight to integrate a public school in Chester County in the middle 1930s, a fight that used public protest as well as the courts. Many black parents went to jail during this protest.

But Alexander was also very involved in machine politics in the city. He worked as a loyal Republican for many years, then switched to the Democrats during the Roosevelt era. Though this sort of client relationship with white political machines may have enabled individual blacks to profit, it yielded blacks as a group very little, which was why Moore so assiduously avoided it. Moore was no doubt profoundly affected by the example of Alexander and men and women like him who were repeatedly frustrated during the 1930s and 1940s because they received so little from the parties they so passionately supported. White ethnic groups, however, were using the political machines in much the same way to great benefit. Alexander was not, by temperament or background, likely to be comfortable with the modern civil rights movement with its emphasis on street demonstrations, militant rhetoric, and cultural interest in things African. His generation, it must be understood, found none of this to be dignified behavior for a black person; nor did they consider such behavior a reflection of achievement, which was an obsession for the middle class of Alexander's generation, who saw merit and achievement as ways of breaking down segregation and racism. Alexander was sincerely interested in getting rid of blackface makeup in the Mummers Parade but he felt he had pushed the issue as far as it could go. He had achieved something of great importance by getting the city to disapprove it officially.

Moore pursued this issue again in 1963; it came to a head in the January 1964 Mummers Parade, eight months before the North Philadelphia riot. The parade had been postponed several times that year because of bad weather. When it was finally held, the mood was ominous. Magistrate Elias Myers, the grand marshal of the 1964 parade, had ruled that blackface was banned and that those who showed up in it would not be permitted to march. This decision mostly affected the comic clubs, not the fancy division or the string bands.[18] But on December 27,

1963, Myers changed his mind and permitted black-face if the performers "behaved themselves and acted like gentlemen."[19] When Moore learned of this, he threatened to boycott the parade and line the route with pickets. The Congress of Racial Equality (CORE) also threatened to demonstrate. There was now real fear of bloodshed because the parade route on Board Street went past Fitzwater, Bainbridge, Catherine, and South streets, the black section of South Phila-delphia where a large number of blacks were expected to watch the parade. Moore was aware of the bargain-ing power that potential violence held, as was CORE. Moore sent the NAACP lawyer Charles Bowser to court to get an injunction, which Bowser succeeded in do-ing, but not quite on the grounds Moore wanted. Moore wanted blackface banned on the grounds that blacks were being forced to pay for their own deni-gration since black tax-payers' money supported the prize money given to the Mummers. This was exactly the argument Raymond Pace Alexander had used ten years earlier. What Moore got was a court injunc-tion against the use of blackface on the grounds of public safety because the likelihood of violence at the parade would be vastly increased were blackface permitted. Moore was afraid that winning the ban on these grounds would have a chilling effect on any public demonstrations by any group.

In any case, what the court ruled was clearly un-constitutional, and after the 1964 parade Mayor Tate sided with Moore, saying that prize money would be withheld if any parade participants denigrated any ethnic, racial, or religious group, which was precisely what Alexander had wanted but could not get back in 1954. At the 1964 parade, under a heavy police presence, the Philip J. Hammond clown unit staged a sit-in at Broad and Fitzwater Streets, mocking the methods of black civil rights demonstrators. They held up the parade for fifteen minutes. They also walked by the black blocks of the parade chanting: "One, Two, Three, Four / We Hate Cecil Moore and CORE / five, Six, Seven, Eight / We Hope They All Disintegrate."[20] When the Hammond unit reached Pine Street, they decided to perform using, oddly enough, an all-black band, members of the O.V. Catto Lodge of Sixteenth and Fitzwater Streets. Band members would not speak to the press about why they were playing for the Hammonds.

It is clear that Moore's success had much to do with his inclination to use pressure politics and the fact that the times permitted him to do so with much greater effect. We also see that Moore was still resorting to the courts, as the NAACP normally did. And he won his day in the courts, not on the streets. But his success in the courts was tied to the threat of demonstrations or street activities, which was a lever that Alexander had lacked. Plus, Moore's opponents and adversaries knew that he was not at all bashful about going to the streets, taking matters outside the court and legal system to gain his objectives. Alexander could never have backed up such a threat, even had he been so foolish as to make it, because he could never have gotten the followers for it. Although he clearly had a theatrical bent, Alexander had neither the personality nor the desire to lead street demonstrations in the way Moore did.

Girard College and Its Wall of Whiteness

Raymond Pace Alexander had a particular passion about the integration of Girard College. It was the issue that probably meant the most to him during his years as a city councilman (1951–59). The modification of Stephen Girard's will was what he wanted to be known for; it would have been his greatest legal victory. Perhaps his great absorption with this case was personal. Girard College was surrounded by a ten-foot-high wall. As Alexander said in a speech in 1931, " 'Walls' have been a problem for the Negro worker, the college graduate, the college professor, the scientist etc. to crack. I hate walls around anything. I refuse to have them, or even fences, anywhere around the place where we call our home on the hills of Chester Country, Pennsylvania. I have spent so much of life on the problem of removal of the walls of prejudice that shut out one's opportunity in life that I believe it is appropriate at this point briefly to read one stanza of the immemorial poem 'Mending Wall' by America's great poet laureate, Robert Frost."[21] Alexander then went on to read the poem. He went on to speak more specifically about Girard College in a May 21, 1948, letter to Earl Shelby of the *Philadelphia Bulletin*:

> *I was born and raised in the shadows of the cold, grey and forbidding walls of Girard College. As a young-ster, I had to walk that long walk down Ridge Avenue past those walls and return daily on my way to the old Central High School. A $.5 cents fare for twenty city blocks was too much to pay for a poor kid, one of six in a poor family. We, as the City's colored population, knew these walls meant discrimination—and I grew up to hate walls. I knew not what they were walling in, and keeping out—but I thought then, and know now, whatever it was, it was not a good omen. I swore, were I ever able to become a lawyer, or legislator, or both, I would try every legal means to break that evidence of segregation and discrimination that Girard College symbolized in the heart of the most populous Negro community in the City of Philadelphia.*

Stephen Girard was a Frenchman, born in 1750, who eventually made Philadelphia his home and made a great deal of money in the shipping and banking business. There is no evidence that he was ever involved in the slave trade, although an arti-cle in the May 8, 1965, *Philadelphia Tribune*, which appeared during the height of the Girard College controversy under Cecil Moore, accused Girard of stealing millions from the Haitian liberator Tous-saint L'Ouverture and of being involved in the slave trade. Few black people have ever believed it possible for anyone to make money during the slavery era without, in some way, being touched by that institution. Most blacks believe that, to paraphrase Balzac, every white antebellum fortune is built on a crime. Girard wrote his will in 1830, leaving the bulk of his estate to charity, most of it to establishing a school for "poor male white orphan children." Although Girard was married (his wife was eventually committed to a mental institution), he had no children. But his relatives did, unsuccessfully, contest the will. What was unusual about the will was that Girard established the school as a public trust to be administered by the city—it was on this ground that Alexander and others were later to fight the will in court. Girard College was opened in 1848 with ninety-five boys attending and was located on a farm that eventually became part of the most congested black neighborhood in the city. Although Girard's will was modified in a number of ways over the years, two provisions remained strictly enforced: no clergymen were permitted on the campus (which has kept Girard College banned to this day from all school athletic leagues, mostly at the insistence of the Catholic Church), and no blacks were permitted to attend the school. President Truman visited Girard College in May 1948; on July 26 of that year he issued Executive Order 9981, which outlawed racial discrimination in the armed services. Outside the college during Truman's visit, a group held a sign that read: "Down with Jim Crow in Girard College."[22]

I am unsure whether they were the first to picket the school, but they were certainly not the last.

Alexander began his campaign against Girard College on July 23, 1953, by introducing to the Philadelphia City Council a resolution to end discrimination at the college. The resolution threatened court action if the school continued to practice segregation; it was unanimously passed on March 27, 1954. This was a good time for Alexander to mount this effort: liberal, reformist Democrats now governed Philadelphia after decades of Republican domination. (Alexander had been a staunch Republican, as were many black professionals, until 1945. He ran for city council in 1951 as a Democrat.) The city charter had been rewritten, and there was a sense of change in the air, indicated as much by the fact that Alexander was on the city council as anything else.

Nothing changed as a result of the resolution, so Alexander decided to challenge the will in Orphans Court. He had six boys apply for admission to Girard College. Other than the fact that they were black, they met every requirement for admission, but the college still rejected all of them. On September 24, 1954, Alexander filed petitions for two plaintiffs in the Orphans Court of Philadelphia. Alexander was relying on the recent Supreme Court decision (*Brown v. Board of Education*), which outlawed segregation in public schools, not as a legal precedent but as something of a moral lever. (Besides, many private schools had abandoned discrimination since the decision.)

More to the point legally, he thought that *Shelley v. Kraemer*, which outlawed racially restrictive housing covenants, would help him win the case, as it outlawed state action in supporting a contract that violated the Constitution. The city of Philadelphia essentially ran the board of trustees of Girard College since the city administered Girard's trust; state involvement in the school was profound. In effect, the plaintiffs argued, Girard was a de facto public school, and the state was involved in administering a trust that violated the Constitution by discriminating on the basis of race. Alexander also challenged the will on the doctrine of cy pres, that is, changing or approximating a particular duty or function in, say, a will, because it cannot be performed in precisely the way the party meant for it to be performed. In other words, Alexander was arguing that times had changed since the will was written in the antebellum nineteenth century and that common sense would dictate that the spirit of the will could still be adhered to by admitting black boys since the letter of the will was repugnant both morally and legally.

The plaintiffs lost in Orphans Court and the Pennsylvania State Supreme Court. On February 12, 1957, the plaintiffs petitioned the U.S. Supreme Court. In what was the biggest legal victory of Alexander's career, the Supreme Court ruled in favor of the plaintiffs on April 29, 1957. "Brother am I happy! Isn't it marvelous?" Alexander told a reporter from the *Philadelphia Bulletin.* "They said that Raymond Pace

Alexander was talking pie in the sky. They said he had illusions. And now we're in. I'm the happiest man in the world." I am not sure who Alexander is referring to when he speaks of "they." Perhaps "they" were doubters in general. Perhaps they were specifically black doubters who were convinced the system was stacked against blacks, that it was crazy to appeal to the system that oppressed you to relieve that oppression through a recognition of the pain it caused. I myself had been taught by older blacks that white people enjoyed our pain. If they didn't, they wouldn't sell tickets to lynchings, would they? But even given this, what else was one to do about oppression? It was better to do something than to do nothing but complain, an art in which most black people I knew, even as a boy, were highly skilled. Most felt that integrating Girard College was not going to make much of a difference in their lives, but it was going to make a difference in some few people's lives, people who might be able to attend the school. And it was certainly going to make a difference in how black people in North Philadelphia felt when they walked by the school. Alexander could not have been alone in how he felt about growing up in the shadows of the walls of the school.

For a time, my mother, who was a widow, began to think that even I might be able to go to Girard College. Since I was only in kindergarten, I was too young to have any thoughts on the matter. As I grew older, I became increasingly uneasy about attending

Girard College and felt a certain relief when, during the height of the controversy in the 1960s, my age rendered me ineligible for admission. I think that for a time my mother respected Alexander, thought he was a great man. This feeling did not last among working-class blacks, particularly with the onset of the civil rights movement. What those in the movement gained from their newfound militancy in self-respect, dignity, and mass action political purpose were deeply impressive, but these things also led them to toss aside a man like Alexander and to dismiss his years of work. This seemed to me many years ago and today still a steep price to pay, but perhaps it was an unavoidable one.

In any case, Alexander's happiness was short-lived. On October 4, 1957, the Orphans Court appointed a new, private board of trustees for Girard College. Since it was no longer administered by the city, the directive to integrate no longer applied. The college was completely private now, or seemingly so. The irony was that the college, which fought so hard in court on the principle that Girard's will was inviolate, violated the will itself by removing the trust from the city in order to keep blacks out. And didn't the Orphans Court's appointment of a private board that would continue to bar blacks constitute a state action that violated the Constitution, the principle on which the Supreme Court decided *Shelley v. Kraemer*? As a teenager, I heard the local Nation of Islam minister shout to his believers, "The white man is the biggest liar on the face of the earth! The white man is the biggest hypocrite on the face of the earth!" There were a lot of people who had good reason to vigorously assent to that.

Of course, nothing is as simple as it seems. The city of Philadelphia and the commonwealth of Pennsylvania joined the plaintiffs in their appeal, so a considerable portion of the white power structure, as it was called, also wanted the school integrated and, doubtless, was vexed by the intractable attitude exhibited by the school's leaders and the head of its board. But if the school could not be reasoned into changing, perhaps it could pressured into it.

The Contrariness of the Goddamn Boss

I'm just an arrogant black son-of-a-bitch. I like bourbon whiskey, good food, good talk, a little respect from my fellow man. I say what I want to say, do what I want to do, won't take no orders. I'm 59, ain't afraid of anythin', and there is no other SOB in Philadelphia like me.

Cecil Moore, *Philadelphia Inquirer*,
December 1, 1974

Who can control Mr. Moore?

Jerry Katz, manager of the Latin Casino,
Philadelphia Tribune, February 27, 1965

On February 7, 1965, the Philadelphia branch of the NAACP held its presidential election at the National

Guard Armory at Thirty-third Street and Lancaster Avenue. It was a chaotic affair, poorly run by the officials of the national office. Many had to wait for hours to vote since membership documents were misfiled or lost. Many who showed up to vote wound up not being able to vote at all, for one reason or another, including not being able to get the registration desk to get a ballot. But everyone who was anyone in black Philadelphia showed up to vote, from Chubby Checker, the king of the twist (one of whose brothers used to date my oldest sister and another of whom went to school with me before the singer hit it big) and the holder of a recently purchased $500 lifetime membership, to Federal District Judge Leon Higginbotham, a former president of the local NAACP, who almost did not get to vote at all in the confusion.

The candidates were the Reverend Henry Nichols and Cecil B. Moore. Nichols, pastor of a Methodist church in Germantown, had led a revolt of the black ministers against the local NAACP wherein they paid their dues directly to the national office instead of the local Philadelphia branch. The object of this revolt was the incumbent, Cecil B. Moore, the hard-drinking, cigar-chomping, profanity-spewing leader who refused to be part of any "black coalition."

It had to be a forgone conclusion who was going to win: in its January 12, 19, 23, and February 6 editions, the *Philadelphia Tribune*, in its "man on the street" column ("The *Tribune* Inquiring Reporter"), asked whether Rev. Nichols could win the presidency from

Moore. Whether male or female, old or young, professional or working class, no one thought Nichols could win and no one wanted him to. Nichols was not considered militant enough, and people thought him too likely to compromise with the "white power structure." He was actually dismissed *because* he was a minister; as Shad Sherman, a construction worker, said, "Ministers should stay in the pulpit."

It is stunning that such sentiments were expressed by a people whose ministers usually wielded such great influence and power and were virtually the sole class of leadership. It is even more stunning that these beliefs were being expressed when the most noted black leader on the national scene was a minister, Dr. Martin Luther King Jr.

Just a little more than a week before the election, Moore and thirty other members of the NAACP staged a demonstration at the radio station WCAU to protest the appearance of the Ku Klux Klan leader Robert Shelton on a radio interview program. Many of the protestors, including the popular disc jockey Georgie Woods, dressed up in Klan garb. There were more police at the event than protestors, and four fire trucks appeared when a rumor spread about a bomb threat. It was just the kind of direct action theater that Moore loved and that his followers craved. During the protest, Moore debated Gil Spencer, a journalist for WCAU, who defended the station's right to have guest like Shelton. When some listening to the debate thought that Spencer might be a member of the

KKK and began to hurl insults, Moore quickly calmed the situation. Few blacks in Philadelphia at the time thought that someone as staid as Rev. Nichols could lead a demonstration like this. And they were right: he almost certainly wouldn't have done such a thing. But this was the new NAACP, and the grassroots blacks that Moore appealed to liked his style a lot better. As the *Tribune* editorialized on February 6, shortly before the election: "[The NAACP] has had to change from its dependence on the orderly processes of the law, with its interminable delays, and to move out into the mainstream of militant protest."

Nichols did not come close to winning. Moore beat him by better than a five to one margin. Notably, among Nichols's supporters was Raymond Pace Alexander, clearly an important figure in the shift locally from black church leadership to black secular leadership. However, Nichols's loss virtually consigned Alexander, and blacks of his ilk, to the margin: they were seen not merely as ineffective but as virtual sellouts. At his victory party at Gus "Silk" Lacey's Third Base Café on Fifty-Second Street, in the heart of black West Philadelphia's business district, Moore announced that the motto for his next two years in office would be not "We Shall Overcome" but "We Shall Overrun."

Moore was in the papers again a few weeks after the election, embroiled in a controversy out of which he emerged, depending on who was speaking, as a protofascist, a racial racketeer, or a savvy politician who knew that most black people desired nothing more than that the most famous and successful among them be forced to acknowledge racial solidarity and racial pride. The controversy started with an article in the February 16, 1965, *Tribune* about how the singer Nancy Wilson had changed management, parting ways with John Levy, an African American, and hiring Joel Cooper, a white, to replace him. She said, "I searched widely and it is almost impossible to find a Negro lawyer with corporate knowledge of the entertainment business." She added: "I had to switch from a Negro accountant to a white-owned firm when I found my earnings demanded better knowledge of the entertainment business from my accounting workers." It was reported later (in the February 27th *Tribune*) that the article was written at Wilson's request to respond to concerns that she was " 'going white.' " The remarks attributed to her in the original article hardly helped her case, although clearly Wilson had the right to hire whomever she wanted on whatever pretext she wished without giving an account of herself to anyone, particularly some local civil rights leader. However, her remarks inflamed Moore, who felt, with some justification, that Wilson had defamed black professionals, a class of which he was a member.

Later in February, Wilson appeared at the Latin Casino, a popular nightclub in Cherry Hill, New Jersey, that attracted most of its clientele from Philadelphia. Moore called the owner of the club to demand that Wilson apologize for her remarks. That evening he, with a party of eighteen, went to the late show. First, he went to Wilson's dressing room, demanding an onstage apology, which she refused to give. He claimed to have used no profanity but did admit to calling her lawyer, Cooper, "a faggot," much in keeping with macho Marine mentality. Wilson said Moore told her: "I'm telling you, you'd better apologize. I'll break your back in Philadelphia. I'll destroy you in show business. I'm worse than two Malcolm X's." During the show, he and others in his party apparently heckled Wilson; Moore's voice booming out, "That damn bitch better prostrate herself up there or we'll get some pickets." He also reportedly said, "You black bitch. You dirty black bitch. You are a disgrace to the Negro race." It is unclear exactly what happened when Moore and his party did this. He clearly had an altercation with several white patrons, but whether they came to blows is uncertain. Moore also claimed to have flattened a black off-duty Philadelphia cop. Despite the disturbance, Wilson managed to keep her composure and finish a shortened show. The manager of the club then came on stage and told everyone to leave, which probably most were glad to do, under the circumstances. Next day, Wednesday, Moore spoke to a crowd of two hundred at the NAACP officer installation ceremony at the Blue Horizon, the Mecca of boxing in Philadelphia (a symbolically appropriate venue): "Yes, I called her a name. You know what name I mean. I would call any woman that name who made a statement like she did. And if you want to impeach me, you can do it now."[23] He was wildly cheered.

At the time, I remember that I did not like what Moore had done. It seemed to be a form of bullying in which blacks were trying as hard as whites to make sure that one could never forget that one was black. There was a certain innocence to this line of thinking, unavoidable for a sheltered thirteen-year-old boy who had experienced racism hardly at all except as expressions of lack of breeding, good taste, or good manners in some ethnic whites. Yet there was a core of skepticism in me, a conviction as principled as anything I ever felt in my life, that binding someone to race through shaming and dishonor seemed both demagogic and exploitative, and that it disguised a lot of numbing conformity and jealousy behind a sense of populist revival and commitment. How liberating it is for a mob, inflamed by a charismatic leader, to destroy someone, particularly when the mob itself had a history of being persecuted? Of course, I was reading books like Richard Wright's *Black Boy* and Salinger's *Catcher in the Rye* in those days and lots of superhero comic books. Enveloped as I was in a haze of boyish fantasy and adolescent romanticism, it is surprising that I could think clearly at all, and certainly I consider my adolescence as a time when I was somewhat mentally ill, being too isolated for my own good. But Moore taught me, through the principles, such as they were, guiding his actions (and I truly believed that he believed in his courage, however stimulated it was by drink, marine bravado, and the fact that most black people believed in him) that it was good to have principles and to stand up for them. I admired him in spite of myself. He was the toughest black man I knew, a man's man, and he was fearless. When you are a teenaged boy consumed by doubts, self-pity, petty hatreds, and the not-unreasonable fear that either black boys or a white cop might kill you, you admire fearlessness all the more when you find it in something that is not a fantasy (even as you distrust it far more than you would any fantasy). I had learned by the time I was thirteen that real life was largely disappointing most of the time.

In 1965, the trustees of Rice University decided unanimously to break William March Rice's will, which stipulated that the school was to admit only whites from the city of Houston and the state of Texas. In *William March Rice University v. Waggoner Carr, Attorney General of Texas, District of Harris County*, the court allowed the change to be made. Nothing had happened with Girard College since the board had been made private in 1959, so Moore decided it was time to reopen the issue of a segregated private school in the middle of a large black urban neighborhood. But he chose a different tactic from Alexander, one that, in fact, Alexander opposed. Alexander was interested in consensus politics, cooperation with the power establishment, the inherent fairness of the justice system in the long run; Moore believed in pressure politics and causing the power establishment discomfort. Moore thought fairness would arrive only after the threat of violence, and that the long run didn't matter, because by then you'd be dead, as the economists say. Moore always assumed, not incorrectly, that blacks like Alexander wanted to be liked by whites. Moore understood that being hated by whites was far more valuable in strengthening his authority and in getting concessions from them, since they knew they couldn't get him to compromise in exchange for their approval. His followers intuitively understood this. Of course, in the heady, heated days of the 1960s, everyone believed in the apocalypse, the social conflagration that would bring down salvation history, and hard bargaining with powerful whites about its imminence was the way things were. On Saturday, May 1, 1965, less than a year after the North Philadelphia riot, Moore and about eighty or so marchers began to picket Girard College, chanting slogans and walking around the wall with signs. They continued this for the entire weekend and were greeted by over six hundred policemen, as there was great fear of another riot. Indeed, the protestors seemed engulfed in a sea of cops, who outnumbered them eight to one. But the protest did not end that weekend, or that week, or even that month. For months on end, Moore had people, sometimes as few as four or five, marching around the school. In effect, he decided that since the school saw itself as an insular institution apart from the neighborhood in which it existed, he would lay siege to it, exposing its racism to the world. In allowing the residents of North Philadelphia to vent their anger and frustration at the school, he was able to threaten it without ever violating the sanctity of its privacy. Grant at Vicksburg seemed to pale in comparison with Moore at Girard College.

What I Saw in Philadelphia

I knew an Italian boy in my neighborhood who went to Girard College. His mother, too, was a widow. I was probably the only black friend he had, or, more likely, the only black friend he wanted. His name was Joey, and he was a nice, generous kid. His mother liked me, too, because I was a good black kid, not one of "those troublemakers," "those good-for-nothings." That's how most of the Italians referred to most of the blacks who didn't clean their homes, work as stock boys in their stores, patronize their produce stands on Ninth Street, or play bingo at the local Catholic churches. That is, when they didn't fall back on tried-and-true epithets like "nigger," "jigaboo," and "coon." I tried to get along with everyone and had the great fortune of succeeding. The Italians rarely called me anything but my name. It was the black kids who had a bunch of irritating names for me that they thought were funny.

I don't recall ever talking to Joey about his school.

Perhaps it was because we played together only in the summer when he was home from school, or perhaps it was because we did not go to the same school. Perhaps school is not such an all-consuming subject for the young as adults like to think. Or perhaps, especially in the later years of our friendship, with all the demonstrations going on outside the school, Joey and I were too awkwardly embarrassed to find a way to deal with our discomfort about it. After all, he knew my mother was a widow and he also knew why I didn't go to Girard College. I also knew why those black folk were marching around the school, and when I was with Joey I always felt ashamed of that. When I was in his presence and thought of those demonstrators, I felt painfully inferior, in much the same way I would feel inferior and ashamed whenever I walked by the neighborhood State Store (in Pennsylvania, only special stores licensed by the state could sell liquor) with my white friends and see a line of derelict blacks waiting to get in. No, it was more than an association by color: I *knew* some of those men and women. I *knew* them and they would call to me as I passed by.

By this time, I was too old to be admitted to Girard, but I knew that even had I not been, I could never go to the college, because, well, how could one go to a school after having won admission in that way, after being forced into a place that didn't want you by people who argued all the while that everything was going to be better as a result? I wanted the world to change and I wanted it to stay the same, because it was not, after all, a bad world for me at that moment. But was my future to join those drunken blacks waiting like docile cattle outside the State Store? I am sure that when they were thirteen they hardly imagined such a future for themselves. And how does one, as a black, wind up with such a future, anyway? I was not being rational, I guess. But the world itself did not seem rational. It was, I suppose, that I began to feel the color of my skin and the color of his.

I wasn't friends with Joey anymore by 1966, when, thanks to the pressure of Moore's demonstrations, both the city and the state had taken Girard College back to court. Any sort of interracial friendship in the neighborhood where I grew up was doomed to die when one hit adolescence, the age at which the world suddenly became a great complexity, because suddenly, one wanted more from it and yet also vaguely realized that it was unlikely to give it to you. And you realized just as suddenly that you and your Italian friends did not quite live in the same world. They overlapped, but they did not converge. A realization swept over me by the time I was a teenager: I never talked about race with my Italian friends. Everyone wanted to avoid it, although I think, at times, that they timidly and tentatively broached the subject with me, perhaps out of curiosity, to get a sense of how I felt, or perhaps because they thought that I was masking something. I never, absolutely never, wanted to know how they felt, probably because I figured I already knew (from other sources), and it was good, a very good thing indeed, not to be reminded of such things by people whom, in many respects, you liked.

I was delivering the *Philadelphia Inquirer* in the neighborhood in those days (until I was sixteen), my route evenly divided between Italians and blacks. I hated collecting what I was owed from the white barbershop, particularly since on Saturdays, when I did all my collecting, the shop would be crowded with patrons. I would be standing there, a lone black in a sea of white men, mostly Italian. Well, not quite alone: a black boy I went to school with named Freddie worked in the shop shining shoes. For some reason, seeing him on his knees made me feel even more ashamed and angry, and I would feel myself infinitely better because I delivered newspapers and didn't kneel before white men, cleaning their shoes. The banter in the shop was like this when I entered:

"Hey, what's that jig Cecil Moore up to now?"

"He'd better keep his ass up there in North Philadelphia in coon town."

"They ought to just move Girard College to the suburbs. They let niggers in there and the whole place is shot."

"Why do the jigs always want to get in to places where they ain't wanted? Why don't the jigs build their own schools?"

"You think some nigger's gonna will some money for a school? Niggers are too busy buying Cadillacs and drinking Chivas Regal to will any goddamn money to anybody."

"Hey, Cecil Moore is turning into another Martin Luther Coon, ain't he? Just integrating everything. Now, they want to integrate wills. If I leave my money to my family, the NAACP will come along and picket, saying I got to leave my money to some poor niggers."

"They ought to get rid of that fucking bleeding heart Leary and let Rizzo clear all those niggers and bleeding heart nigger lovers away from Girard College. They got no business marching around private property. The spooks always want something for nothing."

"Hey, boy, you want to get your haircut here," someone would say to me.

"You can't use scissors to cut a jig's hair. They use lawn mowers, don't they?"

"All the niggers want are white girls. That's why they want all this integration. I bet you want a white girl, don't you, boy," one of the barbers might say to me.

This would go on sometimes for several minutes. Many of the men were amused by what they were saying; others actually worked themselves into a fit of anger and indignation. Freddie would be in a corner shining shoes, smiling wryly, and saying nothing. Sometimes I would be almost insanely angry with him, thinking that he could at least stand with me against this instead of looking like he knew something I didn't, as if he knew how not to provoke these men while I stupidly did it every time I walked into the shop. It seemed like a form of intimidation and like a sort of racial hazing, an initiation of some sort. But Freddie was just a poorly educated black boy like me, and with a bad speech impediment, besides. And he had to work in that shop for eight hours a day on Saturday! He was in no position to help me, and indeed I offered very little that would have attracted help. (It always struck me as funny that when I saw Freddie on the street, we never talked about those encounters in the barbershop. I couldn't stand the idea of raking my humiliation over the coals, and he always exhibited an attitude that seemed to say that he didn't give a shit about any of that.) I certainly didn't debate these men, nor did I want to. Whenever one of them asked my opinion I would say, "I just deliver the papers, mister, I don't read 'em," a lame answer that wasn't remotely true. I read the daily papers voraciously. I knew they really didn't want my opinion; they simply wanted to abuse me with theirs. They also wanted to see if I would quit the job or complain about their insults to my manager. There was something about it all that seemed a bit like a masculine contest of a sort. I didn't complain and I didn't quit.

While all of this was going on, I would try to look as innocuous as possible, not glum or grim but not smiling either. I would arrange my face into an expression of bland, unthinking neutrality.

Finally, before paying me, the head barber, the guy who owned the shop, would say, "Come on, this boy's okay. He's working hard to make something of himself. He's a good-natured kid. He and Freddie are all right. They don't cause no trouble. Give us a big smile, boy. A nice happy smile."

Somehow, the owner wanted to be reassured that I was not offended by all this. I am not sure why, though maybe his need to have me smile suggested that he felt I had a right to be offended and that he wanted to use the leverage he had in the situation to blunt both my inclination and my need to be so. It also suggested that the men in the shop wanted us to participate in our own degradation by pretending that we didn't mind being disrespected so that they wouldn't feel guilty about what they were doing. Moreover, it suggested that despite their feelings that we were just stupid black boys, they knew that we actually understood very well what this whole exercise was about. Indeed, his need to be reassured meant that the barber was, in fact, afraid of what he *knew* we felt and even more afraid of what we really thought of them.

In response to him, I would then give the biggest, cheesiest smile I could, looking more like someone who was grimacing from pain. The barbers were, by far, the biggest tippers on my route. As Frederick Douglass once said, you may not get everything you pay for in this life, but you pay for everything you get.

For various reasons, Girard College and Cecil Moore were big topics in my family's domestic discussions. Some members of my family were participating in the marches around the college, some of my aunts, my older sisters, even my mother. On weekends, especially during the early days of the siege, lots of people would march. It became a bit of a social event, a way for young people, black and white (and a fair number of liberal whites showed up in the first phase of this campaign), to show they were for civil rights; its anti-establishment tenor give it something of the air of a politically meaningful adventure. You could go to "the wall," as the protestors put it, and face down the huge army of police officers there without putting yourself at much risk of being attacked. It had the trappings of Birmingham without remotely being Birmingham.

I never went on any marches around the college. I cannot remember if it was because I didn't want to or because my mother wouldn't let me. I suppose I would have wanted to go. If I didn't want to, I can't remember now why I would have felt that way. My family also went to a number of meetings at the Church of the Advocate in North Philadelphia, a black activist Episcopal church pastored by Father Paul Washington (my family was pretty much high-church Episcopalian for a time), that had speakers like Stokely Carmichael, Rap Brown, and James Foreman. I don't remember ever going to those meetings, either. A lot of pep rallies for the Girard College demonstrators were held at the church because it wasn't very far from the school.

Another reason my family talked about this all the time was because they were, like most black Philadelphians, strong supporters of Cecil Moore. Most of my family, including my mother, became members of the NAACP during the years of Moore's presidency, something they never thought of doing before and something they discontinued after Moore was no longer president.

Also, my mother's boyfriend at this time was a policeman who worked a good deal of overtime at Girard College. It was not a hard duty. Most of the time, the cops sat on buses waiting for something to happen. There were always hundreds of them on duty at the college, even when the number of demonstrators was tiny. As a result of my mother's relationship with the cop, there were always black cops going in and out of my mother's house—young, ambitious men, probably the smartest, most impressive black men I had ever met at that point in my life. This gave me an interesting perspective on the Girard College confrontation, as most of them saw the matter primarily as a way to make extra money. They were convinced that the college would eventually be forced to give in because protecting it from the demonstrators was costing the city such a huge amount of money in police overtime. (Moore knew this, of course, taking advantage of Leary's, and later, when Leary went to New York, Rizzo's fears of another riot. Also, Rizzo's political ambitions necessitated that he display both strength and force, that he was in control of the situation, although he did not do anything differently from Leary.)

The black cops spoke of the police department as biased and corrupt (they spoke so often about so many cops being on the take and about all the crime they knew was going on but could do nothing about that it made me wonder whether police controlled crime or merely institutionalized it). Black cops faced a tough time trying to get promotions, which were all about politics and who you knew and not about what you scored on the test. These were highly cynical men, and that made them seem almost hip and supernaturally masculine to me at the time. Most of them liked Cecil Moore but most of them also liked Frank Rizzo, and for nearly the same reason: the two of them were tough men who spoke up for their constituency in no uncertain terms.

The cops were convinced that Rizzo would be mayor one day: he had the right connections, they always said, not with rancor but with wry admiration.

The Peace That Passes All Understanding

On June 23, 1968, Cecil B. Moore held a peace festival to celebrate the final and complete capitulation of Girard College. The black people of Philadelphia believed that Moore had helped them to a great victory. It was he who kept up the demonstrations in 1965. It was he who recommenced the picketing of the college in the fall of 1966, when he felt unsure about the legal outcome, and against the advice of white liberals, the representatives of the power establishment who were working to integrate the college, and even many high-placed blacks. (The tone of the second round of picketing was far more militant than that of the first: speakers this time around included the Harlem congressman Adam Clayton Powell and the SNCC chairman Stokely Carmichael. Moore was now using the demonstrations to espouse black power. He lost nothing in alienating certain people, even influential members of the black community and powerful white liberals, because they were, after all, already committed to winning the case. Furthermore, they ultimately would have to deal with him again in future racial bargaining sessions because black folk would not accept a deal brokered by anyone else. Moore actually intensified his own grip on the black grassroots by alienating these certain people.) Girard's final appeal to the Supreme Court was denied and so, after three years of legal wrangling and court decisions, the school had to integrate. Moore's demonstrations had forced the issue. By the end of the summer of 1965, Pennsylvania governor William Scranton met with members of the Girard Board of Trustees to try to find a solution. (Moore was not invited to this meeting because he insisted that no other civil rights representatives could be there. Also, the chair of the Girard board insisted that Moore not be there.) There was even a plan to integrate the school without attacking the will: the city of Philadelphia offered to buy scholarships to Girard College to be given to children of all races. Shortly after the meeting with the governor, the board rejected this offer. In December 1965, the city of Philadelphia and the commonwealth of Pennsylvania brought suit against Girard College in federal district court. Oddly, the NAACP never joined the suit or participated in any way in the legal battle because the Philadelphia local had no money. This, in part, explains Moore's populist, to-the-ramparts approach. But eight months of daily demonstrations had had their effect: Girard College had become one huge nuisance, and the state was determined to integrate the school at whatever cost and end the controversy. In the fall of 1966 the federal court ruled in favor of the plaintiffs. The defendants tried to get the case moved to the Pennsylvania Supreme Court but failed. They lost on appeal in the federal courts. Finally, on April 17, 1968, the Girard trustees appealed to the U.S. Supreme Court. On May 20, their writ of certiorari was denied.

Raymond Pace Alexander showed up at the peace festival. He and Moore had had their run-ins during the Girard College ordeal: Alexander had wanted Moore to stop the demonstrations back in 1965, thinking them counterproductive, and Moore had criticized Alexander for not supporting the demonstrations and for passively accepting the first set of court decisions that allowed Girard College to escape integration. Many in the crowd began to boo Alexander when he appeared, but Moore quickly hushed the gathering and permitted Alexander to recite his account of the 1950s court battle. At the time, when I read about that in the papers, I thought it was good that some momentary peace and reconciliation had come, that Moore was a large enough man to realize that Alexander deserved something infinitely more for his extraordinary effort than just another form of heartbreak.

Notes

Introduction

1. It is interesting to note that the word *activist* replaced both *advocate* (as in *peace advocates*) and *agitator* (as in *outside agitators*) in the official newspeak as the 1960s progressed, blurring the important distinction between the two while seeming nonjudgmental.

Muhammad Ali as Third World Hero

1. Of course, Ali, like nearly all champion boxers, enjoyed the indulgences that are considered the perks of his trade: sex with numerous beautiful women, conspicuous consumption, and an army of flunkies and yesmen to placate his temper, satisfy his whims, protect him from his fans, and keep him from being lonely. The behavior that accompanies the aristocratic status conferred upon our most successful male pop culture figures was expected and,

indeed, appreciated by Ali's public. Anything less would have been considered strangely amiss.

2. Kid Gavilan (real name: Gerardo Gonzalez), born (1926) and reared in Cuba, was named after a Havana café called El Gavilan (the hawk). He fought nearly 150 professional fights over a period of fifteen years and was very popular with the audiences of early television. He held the welterweight title from 1951 to 1954. He was a fast, stylish boxer known for his bolo punch, a kind of windup uppercut, which Ali affected to much comic effect in the latter days of his career.

3. LeRoi Jones, "The Legacy of Malcolm X and the Coming of the Black Nation," in *Home: Social Essays* (New York: William Morrow, 1966), p. 238.

4. For discussion of the relationship between Ali and Malcolm X, see Mike Marqusee, *Redemption Song: Muhammad Ali and the Spirit of the Sixties* (London: Verso, 2000); Melani McAlister, *Epic Encounters: Culture, Media, and U.S. Interests in the Middle East, 1945–2000* (Berkeley: University of California Press, 2001), pp. 91–93; David Remnick, *King of the World: Muhammad Ali and the Rise of an American Hero* (New York: Vintage, 1999). Oddly, Ali scarcely mentions Malcolm X in his own autobiography, *The Greatest: My Own Story* (New York: Random House, 1975).

5. Thomas Hauser, *Muhammad Ali: His Life and Times* (New York: Simon and Schuster, 1991), p. 97.

6. Hauser, *Muhammad Ali*, p. 97.

7. Hauser, *Muhammad Ali*, p. 102. Ali still considers the name change one of the most important acts of

his career. See Howard Bingham, "Face to Face with Muhammad Ali," *Reader's Digest*, December 2001, pp. 90–97.

8. Hauser, *Muhammad Ali*, p. 109.

9. Malcolm's first 1964 African trip started on April 13 and ended on May 21. His second trip started on July 9, 1964, and ended on November 24, 1964.

10. The May 20, 1964, headline in the *Evening News* reads "Ring Poet Sings the Glory of Dedicated Leadership / 'I am Great but Osagyefo [Nkrumah] Is Greatest'—Clay."

11. Mark Kram, *Ghosts of Manila: The Fateful Blood Feud between Muhammad Ali and Joe Frazier* (New York: HarperCollins, 2001), p. 40.

12. Photos in the *Daily Times* on June 3, 1964.

13. As Malcolm X once said: "You cannot read anything that Elijah Muhammad has ever written that's pro-African. I defy you to find one word in his direct writings that's pro-African." Quoted in William W. Sales Jr., *From Civil Rights to Black Liberation: Malcolm X and the Organization of Afro-American Unity* (Boston: South End Press, 1994), p. 163.

14. William W. Sales Jr. estimates that Malcolm passed through thirty African countries on his two 1964 tours (*Civil Rights to Black Liberation*, p. 100).

15. For more on African American jazz musicians and Islam, see Richard Brent Turner, *Islam in the African American Experience* (Bloomington: Indiana University Press, 1997), pp. 138–40.

16. *Playboy Magazine*, November 1964.

17. Nation of Islam leader Elijah Muhammad traveled in the Middle East in the late 1950s as well: "On visiting with a couple of my sons in what they call the Near East, in 1959, I began in Turkey. We traveled from Turkey down to Africa to Ethiopia and the Sudan. We visited Arabia (Mecca and Medina), and we visited Pakistan. We returned home from Lehore, Pakistan, on about the 6th of January, 1960." (Elijah Muhammad, *Message to the Blackman in America* [Chicago: Muhammad's Temple No. 2, 1965], p. 59.) Muhammad did not take the hajj during his visit, although he was invited to do so.

18. Hauser, *Muhammad Ali*, p. 97.

19. George Breitman, *Malcolm X Speaks: Selected Speeches and Statements* (New York: Grove Weidenfeld, 1990), p. 21.

20. Quoted in Karl Evanzz, *The Messenger: The Rise and Fall of Elijah Muhammad* (New York: Pantheon Books, 1999), p. 169.

21. Ali was hardly free or independent, as he was mostly trapped in the NOI, who exploited him when it served their purposes.

22. Hauser, *Muhammad Ali*, p. 103.

Sammy Davis Jr., Establishment Rebel

1. Quote in Craig Werner, *A Change Is Gonna Come: Music, Race, and the Soul of America* (New York:, Plume, 1999), p. 37.

2. Like Sammy Davis Jr., Miles Davis managed to

redefine his art through an association with whites and a "white" sound.

3. In Daniel Bell, *The End of Ideology: On the Exhaustion of Political Ideas in the Fifties* (Cambridge: Harvard University Press, 2000).

Cecil B. Moore and the Rise of Black Philadelphia, 1964–1968

1. Marshall Frady, *Martin Luther King, Jr.* (New York: Penguin, 2002), pp. 135–56.

2. Clayborne Carson, *In Struggle: SNCC and the Black Awakening of the 1960s* (Cambridge: Harvard University Press, 1981), p. 100.

3. "NAACP Prexy Outlines Militant Program," *Philadelphia Tribune*, January 6, 1963.

4. A full account of the Philadelphia race riot of 1964 can be found in Lenora E. Berson, *Case Study of a Riot: The Philadelphia Story* (New York: Institute of Human Relations Press, 1966).

5. "Tribune Photog Gives Blow-by-Blow Account of Columbia Ave. Rioting," *Philadelphia Tribune*, September 1, 1964.

6. Muhammad Hassan was most famous for, in June 1963, having knocked the WDAS disc jockey Joe Rainey, a frail man, twenty feet when Rainey condemned his political ideas on "The Listening Post" and refused to offer him an opportunity to rebut the criticism on the show. I doubt the assault made Rainey any more disposed to have Muhammad Hassan on his show.

7. "Muslim Leader Denies Traffic Tiff Was Trigger," *Philadelphia Tribune*, February 6, 1965.

8. "Tribune Photog Gives Blow-by-Blow Account of Columbia Ave. Rioting," *Philadelphia Tribune*, September 1, 1964.

9. "Tribune Photog Gives Blow-by-Blow Account of Columbia Ave. Rioting," *Philadelphia Tribune*, September 1, 1964.

10. S. A. Paolantonio, *Frank Rizzo: The Last Big Man in Big City America* (Philadelphia: Camino Books, 1993), p. 78.

11. E. Digby Baltzell, introduction to *The Philadelphia Negro* by W. E. B. Du Bois (New York: Schocken Books, 1967).

12. "Tribune Photog Gives Blow-by-Blow Account of Columbia Ave. Rioting," *Philadelphia Tribune*, September 1, 1964.

13. Quoted in Arthur C. Willis, *Cecil's City: A History of Blacks in Philadelphia, 1638–1979* (New York: Carlton Press, 1990), p. 107.

14. Quoted in Willis, *Cecil's City*, p. 93.

15. "The Goddamn Boss," *Time Magazine*, September 11, 1964, p. 24.

16. Quoted in Willis, *Cecil's City*, p. 76.

17. The Boule is a highly selective fraternity of successful black professionals. One can join only by invitation, and only after one has achieved eminence in one's field.

18. The Mummers Parade has three divisions, or parade groups: the comic division, the fancy divi-

sion, and the string bands. Each division has its own performance style and costume tradition.

19. Quoted in Willis, *Cecil's City*, p. 133.

20. Quoted in Willis, *Cecil's City*, p. 136. Also see "Mummers Unit Jeers Negroes but Police Prevent Clash," *Philadelphia Tribune*, January 7, 1964.

21. Quoted in Paul Luang, "Raymond Pace Alexander: Realizing the Middle-Class Dream in the Face of Racial Oppression," (senior thesis, University of Pennsylvania, 1993), frontispiece.

22. Deborah P. Samuel, "The fight for Equality: Racial Integration of Girard College" (senior honors thesis, Girard College, 1990), p. 24.

23. "Controversial Tribune Story Written at Singer's Request," *Philadelphia Tribune*, February 27, 1965; "Singer Nancy Wilson Shucks Negro Management As She Moves Up to Big Time and Big Money," *Philadelphia Tribune*, February 16, 1965; "Latin Casino Manager Says He Called Cops," *Philadelphia Tribune*, February 27, 1965; "Moore Says He Is Victim of Loud White Man," *Philadelphia Tribune*, February 27, 1965; "Singer Tried to Quiet Club Row with Song Pleas," *Philadelphia Tribune*, February 27, 1965.

Art Ensemble of Chicago, 4

Baldwin, James, 85
Bandung Conference, 2, 25
Baraka, Amiri, 6
Belafonte, Harry, 59
Bell, Daniel, 61
Bishop, Joey, 63
Black Bourgeoisie (Frazier), 85
black entrepreneurialism, 4
blackface performers, 93–94, 96,
    98, 99
black middle class, 96
black militant activism, 77, 78
black nationalism, 2, 4, 24; and
    masculinity, 29
black nationalist rhetoric: as used
    by Cecil Bassett Moore, 88
Black Power, 88
black vaudeville, 39–40, 42, 46,
    50
black working class, 107
Blakey, Art, 20
Boule, 96, 136 n.17
Bowser, Charles, 99
boxing, 28, 33; as romanticized
    notion of social Darwinism,
    27–28. *See also* Ali, Muham-
    mad: and boxing opponents
boycotts: of products by blacks in
    Philadelphia, 92
Bradford, Odessa, 75–76, 85: ru-
    mors of pregnancy of, 77
Bradford, Rush, 6
Britt, May, 49, 52, 56, 58
Brown v. Board of Education, 104
Burse, Dr. Frank: and ban of

blackface performers in 1954,
    94

Cameron, Lucille, 49
civil rights movement, 73, 74,
    82, 97, 107; and black middle
    class, 96
Clark, Joseph, 83
Clay, Cassius Marcellus, 7, 8–
    9; and announcement of
    new name, 10. *See also* Ali,
    Muhammad
Cole, Nat King, 59
Coltrane, John, 4
Confidential: article about Sammy
    Davis Jr. in, 60
Congress of Racial Equality
    (CORE), 99
Cooke, Sam, 38–39
Cunningham, Evelyn, 48

Daily Times (Nigeria): reports of
    Muhammad Ali in, 15–16
Daniels, Billy, 59, 60
Davis, Miles, 60
Davis, Sammy, Jr.: and the army,
    50–52; autobiographies of, 44,
    58; Broadway performances
    of, 44, 47; childhood of, 50;
    and civil rights, 45, 47, 48;
    and *Ebony* interview, 48; and
    fan base, 39; films appeared
    in, 37, 38, 40–41, 45, 46–
    47, 48, 63, 64; and Jewish
    identity, 57; as link between
    vaudeville and jazz, 46; mar-

Human Relations Commission, 71, 78–79; and blackface performers debate, 94–95

integration, 39, 51
interracial liaisons: significance of those of Sammy Davis Jr., 60
interracial marriage: as viewed by some blacks, 19–20, 49
Islam, 3, 9; and musicians, 20, 133 n.15; and NOI, 23; and Orientalism, 4; and racialization of, 20, 21, 22, 23

Jamal, Ahmad, 20
jazz, 4, 46, 47; and link with civil rights, 49; musicians, 46–47, 48; musicians and Islam, 20, 133 n.15
Jeffries, Herb, 59
Johnson, Jack, 29, 49

Karriem, Osman, 12
Kawaida philosophy, 4
Kennedy, Jack (John Fitzgerald), 56
King, Martin Luther, Jr., 72
Kitt, Eartha, 51
Kwanzaa, 4

Lateef, Yusef, 20
Lawford, Peter, 63, 64
Leary, Howard R., 69–70, 79, 84
Liston, Sonny, 6, 7
Louis, Joe, 29

Malcolm X, 6, 8, 34, 44, 62; in Africa, 12, 19; death of, 11; and Middle Eastern Muslims, 22–23; and Muslim Mosque, Inc., 21–22, 25; Organization of Afro-American Unity, 22; and racialization of Islam, 21, 22, 23; and reasons for leaving NOI, 9; and relationship with Elijah Muhammad, 10–11, 133 n.13; and rift with Muhammad Ali, 12; and suspension from NOI, 7. See also Muslim Mosque, Inc.; Organization of Afro-American Unity
Martin, Dean, 56, 61, 62, 63
Mastin, Will, 50, 51
Mathis, Johnny, 59
Mettles, James, 76
The Mis-Education of the Negro (Woodson), 85
Mississippi Freedom Democratic Party, 72, 73
Mobley, Florence, 77
Moore, Cecil Bassett: activism of, 110; and attempt to disperse rioters, 84–86; and blackface performers in Mummers Day Parade, 94, 98–100; and Black Power, 88; and integration of Girard College, 88, 115–17, 126–28; as leader, 87; and Philadelphia branch of NAACP, 74, 86, 91, 109–10, 111; political stance of, 91; and protest of Ford Foundation study, 92; and pressure politics, 91, 93;

In the Abraham Lincoln Lecture Series

Sander L. Gilman
Smart Jews: The Construction of the
Image of Jewish Superior Intelligence

Gerald Vizenor
Fugitive Poses: Native American Indian
Scenes of Absence and Presence

Linda Hutcheon and Michael Hutcheon
Bodily Charm: Living Opera

Bernice Johnson Reagon
If You Don't Go, Don't Hinder Me:
The African American Sacred Song Tradition

Gerald L. Early
This Is Where I Came In:
Black America in the 1960s